The Turbo Years

THE TURBO YEARS

Grand Prix Racing's
Battle for Power

ALAN HENRY

**Foreword by
Niki Lauda**

The Crowood Press

First published in 1990 by
The Crowood Press
Gipsy Lane, Swindon
Wiltshire SN2 6DQ

British Library Cataloguing in Publication Data

Henry, Alan, *1947–*
    The turbo years.
    1. Formula 1 racing cars, history
    I. Title
    629.228

ISBN 1 85223 397 4

Typeset by Columns of Reading
Printed in Great Britain by Butler & Tanner Ltd, Frome

ACKNOWLEDGEMENTS

The author would like to acknowledge the advice and assistance of the following key people during the writing of this book: Frank Williams, Patrick Head, Peter Warr, Keke Rosberg, Steve Nichols, Harvey Postlethwaite, John Watson, Charlie Whiting, the Honda Formula 1 Team, Nigel Roebuck and David Phipps.

CAESARS

CONTENTS

FOREWORD

The turbo years in Formula 1 were fascinating from a technical standpoint, but plagued by many off-track political controversies which helped to gain Grand Prix racing a considerable amount of media exposure. The very nature of the cars, developing around 1,000bhp in their heyday, produced a generation of extremely strong and safe racing cars and circuit safety facilities, in the main, were also improved to match that increased level of performance.

In that crucial respect, the turbo years left a legacy which has endured into the new era of naturally-aspirated engines that followed in 1989. *The Turbo Years* tells you how it all came about.

Niki Lauda
Vienna, January 1990

INTRODUCTION

What does the word 'turbo' conjure up in the mind of the average motorist? A badge, a cachet conferring exclusivity and high performance? Or merely a trendy, 'go-faster' label reflecting some hasty upgrading in the specification of a run-of-the-mill production car?

In relation to road cars, the answer is probably 'both'. In the late 1970s and early 1980s, turbocharged road cars proliferated. Instant performance was available to anybody who wanted to pay the extra price. The turbocharged car grew in popularity with only a few observers wondering whether it accurately reflected the direction in which the motor industry wanted to go. Were the manufacturers simply cashing in on the high performance image of the turbocharged competition car, notably the phenomenally fast and powerful generation of Grand Prix cars which reached its zenith in the mid-1980s?

The age of the Grand Prix turbo in Formula 1 was a wild and turbulent one, racked by controversy both on and off the circuit. Condemned by their critics at the outset as fuel-squandering monsters, inefficient and unreliable, the turbos developed into the most powerful, spectacular and remarkably fuel efficient Grand Prix cars of all time. Their very existence wrought a fundamental sea change within the Grand Prix community, raising the technical stakes to levels of hitherto unimaginable complexity.

Yet they were legislated off the circuits with quite remarkable suddenness by the same governing body which had defended them in their fledgeling years with a zeal so intense that its impartiality was severely called into question.

Not for nothing is this book sub-titled 'Grand Prix racing's battle for power'. The 1980s saw the struggle for organisational and commercial pre-eminence in Formula 1 contested with the same uncompromising ruthlessness as that applied by the rival engine manufacturers and racing teams.

I hope this book reflects the piquant flavour of Formula 1 racing in the 1980s, not simply an account of the events that took place. Reading the proofs, I sometimes find it hard to believe that many of the episodes occurred; the pseudo-political back-biting, the anarchical decision making, the juvenile lines of argument. Yet the sport survived, undeniably stronger but no better equipped to deal with, or control, its own irresistible urge for public self-mutilation.

By the end of the last chapter it is possible the reader will have reached the conclusion that nothing much has changed, that few mistakes of the past have produced any increase in the accumulated wisdom of the key players in the story. The technology may have changed beyond all recognition, but the human element involved remains as vulnerable, inconsistent and unpredictable as ever.

That is what makes this business so uniquely compelling – as well as bewilderingly complex . . .

Alan Henry
Tillingham, Essex, June 1990

PROLOGUE

Saturday, 16 July 1977, was one of those glorious summer days that our memories always trick us into believing were the norm in bygone times. For the thousands of motor racing fans who crammed round a former wartime RAF base near Towcester, it was also to prove an historic day in the history of Grand Prix motor racing, although few could have been expected to recognise its significance as such.

James Hunt, reigning World Champion, went into this race at the absolute zenith of his career. His McLaren M26 was to start the tenth round of the Championship from pole position. Ahead lay sixty-eight laps of what was once Silverstone airfield's perimeter track, now the circuit popularly regarded as the home of British motor racing. But alongside Hunt on the front row was the glorious scarlet Brabham-Alfa Romeo driven by John Watson and it was the popular Ulsterman who seized the lead at the start as the pack jostled into the first corner.

Thirteen days before, Watson had held victory in the French Grand Prix in the palm of his hand. He was thwarted only on the very last lap when the Brabham hesitated, low on fuel. Mario Andretti's Lotus 78 nipped through to win, leaving a dejected Watson to trail home second. Now, on the fast open sweeps of Silverstone, 'Wattie' seemed to be making the most of a second chance. Again, it was destined to end in bitter disappointment.

The sleek Brabham BT45 led for forty-nine laps before scurrying into the pit lane with yet another fuel feed problem. Hunt swept by into the lead to win from Niki Lauda's Ferrari. Watson resumed twelfth, but eventually succumbed for good to a major fuel system malfunction.

On the face of it, the Silverstone race was just another re-run of a well-thumbed script. A 'kit car' from a specialist constructor, powered by one of the ubiquitous Cosworth-Ford DFV 3 litre V8 engines had just won another Grand Prix. It could just as easily have been Jody Scheckter's Wolf or Mario Andretti's Lotus, other top DFV runners of that era. Lauda's Ferrari and Watson's Brabham-Alfa were very much the interlopers with their flat-12 engines.

However, a glance down to the eleventh row of the starting

Where the story started. The shimmering heat haze following Jean-Pierre Jabouille's Renault RS01 as the Frenchman hurls it through the Woodcote chicane during practice for the 1977 British Brand Prix at Silverstone.

grid would provide the real news of the weekend. Starting from twenty-first position, sandwiched between Jean-Pierre Jarier's Penske PC4 and fading champion Emerson Fittipaldi's Copersucar, was the Renault Elf RS01 driven by Jean-Pierre Jabouille. This was the first turbocharged Grand Prix car to see the competitive light of day since an unobtrusive loophole had been created in the Formula 1 technical regulations fourteen years before. It spluttered round at the back of the field for sixteen precarious laps before Jabouille retired, loss of boost pressure having reduced the turbo engine to a naturally-aspirated 1½ litre V6 in a field of 3 litre cars. Only Formula 1 visionairies took the Renault seriously. They realised the long-term implications of its faltering debut.

The trouble began — and trouble is the right word in view of the long-term controversy the turbo's presence would stir up — at a meeting of the sport's governing body, the Commission Sportif Internationale (CSI) in January 1963. The 1½ litre Formula 1 was scheduled to run to the end of 1965, after which the introduction of a 3 litre naturally-aspirated engine category was envisaged. But a great deal of short-term nervousness manifested itself amongst the rule makers. Would there be a sufficient number of engine manufacturers interested? What would be the expense involved?

In providing a possible interim solution, the new technical rules were framed to provide for 3 litre naturally-aspirated engines or 1½ litre supercharged units. Thus was born the 'equivalency formula'. Years later, eminent engineers, including the likes of Cosworth co-founder Keith Duckworth, would argue that such an equivalency formula was nonsense. The notion of equating the performance of a 3 litre atmospheric engine with a 1½ litre forced-induction unit had no basis in reality. And they were correct.

The roots of the regulation were firmly embedded in well-meaning, short-term expediency. Just as Cosworth have ruled the Formula 1 'customer engine' roost for the past twenty years, so Coventry-Climax fulfilled a similar role in the early 1960s. It was widely anticipated that many private teams would opt for supercharged versions of the redundant Climax 1½ litre V8s to get up and running under the 1966 Formula 1 regulations.

In the event there was no need for anybody to take advantage of these provisions. There were more than sufficient new 3 litre engines to go round with Repco, Maserati, Weslake, Honda and Cosworth-Ford all throwing their hats into the arena in the early months of the new formula. But the forced induction regulation remained on the statute book as a 'sleeper' for more than a decade before Renault reactivated it to devastating effect.

Renault Sport, the competitions arm of the French national car company, started its motor racing involvement in a relatively low-key manner. Using an iron block, four-cam 2 litre V6, developed by a team headed by François Castaing, Renault contested the European 2 litre Sports Car Championship during the early 1970s, dominating the category in 1974, and this engine was used to propel Jabouille's Elf 2 single seater to victory in the 1976 European Formula 2 Championship. Formula 1 was increasingly seen as an important item on the motor sport agenda, but the number one priority was victory at Le Mans. Renault would achieve this goal in 1978 thanks to prodigious engineering effort and the driving talents of Didier Pironi and Jean-Pierre Jaussaud. Only after this success had been achieved did Renault Sport focus its entire effort on to the fledgeling Formula 1 programme.

Engineer Bernard Dudot was probably the most significant key individual involved in the early development of Renault's 1½ litre version of the V6, reducing the stroke of the 2 litre V6 to produce the necessary capacity. Jabouille did all the donkey work when it came to initial testing, reporting that the engine was very promising whilst adding that there was clearly a great deal of ground to cover before it could be regarded as truly competitive. And there was one major problem, absolutely fundamental to those early turbos, that became a top priority to resolve.

At an early test session at Jarama, the sinuous little circuit just north of Madrid which intermittently played host to the Spanish Grand Prix, the French driver found that the short straights between the corners were not long enough for the turbo boost pressure to build up again before he needed to brake for the next turn. Thus the Formula 1 world was introduced to the dreaded 'turbo lag' which was to prove enormously frustrating for drivers

Jabouille watches his mirrors during his brief maiden race outing with the car that was to reshape a generation of Grand Prix car design. Following are Emerson Fittipaldi's Copersucar, Brett Lunger's McLaren M23 and Patrick Neve's Frank Williams Team March 761.

'It'll never bloody work – and if it does it should be banned.' Cosworth founding father, Keith Duckworth (in pale open necked shirt), the High Priest of naturally-aspirated engine technology, looks suitably disapproving as Renault technicians buckle down to working on their new V6 baby.

grappling with the new generation of forced-induction racers for the next few years.

Initially, of course, the presence of a major motor manufacturer on the Grand Prix grids was regarded as a positive development for the credibility of Formula 1 as a whole. But, of course, that tolerant attitude would soon start to change once the Renault turbo began demonstrating its undeniable pace in 1979. It was supremely ironic that possibly the most consistently vociferous opponent would be British team owner Ken Tyrrell.

On 18 December 1976, Tyrrell had hedged his bets by signing an option to use the Renault turbo to the end of the decade. In the event, he declined to pursue that option, preferring to concentrate on the proven Cosworth naturally-aspirated formula. The increasing vehemence of his objections as the years rolled by must have been fuelled by frustration over his own lack of prescience!

In the meantime, it was left to a thoughtful handful of engineers privately to consider a major potential problem area. The regulations for 1½ litre engines stated that they be supercharged. This implied a direct-drive, mechanical system. The Renault relied on exhaust gas turbocharging for its forced-induction system. Was it the same thing?

Clearly not. Turbocharging was originally evolved by the aviation industry as a means to sustain intake manifold pressure at altitude on piston-engined aircraft. As the production of power within a combustion chamber depends on the rate at which air can be introduced into the engine to mix with the incoming fuel, the higher the altitude the less the power output of a naturally-aspirated engine. That is because barometric pressure falls with altitude. The density of the air around us at sea level is 1 bar — about 14lb per square inch. But at even the relatively modest 5,000ft (1,500m) above sea level (the level at which the Kyalami circuit near Johannesburg is situated) the density of the air drops to 0.85 bar. From this it can be readily understood how the potential performance of a non-turbocharged piston-engine aircraft drops away the higher it climbs.

An exhaust-driven turbocharger linked to a centrifugal compressor pressurises the air entering the engine. A turbine within the exhaust system harnesses the engine's waste gases to drive that compressor, forcing dense air into the engine where it is matched by a correspondingly increased amount of fuel. In the immediate post-war years this technology was harnessed to produce more power from diesel engines used in large commercial vehicles, but this involved relatively crude detailed engineering compared with the specialist demands of a precision-built racing engine operating to extremes of temperature and revs.

After missing the German and Austrian Grands Prix, Jabouille's Renault appeared again at Zandvoort for the Dutch Grand Prix where it displayed much-improved form. Mario Andretti's Lotus 78 qualified on pole position with a lap in 1min 18.65sec for the 1.626 mile (2.617km) Dutch seaside circuit, Jabouille lining up tenth on 1min 20.13sec. Considering this RS01 was little more than a testing 'hack', and the driver a willing journeyman, this was really a very promising performance. The French car was still running at the finish, many laps behind.

It ran again in the Italian Grand Prix at Monza, retiring with engine trouble after twenty-three laps, then contested the two North American races at Watkins Glen (USA) and Mosport Park (Canada), respectively retiring with a broken alternator and failing to qualify.

The Renault failed to make the trip to Japan for the last race of the year, but the Regie's popular team manager, Jean Sage, went along just to keep his eye on what the opposition was up to. I well recall bumping into him in the shopping plaza of Tokyo's Keio Plaza hotel where he was buying himself a kimono. We chatted for a while and, jokingly, I asked him where on earth he thought he was going to wear it.

'I will walk down the starting grid in it when the Renault first qualifies on pole position.'

As I recall, he didn't when the moment came. But then I doubt he thought that occasion would arrive as quickly as it did.

1978

The summer of 1978 saw the moustachioed figure of Anthony Colin Bruce Chapman at the absolute peak of his achievement. Team Lotus had been a Grand Prix force for exactly twenty years and, some lean spells during the mid-1970s notwithstanding, Chapman's remarkable far-sightedness continued to add layer after lustrous layer to his reputation as the sport's most innovative technical thinker. Moreover, just as in the 1960s he had forged a unique personal bond with the great Jim Clark, by 1978 it seemed as though he had managed to strike a similar chord with the enormously charismatic Mario Andretti. Nothing seemed impossible for Team Lotus.

On reflection, it still seems almost unbelievable how events were to unfold over the following few years. Lotus would fall from the high wire, their technical pre-eminence evaporating in 1979 and 1980. Lengthy shadows would be cast over the company's future after Chapman's sudden death in December 1982, while the spectre of Lotus's dealings with the ill-starred DeLorean car company would resurface to haunt the racing team as much as a decade later. But in 1978, Chapman had the Formula 1 world at his feet. And the reason could be summed up in two words: ground effect.

The development of ground effect, the harnessing of the airflow under the car to produce aerodynamic downforce, is an absolutely integral facet of the turbo years. The development of this chassis technology was to become inextricably interwoven with the development of forced-induction engines, and the eventual restrictions on under-car aerodynamics would be the by-product of an internal dispute which would bring the Grand Prix business to the brink of anarchy in the early 1980s. Silly, really, when you look back on it.

Chapman's design team first harnessed ground effect with the Lotus 78 'wing car' in 1977. In basic terms, this was a conventional Cosworth V8-engined Grand Prix car with a slim central fuselage, on to which were grafted inverted 'wing profile' side pods. Team Lotus developed the concept in conditions of great secrecy, enveloping the type 78 with plenty of hi-tech, hush-hush melodrama. The press played its part too, as I recall.

When the late Gunnar Nilsson was snapped by an eagle-eyed lensman giving the 78 its preliminary shake-down run at Snetterton in Norfolk, several observers concluded that there seemed to be some 'central aperture' within the car that somehow ducted airflow from beneath the vehicle out over the top.

What were we thinking about? As was customary with Chapman, his latest brainchild was awesome in the uncluttered simplicity of its concept. Even when the 78 was unveiled at a ritzy London press conference, just before Christmas 1976, many people failed to grasp the significance of the machine. Only when it was out racing in 1977 did we see what ground effect was all about.

Chapman and Andretti, meanwhile, spent much of the summer trying to throw rival designers off the scent, publicly attributing much of the 78's success to a special differential used in the transmission system, or to its preferential tank-draining system which allowed Andretti to delicately balance the car's handling characteristics in different ways on different circuits.

In fact, as the opposition was to discover in 1978, the Lotus wing car represented merely the first staging post on Chapman's latest innovative journey. What he had in mind for 1978 was a full ground effect car, the aerodynamic underbody of which extended right back to the tail of the car, fully shrouding its rear suspension. This was the glorious Lotus 79 – or Black Beauty as it became affectionately known – and to drive her, Chapman would partner Ronnie Peterson alongside Andretti to present the world with one of the most formidable Formula 1 driver partnerships of the post-war era.

At about the same time as Jabouille was struggling the Renault turbo test bed through its final pre-race debut tests, Andretti was finally consolidating his reputation as a World Championship challenger. Writing now, the best part of a decade after his full-time Formula 1 career came to an end, I believe that Andretti is still rightly regarded as one of the most mesmeric personalities to whom international motor racing has ever played host.

Mario Andretti was born in 1940 in Trieste, in that north-east corner of Italy which was ceded to Yugoslavia after the Second World War. As a direct result of this arbitrary re-drawing of European boundaries, Mario and his family were to spend seven years of their post-war life in a displaced persons' camp at Lucca, near Florence. It was from Lucca, at the age of 15, that he cycled the short distance to Florence and stood, entranced, behind the straw bales in one of the broad piazzas as Stirling Moss's Mercedes-Benz roared through on its way to victory in the epic Mille Miglia road race.

*The alliance of Colin Chapman (*left)*, Mario Andretti and Ronnie Peterson ensured that the Lotus 79 was a ground-effect sensation throughout its short summer of 1978.*

His imagination had earlier been fired by the sight of the great Alberto Ascari at Monza and he knew, somehow, that he would make motor racing his life. Within weeks, he and his family had turned their back on Italy. With a wide-eyed optimism shared by thousands of others, they joined the exodus to the United States. Mario's childhood experiences not surprisingly put a sharp focus on his sense of ambition.

Andretti and Chapman briefly worked together in 1968, only months after Jim Clark's death. Mario planted the works Lotus 49B on pole position for the United States Grand Prix at Watkins Glen and enjoyed a few intermittent drives for Lotus the following season. But his commitment to American racing, and the lure of Ferrari, kept him away from Lotus until the mid-1970s. Then Chapman and Andretti were thrown together when both needed each other most.

The trend-setting Lotus 72 had been the car to beat throughout the first few seasons of the new decade, but Chapman's efforts to replace it with something more sophisticated went badly awry. The net result was that the type 72 struggled on beyond its competitive life. Lotus's Formula 1 fortunes faded as a result, hitting rock bottom in 1976 with the type 77. Unusually for Lotus, it was a dud — to start with, at any rate.

Mario, meanwhile, had been effectively turned out on to the street as far as Formula 1 was concerned when the ambitious Vel's Parnelli Grand Prix team closed its doors early the same year. He switched to join the up-and-coming Swedish driver Gunnar Nilsson at Lotus. Progress was made. Everybody recalls that James Hunt clinched the World Championship in the final race of the season, the Japanese Grand Prix. Fewer, perhaps, recall that Mario Andretti won the race in a Lotus 76.

Ironically, that success could be directly attributable to the type 76's fundamental chassis shortcomings. A few weeks later, relishing the irony, Chapman explained that the 76 just didn't use its tyres to best effect. That quality had helped it at Mount Fuji where the field was running on soft rain tyres on a fast-drying surface.

'The fact that it didn't work its tyres hard enough enabled them to stay in one piece on this occasion,' recounted Chapman with a mix of glee and frustration. By the start of the 1978 season, all these problems were history. The type 78 was a winning tool, but the forthcoming 79 proved to be even better.

Andretti, though, hankered to drive for Ferrari once again. He had driven for the famous Italian team during 1971 on an ad-hoc basis, winning the South African Grand Prix at Kyalami. Noting his apparently revitalised 1977 form, Maranello made an offer. Even though Andretti had agreed a deal with Chapman, they talked it through once more. Chapman matched Ferrari's offer, but needed outside sponsorship in order to do so. That was achieved by taking on Ronnie Peterson.

Andretti's Lotus 79 keeps ahead of Niki Lauda's oversteering Brabham BT46 'fan car' in the 1978 Swedish Grand Prix at Anderstorp, but not for long. Once the track became coated with oil, however, the Austrian came surging by into the lead...

Ronnie had previously driven for Chapman in the early 1970s at a time when he was rightly regarded as one of the few seat-of-the-pants contenders cast from the heroic mould. After serving his Formula 1 apprenticeship with March, he switched to Lotus in 1973 and won a lot of races for Chapman before they fell out in 1976.

Ronnie rejoined the March team. Chapman scathingly described him as a 'ninety per center' at the time. But the Lotus boss was more frustrated by Ronnie's lack of car-sorting ability rather than any doubt over his out-and-out speed. Even though a couple more years had passed, Ronnie was clearly still quick. And he could bring some outside sponsorship to ease the burden of Andretti's upgraded financial aspirations.

Jabouille on his way to scoring the first points for a turbocharged Grand Prix car, when he took his Renault to fourth place in the 1978 United States Grand Prix at Watkins Glen.

The elegant profile of the Lotus 79 – seen here with Mario Andretti at speed during practice for the Austrian Grand Prix – became the shape to beat in 1978, although the opposition took a surprising amount of time to appreciate just what aerodynamic secrets lay beneath those long side pods.

Mario was apprehensive. 'I'd like to know where it's written that we need two number ones in this team,' he growled when he heard that Ronnie had been signed. Happily, their relationship was not only productive, but highly enjoyable for the two men. Not for them any of the juvenile internecine back-stabbing which would later characterise the pairing of Nelson Piquet and Nigel Mansell at Williams, or Ayrton Senna and Alain Prost at McLaren, during the decade that followed. Ronnie and Mario were adults operating in an environment soon to be populated by what many people regarded as an increasing number of spoilt brats.

Chapman had always been a chassis man and the onset of his ground-effect technology absolutely characterised that philosophy. He was happy to let the car do the work, figuring that superior chassis engineering would enable his drivers to extract more from the engine's performance. At the time, the Cosworth DFVs were producing something in the order of 495bhp when Ferrari's flat-12 peaked at around 520bhp. But Chapman shrugged aside that power differential.

'Give me a nice DFV V8 with plenty of reliability, and I'll get it to move through the air as quickly as a 525bhp flat-12,' he promised. 'That's what I think we should all be concentrating on in Formula 1; getting the best out of a nice reliable power unit. What I want is to make power have less work to do, or have more of that power working more often.'

This was the nature of the underlying philosophy propounded by Grand Prix racing's top designer at the start of the 1978 season. That was what Renault was up against.

Back at Renault Sport the small French team was preparing for a more concerted assault on the Formula 1 Championship. Dudot and his team had learned a great deal about the behaviour of their tiny turbocharged V6 over the winter and, while not taking part in every race, they would achieve sufficient success to raise a few eyebrows amongst the doubters. Once Le Mans, that long-awaited endurance victory, was in the bag and out of the way, the opposition would notice the tempo of Renault's Formula 1 effort go up a gear. Even at the start of 1978, the turbo revolution was now unstoppable.

Renault did not bother to contest the first two races of the season, in Argentina and Brazil. They fell respectively to Mario Andretti's Lotus 78 and Carlos Reutemann's Ferrari 312T2, both these cars being throwbacks to the previous season. Renault now had assistance on the tyre front given that Michelin had also signed up with Ferrari, indirectly providing the fledgeling French team with technical feedback from an established outfit which was regularly running at the front of the field.

Kyalami's altitude helped enhance the Renault's potential, Jabouille qualifying sixth on 1min 15.36sec, 0.7sec slower than Niki Lauda's pole position at the wheel of the Brabham-Alfa BT46. The Austrian driver had left the Ferrari team at the end of the previous season, tired of the politicking directed at him ever since he had survived his terrible, fiery accident in the 1976 German Grand Prix. Assessing the options open to him in typically pragmatic fashion, Lauda reached the conclusion that the Bernie Ecclestone-owned Brabham team, under the technical stewardship of the talented Gordon Murray, would be the most appropriate new berth.

Even though he was on pole at Kyalami, Lauda had begun to realise that the Brabham option was not necessarily going to be the unqualified success he had anticipated. Murray's plans for 1978 involved a complex system of 'surface cooling' for the striking new BT46-Alfa, whereby the sides of its monocoque would in effect become a giant heat exchanger. Suffice it to say, when the car overheated in the bitter conditions at Donington Park during a mid-winter test, it was fair to conclude it might be a shade under-cooled for the 100°F (38°C) plus of Buenos Aires or Rio at the height of a South American summer. The surface cooling concept was shelved, the BT46 revised with nose-mounted water radiators and its race debut deferred to Kyalami. Lauda and team-mate John Watson used uprated versions of the previous season's BT45 in the first two races of the year.

Lauda missed a gear getting off the line at the start of the South African Grand Prix, allowing Andretti to take an early lead. Jabouille held the Renault in a promising fifth place for the first few laps before fading gently back through the field, retiring after thirty-eight laps with a terminal misfire.

Meanwhile, the race for the lead had been absolutely electrifying. After that early spurt, Mario eased back to conserve his tyres, allowing the rest of the leading bunch to close up. This was traditionally a race marginal on fuel, so when Andretti, running second to Patrick Depailler's Tyrrell, pulled into the pit lane for a top-up with only three laps to go, the folly of Chapman's pre-race strategy was thrown into sharp relief.

The Lotus boss was absolutely obsessional about his racing cars starting races at as low an all-up weight as possible, so on the starting grid he instructed his mechanics to pump a couple of gallons from Mario's tank. He told Peterson's mechanics to do likewise, but they ignored him only pretending to remove the fuel. Ronnie lasted the distance, snatching victory in a brilliant last-lap scramble past Depailler's Tyrrell. Mario trailed home seventh, fit to be tied. On this occasion, Chapman made himself scarce . . .

Renault then made the trip to Long Beach, but the French car's poor throttle response handicapped Jabouille's performance through the many tight corners. But he was still far from last on the grid, although his thirteenth fastest 1min 22.491sec was over two seconds away from Carlos Reutemann's pole with the promising Ferrari 312T3 which had made its race debut at Kyalami.

Alongside Carlos on the front row was his dynamic young team-mate, Gilles Villeneuve, destined to become one of the legendary figures of his era and a star player, for one fleeting season, in the Formula 1 turbo story. Getting a perspective on Villeneuve's talent is a task that has occupied many writers in recent times. It is over eight years since he died, yet his deification as one of motor racing's all-time heroes is complete.

Those who believe that Formula 1 World Championship racing is solely about accumulating points, working the permutations, keeping score, tend to dismiss Villeneuve contemptuously as an impulsive fool who squandered his opportunities. Yet nobody with a feel for the sport's emotional roots can fail to be touched by memories of his unquenchable zeal. Years later, Ayrton Senna would produce similar qualities behind the wheel, but accompanied by a character unleavened by Gilles' humour, outward passion or approachability.

Villeneuve's credentials from the US Formula Atlantic scene convinced most of us he was good, but how good we were not to know until Long Beach, 1978. Gilles went straight into the lead from the start, staying ahead for thirty-eight of the race's eighty laps before his inexperience took its toll. Lapping Clay Regazoni's tail-end Shadow DN8, Gilles misjudged his braking, vaulted over the back of the slower car and bounced into a tyre barrier. Reutemann went on to win. Jabouille's Renault suffered a turbo failure after forty-three laps.

Back in Europe, Patrick Depailler scored a glorious win at Monaco, but the new Lotus 79 made its first World Championship appearance during practice. In the claustrophobic and confined surroundings of this famous, yet increasingly pointless, street circuit, Chapman and Andretti agreed they would not risk their new creation in combat. Come the race, neither of the Lotus 78s had a trouble-free run, the main issue being fought out between the two Brabham-Alfas and Depailler, the Frenchman winning his first Grand Prix. Jabouille made it to the finish in tenth place for Renault.

On Sunday, 21 May 1978, the Lotus 79 made its race debut in the Belgian Grand Prix at Zolder. Instantly, the parameters of Grand Prix chassis performance were re-written. Chapman had moved the goal posts yet again. Throughout practice, Mario was unable to conceal his excitement. 'If it hugged the road any closer it would be a white line,' was his most famous crack about the car. 'It feels as though it is painted to the track!'

It looked that way, too. Qualifying on pole position a full second ahead of Reutemann's Ferrari, Mario simply ran away with the race. Peterson, delayed by a late race pit stop to change a blistered front tyre, pounded home second in the old Lotus 78.

Andretti on the Lotus Advantage

Mario's victory in the 1976 Japanese Grand Prix, although swamped by the excitement of James Hunt's World Championship victory, was a crucial staging post on the road to re-establishing Team Lotus as a winning force throughout the following two years.

In 1977, the lessons learned from the Fuji-winning Lotus 77 were incorporated into the type 78 'wing car'. Andretti's affinity for the new car was instant and overwhelming.

'I loved it from the start,' he reflected. 'It's always been my experience that any race car that's well born sends you a message of its quality pretty early in its development. The 78, right out of the box, was able to equal the 77's times without any work being done on it, so that obviously tells you a story right there. But we paid a severe penalty on poor straight-line speed.

'The centre of pressure was too far forward, so we were having to run more conventional rear wing to prevent the car oversteering too much. But we were learning all the time and those lessons would be incorporated in the Lotus 79 which we used the following season.

'The 79 was a fantastic car, although it took a little time to massage into shape. We started the season with the 78, but as early as Monaco I knew we had to go with the new car as soon as possible. It turned out to be fantastic, although it was extremely critical to adjust as far as chassis settings were concerned. When you got it wrong, you really had to go back to square one and begin again.

'But when we got it right, it was tremendous. That car really talked to me, no question about it.'

Jabouille was still running at the finish, but unclassified. The Renault had been dogged with brake troubles throughout the race, requiring several pit stops. But the V6 engine hadn't missed a beat all afternoon. That largely overlooked fact was, in its own way, almost as significant as the dominant performance of the Lotus 79.

In a world as clearly fast-moving as Formula 1, it is instructive to view the overall landscape as it was immediately following Mario's maiden victory with the Lotus 79. Chapman's ground-effect technology was well into its second season, yet remarkably few rival constructors had got the message. Most were still plugging away with extremely conventional, flat-bottomed cars. McLaren, for example, which was later to emerge as one of the super-teams of the 1980s, was busy developing James Hunt's undoubted talents with the ageing M26, a design which owed its pedigree to the 5-year-old M23 which had won the World Championship in 1974 and 1976. When the team finally took the ground-effect route at the start of 1979, it would be a disaster . . .

Ferrari's T3 relied on the lusty output from its powerful flat-12 cylinder engine and on the grip from Michelin's effective radial rubber. Like Brabham, the flat-12 engine configuration did not lend itself to ground-effect packaging. But Williams, Tyrrell, Ligier and McLaren were all clinging to out-moded technical concepts. Only Shadow and Arrows (the same design, as a major High Court action in London later that summer would embarrassingly establish), Fittipaldi and Wolf had started to dabble with ground-effect designs, and all these were already one year down on Lotus in terms of development know-how.

Downforce was now the priority in the design of any contemporary Grand Prix car, as Lotus continued to underline as the 79 reeled its way to victory throughout the summer. Mario would be first past the flag again in Spain, France, Germany, Holland and Italy, although a penalty for an over-eager start in that tragic last-mentioned event would drop him to sixth in the official classification. Peterson would win in Austria, giving Lotus a total of eight wins out of sixteen races.

Gordon Murray, meanwhile, fully appreciated that something out of the ordinary would be required to get the upper hand over the Lotus 79s. So he put on his thinking cap to evolve one of the most remarkable pieces of Formula 1 engineering ingenuity seen for many years. The result was the Brabham 'fan car' which had its sole race outing in the 1978 Swedish Grand Prix at Anderstorp.

Gordon had earlier been concerned, and not a little bemused, when Lauda reported at Rio and Buenos Aires that the interim

BT45C, then fitted with a full-width nose section, was suffering from acute oversteer. Murray had touched on ground-effect theory three years earlier with a system of vee-profile plexiglass skirts on the underside of the Cosworth-engined Brabham BT44 and was more keenly aware than most that Chapman had a few aerodynamic tricks up his sleeve.

'What we hadn't fully appreciated about the BT45C was that the full-width nose section was creating ground-effect downforce, and the car was simply pivoting around its front end,' Gordon recalled. 'That's why Niki complained of oversteer. Then, when I saw the Lotus 79 at Monaco, it clicked into place in my mind. Suddenly, I knew what Chapman was up to. I went to Bernie and said, "Look, we're finished. Unless..."'

For the Swedish race, Murray fitted a huge, gearbox-driven fan to the back of the BT46, sealing off the area beneath the chassis with a complex system of skirts. The fan sucked air out from beneath the car, creating a low pressure area which literally glued the car to the circuit. The gearbox drive system was immensely complex, several clutches being designed into it at several points to lighten the sudden load which would be imposed on it when a driver took off from a racing start, and the Brabham design team encountered all manner of problems with it during testing in conditions of enormous secrecy at Brands Hatch.

On-track, it proved just the job, however. Lauda drove with great determination to beat Mario fair and square at Anderstorp. 'It was the easiest win ever,' grinned the Austrian. 'You could do absolutely anything with that car. When the track was oily after one of the slower cars dropped some of its lubricant, my Brabham felt it was on rails. I just drove past Andretti with no problem at all...'

Word had it that Chapman was already sketching plans on a pad for a 'twin fan' version of the Lotus 79 even before flying home to Norfolk the evening after the Swedish race, but motor racing's rule makers were already hot on the heels of the BT46. Deep amongst the technical regulations it stated that 'aerodynamic devices must comply with the rules relating to coachwork and must be firmly fixed while the car is in motion...' Further, an aerodynamic device was defined as 'any part of the car whose primary function is to influence aerodynamic performance...'

Despite Murray's protestations that the fan had been installed primarily for the purposes of engine cooling, the Brabham 'fan car' concept had clearly been rumbled. Ecclestone deferred with good grace and withdrew the car, his commercial savvy subtly appreciating that a short-term performance advantage was not a good enough reason for compromising the collective strength of

High Achievers. Although Niki Lauda and Brabham boss Bernie Ecclestone (right) did not enjoy great success during their alliance in 1978, both men made a considerable impact on Formula 1 in general and the turbo era in particular.

the Formula One Constructors' Association (FOCA), that influential caucus of which he was the President. As will be revealed in Chapter 2, Ecclestone and FOCA would need to conserve all their energy for a dispute of a very different kind.

Renault's turbo, meanwhile, was quietly bowling along in Jabouille's reliable hands. Thirteenth in Spain, it retired with engine trouble at Anderstorp and at Circuit Paul Ricard (on the opening lap of the French race, much to the crowd's disgust!), a spectacular turbo breakage at Brands Hatch, another engine failure at Hockenheim, gearbox gremlins in Austria, and so-on. Eventually, in the United States Grand Prix at Watkins Glen, Jabouille would come pounding forth to score the French team's first helping of Grand Prix points.

By that time, however, Formula 1 had been touched by tragedy with the death of Ronnie Peterson, the result of injuries sustained in a startline pile-up at Monza. Driving the older Lotus 78 on this occasion after crashing his 79 in the race morning warm-up session, Peterson was side-swiped by another car into a badly positioned barrier as the pack sprinted for the first chicane. A massive impact ripped the alloy monocoque of the Lotus asunder. It was the sort of accident which, ten years later, a bruised and shaken driver might well have walked away from, but Ronnie was removed to hospital with badly shattered legs. Badly hurt, his life seemed in no immediate danger, but a bone marrow embolism got into his bloodstream. In the early hours of Monday morning, this gentle giant of a man passed away.

The world of Formula 1 was pole-axed. Andretti felt crushed. Overcome with remorse, for the moment he had no feeling for the World Championship title he had clinched the previous afternoon. Yet an unfortunate sequence of events now followed which would effectively point the finger of responsibility at Italian driver Riccardo Patrese, the young Italian Arrows driver whose cocky arrogance had, quite simply, got up the Establishment's collective nose during the course of the summer.

At the time of writing, Patrese stands as the most experienced Grand Prix driver of all time with over 180 Grand Prix starts to his credit. A respected member of the Williams-Renault team he has matured, is well-liked and extremely affable. Now 35, it is sometimes difficult to believe that this can be the same person as the conceited, immature 23-year-old with the self-satisfied smirk who very nearly got himself punched on the nose by a furious Peterson after weaving ferociously to keep the Lotus driver back in third place on the final lap of the 1978 Swedish Grand Prix.

In fact, Patrese's unpredictable track performance had been getting on everybody's nerves through much of the 1978 season and, on the eve of the Italian Grand Prix, the Formula 1 Safety Committee convened a meeting to discuss the matter. It was decided that Patrese had to be punished, so the drivers agreed that they would inform the organisers of the United States Grand Prix that if Riccardo's entry was accepted, the race would be boycotted by the rest of them.

In retrospect this was Kangaroo Court justice at its most arbitrary and unreasonable. To this day, Mario Andretti looks back on it as an episode about which he still feels extremely uncomfortable. The organisers caved in, and Patrese was suspended. But the lines became blurred and, to many people, it seemed as though Patrese was being blamed for the Peterson accident.

I have heard a first-hand account, from somebody I regard as a reliable eye-witness, that Patrese flustered the Monza starter by keeping his Arrows rolling gently forward just before the green light was shown to unleash the field. Yet no official blame was ever attached to him, and by all fundamental rules of justice, the penalty suffered by the Italian driver was a disgrace and remains so.

The last two races of the 1978 season were somewhat anti-climactic, although Renault's fourth place in the US race boosted the French team's morale after eighteen months of pioneering effort. Andretti, his Championship title in the bag, would not win again that season, retiring at Watkins Glen when he lost a wheel and at Montreal after a collision with John Watson. The Lotus seat made vacant by Peterson's untimely death went to the Frenchman Jean-Pierre Jarier for these last two races, won respectively by Reutemann and Villeneuve in their Ferrari T3s.

Mario Andretti, World Champion in 1978, in company with newly-elected FISA president Jean-Marie Balestre (right). Balestre would stamp his identity on the following decade every bit as much as the turbo engine – but for even more controversial reasons.

The 'Accident' of Ground Effect

Like so many of motor racing's epochal technical developments, the implications and wider possibilities for the evolution of ground-effect technology happened almost by accident. For while it was Colin Chapman who had the 'blinding flash' of inspiration, it was one of his engineers, Peter Wright, who made the crucial discovery that led to the full realisation of the concept's potential.

Working on scale models of the still-secret Lotus 78 in the wind tunnel at London's Imperial College, research and development boffin Peter Wright became slightly baffled when the instrumentation began producing non-repeatable results.

'We were carrying out tests to assess the feasibility of installing the water radiators within the leading edge of the side pods, a method used during the last war with great success in the Mosquito fighter,' he recalls. 'At first I couldn't understand why we were getting this variation, but on closer examination it seemed that the side pods on our model were sagging. As they got closer to the floor of the wind tunnel, so the downforce increased.

'Obviously, we considered this was something which merited further investigation, so we cut up a piece of cardboard and made side panels to extend the model's side pods right down to the ground. Immediately, the downforce recorded doubled. That was the accidental breakthrough which opened our eyes to how crucial maintaining an air-tight seal along the bottom of the pod would become...'

The sagging side pods on that wind-tunnel model would also be repeated on the full-sized Lotus 79 a couple of years later, alerting Chapman and his team to the need for added structural chassis stiffness in years to come. That legacy would benefit the next generation of post-ground-effect Grand Prix cars as turbocharged engines made chassis stiffness a pressing requirement for subtly different reasons.

Yet as Jarier walked away from the opposition in the early stages of the inaugural Canadian race to be held on the superb Ile Notre Dame circuit, the chill wind blowing off the St Lawrence River signalled not only the onset of a bitter North American winter but also the end of Team Lotus as a consistent Grand Prix winning force.

Amazingly, the Lotus 79 would not win another race. Indeed Lotus would be away from the winner's rostrum for nearly four bleak years. By the time Chapman's team returned, it would be reduced to the role of fortuitous winners, just another normally-aspirated Cosworth customer flattened by the turbo revolution.

THE TURBO YEARS' RESULTS 1978

Winner's average speed

January 15, ARGENTINE GRAND PRIX, Buenos Aires

1	Mario Andretti	Lotus-Cosworth 78
2	Niki Lauda	Brabham-Alfa Romeo BT45C
3	Patrick Depailler	Tyrrell-Cosworth 008
4	James Hunt	McLaren-Cosworth M26
5	Ronnie Peterson	Lotus-Cosworth 78
6	Patrick Tambay	McLaren-Cosworth M26

(119.19mph)

January 19, BRAZILIAN GRAND PRIX, Rio

1	Carlos Reutemann	Ferrari 312T2
2	Emerson Fittipaldi	Fittipaldi-Cosworth F5A
3	Niki Lauda	Brabham-Alfa Romeo BT45C
4	Mario Andretti	Lotus-Cosworth 78
5	Clay Regazzoni	Shadow-Cosworth DN8
6	Didier Pironi	Tyrrell-Cosworth 008

(107.43mph)

March 4, SOUTH AFRICAN GRAND PRIX, Kyalami

1	Ronnie Peterson	Lotus-Cosworth 78
2	Patrick Depailler	Tyrrell-Cosworth 008
3	John Watson	Brabham-Alfa Romeo BT46
4	Alan Jones	Williams-Cosworth FW06
5	Jacques Laffite	Ligier-Matra JS7
6	Didier Pironi	Tyrrell-Cosworth 008

(116.70mph)

April 2, UNITED STATES GRAND PRIX WEST, Long Beach

1	Carlos Reutemann	Ferrari 312T3
2	Mario Andretti	Lotus-Cosworth 78
3	Patrick Depailler	Tyrrell-Cosworth 008
4	Ronnie Peterson	Lotus-Cosworth 78
5	Jacques Laffite	Ligier-Matra JS7
6	Riccardo Patrese	Arrows-Cosworth FA1

(87.10mph)

May 7, MONACO GRAND PRIX, Monte Carlo

1	Patrick Depailler	Tyrrell-Cosworth 008
2	Niki Lauda	Brabham-Alfa Romeo BT46
3	Jody Scheckter	Wolf-Cosworth WR1
4	John Watson	Brabham-Alfa Romeo BT46
5	Didier Pironi	Tyrrell-Cosworth 008
6	Riccaro Patrese	Arrows-Cosworth FA1

(80.36mph)

May 21, BELGIAN GRAND PRIX, Zolder

1	Mario Andretti	Lotus-Cosworth 79
2	Ronnie Peterson	Lotus-Cosworth 78
3	Carlos Reuteman	Ferrari 312T3
4	Gilles Villeneuve	Ferrari 312T3
5	Jacques Laffite	Ligier-Matra JS7
6	Didier Pironi	Tyrrell-Cosworth 008

(110.31mph)

June 4, SPANISH GRAND PRIX, Jarama
1	Mario Andretti	Lotus-Cosworth 79	(93.53mph)
2	Ronnie Peterson	Lotus-Cosworth 79	
3	Jacques Laffite	Ligier-Matra JS7	
4	Jody Scheckter	Wolf-Cosworth WR5	
5	John Watson	Brabham-Alfa Romeo BT46	
6	James Hunt	McLaren-Cosworth M26	

June 17, SWEDISH GRAND PRIX, Anderstorp
1	Niki Lauda	Brabham-Alfa Romeo BT46B	(104.15mph)
2	Riccardo Patrese	Arrows-Cosworth FA1	
3	Ronnie Peterson	Lotus-Cosworth 79	
4	Patrick Tambay	McLaren-Cosworth M26	
5	Clay Regazzoni	Shadow-Cosworth DN9	
6	Emerson Fittipaldi	Fittipaldi-Cosworth F5A	

July 1, FRENCH GRAND PRIX, Paul Ricard
1	Mario Andretti	Lotus-Cosworth 79	(118.31mph)
2	Ronnie Peterson	Lotus-Cosworth 79	
3	James Hunt	McLaren-Cosworth M26	
4	John Watson	Brabham-Alfa Romeo MT46	
5	Alan Jones	Williams-Cosworth FW06	
6	Jody Scheckter	Wolf-Cosworth WR5	

July 16, BRITISH GRAND PRIX, Brands Hatch
1	Carlos Reutemann	Ferrari 312T3	(116.61mph)
2	Niki Lauda	Brabham-Alfa Romeo BT46	
3	John Watson	Brabham-Alfa Romeo BT46	
4	Patrick Depailler	Tyrrell-Cosworth 008	
5	Hans Stuck	Shadow-Cosworth DN9	
6	Patrick Tambay	McLaren-Cosworth M26	

July 30, GERMAN GRAND PRIX, Hockenheim
1	Mario Andretti	Lotus-Cosworth 79	(129.39mph)
2	Jody Scheckter	Wolf-Cosworth WR5	
3	Jacques Laffite	Ligier-Matra JS9	
4	Emerson Fittipaldi	Fittipaldi-Cosworth F5A	
5	Didier Pironi	Tyrrell-Cosworth 008	
6	Hector Rebaque	Lotus-Cosworth 78	

August 13, AUSTRIAN GRAND PRIX, Osterreichring
1	Ronnie Peterson	Lotus-Cosworth 79	(118.03mph)
2	Patrick Depailler	Tyrrell-Cosworth 008	
3	Gilles Villeneuve	Ferrari 312T3	
4	Emerson Fittipaldi	Fittipaldi-Cosworth F5A	
5	Jacques Laffite	Ligier-Matra JS9	
6	Vittorio Brambilla	Surtees-Cosworth TS20	

August 27, DUTCH GRAND PRIX, Zandvoort
1	Mario Andretti	Lotus-Cosworth 79	(116.92mph)
2	Ronnie Peterson	Lotus-Cosworth 79	
3	Niki Lauda	Brabham-Alfa Romeo BT46	
4	John Watson	Brabham-Alfa Romeo BT46	
5	Emerson Fittipaldi	Fittipaldi-Cosworth F5A	
6	Gilles Villeneuve	Ferrari 312T3	

September 10, ITALIAN GRAND PRIX, Monza

1	Niki Lauda	Brabham-Alfa Romeo BT46	(128.95mph)
2	John Watson	Brabham-Alfa Romeo BT46	
3	Carlos Reutemann	Ferrari 3132T3	
4	Jacques Laffite	Ligier-Matra JS9	
5	Patrick Tambay	McLaren-Cosworth M26	
6	Mario Andretti	Lotus-Cosworth 79	

October 1, UNITED STATES GRAND PRIX, Watkins Glen

1	Carlos Reutemann	Ferrari 312T2	(118.58mph)
2	Alan Jones	Williams-Cosworth FW06	
3	Jody Scheckter	Wolf-Cosworth WR5	
4	J-P. Jabouille	Renault RS01 turbo	
5	Emerson Fittipaldi	Fittipaldi-Cosworth F5A	
6	Patrick Tambay	McLaren-Cosworth M26	

October 8, CANADIAN GRAND PRIX, Montreal

1	Gilles Villeneuve	Ferrari 312T3	(99.67mph)
2	Jody Scheckter	Wolf-Cosworth WR5	
3	Carlos Reutemann	Ferrari 312T3	
4	Riccardo Patrese	Arrows A1	
5	Patrick Depailler	Tyrrell-Cosworth 008	
6	Derek Daly	Ensign-Cosworth MN06	

DRIVERS' WORLD CHAMPIONSHIP

Posn	Driver	Points
1	Mario Andretti	64
2	Ronnie Peterson	51
3	Carlos Reutemann	48
4	Niki Lauda	44
5	Patrick Depailler	34
6	John Watson	25
7	Jody Scheckter	24
8	Jacques Laffite	19
9	Gilles Villeneuve	17
	Emerson Fittipaldi	
11	Alan Jones	11
	Riccardo Patrese	
13	James Hunt	8
	Patrick Tambay	
15	Didier Pironi	7
16	Clay Regazzoni	4
17	Jean-Pierre Jabouille	3
18	Hans Stuck	2
19	Hector Rebaque	1
	Vittorio Brambilla	
	Derek Daly	

CONSTRUCTORS' CHAMPIONSHIP

Posn	Constructor	Points
1	Lotus	86
2	Ferrari	58
3	Brabham	53
4	Tyrrell	38
5	Wolf	24
6	Ligier	19
7	Fittipaldi	17
8	McLaren	15
9	Williams	11
	Arrows	
11	Shadow	6
12	Renault	3
13	Surtees	1
	Ensign	

1979

The 1979 season proved to be something of a scene setter. On-track, the increasing level of Renault competitiveness served as a strong reminder that, whatever else happened, the turbo was not going to disappear quietly. Off-track, the administration of Formula 1 racing looked severely threatened by the arrival on the scene of Jean-Marie Balestre as president of the sport's governing body, Fédération Internationale du Sport Automobile (FISA, formerly the CSI).

Ten years further down the road, it is instructive to recall how events unfolded during the summer of 1979. Few involved at the time could appreciate the long-term ramifications – how a power struggle would develop between FISA and FOCA and how that battle would polarise round the question of technical regulations which either did, or did not, favour the burgeoning turbo brigade. For three seasons a mood of confrontation and conflict would exist behind the scenes of Formula 1 while the sport apparently purged itself, painfully and excruciatingly slowly, of all its pseudo-political problems. Those had started, symbolically, on the first lap of the first race of 1979.

A multiple collision at the first corner of the Argentine Grand Prix at Buenos Aires resulted in the race being red-flagged to a halt. Balestre, apparently revelling in his new-found power as the elected emissary of FISA, was the most vocal member of a committee of 'blue blazers' who dished out a 10,000 Swiss franc fine to the unfortunate Watson, at the time of the accident a few hundred yards into his first race with Marlboro McLaren.

'Going into the first right-hander, I was on the outside, nosing ahead of Scheckter's Ferrari and decided I had the line,' John remembers. 'Trouble was, Jody did as well. We touched and both spun, but while I ended up facing the right direction, with only minor damage, he effectively spun the width of the track and ended up on the exit of the corner.

'By this stage his Ferrari only had three wheels left on it, but he still attempted to drive it back on to the tarmac. Heaven knows how he even got it to move on the grass, but the moment it hit the tarmac it spun again. That was when Nelson Piquet's Brabham hit it really hard.'

Unloved McLaren. The gormless ground-effect M28, here with John Watson struggling to make sense of its track performance, was another nail in the coffin of the old McLaren regime during the first half of 1979. It was too big, too heavy and developed too much aerodynamic drag.

During the events that followed, Watson formed the strong impression that Balestre was simply attempting to assert his presence. 'I felt that his stance influenced the stewards of the meeting,' says Watson, 'although I was never even allowed a hearing. Nobody was interested in my side of the case. Initially I was going to be banned for the rest of the season, then from the next race in Brazil and, by the end of the week immediately after the race, it was finally settled that I would pay a fine of 10,000 Swiss francs. That was around £4,000 at the time and certainly seemed like a lot of money. It also represented the start of this trend towards fining drivers for errors made out on the circuit . . .'

To understand how this incident triggered the start of a major deterioration of the relationship between FISA and FOCA, it is necessary to understand the way that Formula 1 had developed throughout the 1970s. Moreover, there is one man who remains absolutely central to the entire theme. His name is Bernard Ecclestone.

For almost two decades, Ecclestone has been the powerhouse of Formula 1 progress. In his role as president of FOCA he formed this grouping of predominantly British teams into the single most powerful lobby in Grand Prix racing during the mid-1970s. Moreover, the rise of Ecclestone's influence seldom seemed to be impeded in any way by the sport's governing body. The CSI, as it then was, proved a rather unobtrusive organisation, compliant and docile. Ecclestone and FOCA were left alone to make the commercial running in the Formula 1 arena and, increasingly, began to exert an oblique influence on the sporting power.

'I think I first met Bernie knocking around the Formula 2 scene in 1969,' recalls Frank Williams. 'He was a friend of Jochen Rindt's, but it obviously wasn't until he'd bought the Brabham team in 1972 that he became a major influence on the Formula 1 scene. His contribution to Grand Prix racing since then has been one hundred times more than that of any other individual, no question about it. All the rest of us have been players, but he has been the leader...'

Ecclestone became a convert to motor racing at a young age. As a teenager in the late 1940s, he was motorcycle scrambling at Brands Hatch when the Kent circuit was little more than a grass track in a leafy dell. He graduated to car racing in the early 1950s, but it was as a shrewd businessman that he made his name. He started selling motorcycle spares out of his mother's kitchen in a South London suburb, thereby setting off on a business career which would see him first train as a chemist before becoming a millionaire many times over from dealing in motorcycles, cars, aeroplanes and property. He also became business manager to Rindt, who went on to win the 1970 World Championship, albeit posthumously. Ecclestone moved into Formula 1 in a major way when he bought the Brabham Grand Prix team from Ron Tauranac, Jack Brabham's former partner, at the end of 1971.

There should be no mistake about it, Bernie quickly came to see the commercial possibilities of Grand Prix racing as a multi-million dollar internationally televised sport. Once entrenched as a team owner, he worked tirelessly towards that end. An autocratic workaholic with a totally determined nature, he could also be charming, witty, tactless, diplomatic and shrewd, depending on his mood and the exigencies of the moment.

He was Grand Prix racing's answer to Mickey Duff and Mark McCormack rolled up in one dapper, irascible ball of energy. He combined the energy and ambition of a politician with the guile and streetwise savvy of a secondhand-car salesman. When Balestre arrived on the scene, instantly each recognised the other as being out of the same mould. The trouble was, of course, they were operating from opposite sides of this particular divide.

By the late 1970s, immediately pre-Balestre, Ecclestone had pushed FOCA to the forefront of the sport's commercial activities. It was FOCA who dealt with the race organisers when it came to prize funds, FOCA who made the international air cargo arrangements for those races outside Europe, and FOCA who effectively decided who could play and who stayed at home.

Had Lewis Carroll written 'Alice goes to the Grand Prix', he might well have considered the following scenario:

'How do you get an entry for all the Formula 1 Grands Prix?' the boss of a small team might ask in the mid-1970s.

'By becoming a member of the Formula One Constructors' Association,' came the corporate reply.

'But how do we become members of the Formula One Constructors' Association,' continued the team boss.

'Quite simple. To qualify for that, you have to take part in all the Grands Prix...'

Even now, some people believe the foregoing was a joke...

Balestre is a wealthy, self-made man whose fortune was made in publishing and in other business interests. He had been through a controversial war. He joined the volunteer pro-Nazi *Legion Charlemagne* and first actually directed the deportation of his countrymen, only later to be jailed himself. In the immediate post-war years it was established that Balestre had been, in reality, an infiltrator, and was duly feted as a Resistance hero.

Initially, most motor racing observers believed him to have aspirations beyond the sport's boundaries, using FISA as a springboard to a full-blown political career. If that was the case or not at the start of the 1979 season, it certainly didn't turn out that way. Over a decade later, Balestre remains firmly entrenched as FISA president, despite – or because of – presiding over the most politically lurid period in the sport's history. Moreover, despite surviving major heart surgery, he continues to display the constitution of an ox, repeatedly getting himself re-elected to the FISA presidency and continuing to occupy a prime spot at the centre of any Formula 1 storm that might be brewing.

The controversy surrounding Nigel Mansell's suspension from the 1989 Spanish Grand Prix, and Ayrton Senna being pilloried as an overtly dangerous driver following his disqualification from the Japanese Grand Prix a few weeks later, involved Balestre in a vociferous, leading role. On the strength of these episodes, you might have been forgiven for thinking that nothing had changed since the FOCA/FISA wars almost a decade earlier. In some respects, you would be right.

By the time the field assembled in the Buenos Aires paddock in January 1979, it was clear that Balestre's mission was to re-establish FISA's authority to administer motor racing. From now on, he made it clear, the sport's governing body would not continue acting effectively as a back-up organisation for FOCA, allowing them unfettered commercial control.

It was against this backdrop of potential political intrigue that the 1979 season got underway. Many people were surprised to find that the Lotus 79's advantage had ebbed away and the the French Ligier team suddenly had the upper hand with its sleek new JS11 driven by the all-French pairing of Jacques Laffite and Patrick Depailler.

In the quest for ever-increasing amounts of downforce, Ligier designer Gérard Ducarouge had appreciated that chassis rigidity was an increasingly crucial element in any Formula 1 car design.

After Alan Jones led and retired, popular Swiss Clay Regazzoni surged to a splendid victory in the 1979 British Grand Prix at Silverstone in the splendid Patrick Head-designed Williams FW07. It was the first win for the Williams marque, ten years since Piers Courage had given the team its British Grand Prix debut in a private Brabham.

Laffite would win, commandingly, not only in Argentina, but also in the following Brazilian Grand Prix at Sao Paulo's splendid Interlagos circuit. Following a third victory, in the Spanish Grand Prix at Jarama, which fell to Depailler after Jacques over-revved his Cosworth engine, Ligier suddenly lost its competitive edge.

From the touchline, it appeared the season was relatively straightforward. The new Patrick Head-designed Williams FW07 had appeared on the scene. And Ligier had somehow contrived to lose the setting-up instructions for the JS11 chassis. This gem of information was revealed many years later by a highly amused Laffite. Apparently Ducarouge had noted them down carefully on the Ligier equivalent of a cigarette packet. And then lost it.

This delightful tale is absolutely typical of this endearingly shambolic French team named after its patron, the rumbustious former international rugby player and amateur Formula 1 driver Guy Ligier. Time and again during the 1979 season, the Ligiers would go like the wind on the first morning of practice. Suitably elated, the team would then settle down to a lavish lunch, where the wine flowed freely, while the opposition would be beavering away trying to improve their cars. This was a constant source of amazement to the Williams number one driver, Alan Jones, the man who would help topple the Ligiers from their early season pre-eminence.

The rise of the Williams team to a position of near-dominance in 1979 represented the realisation of a dream for the team's owner, Frank Williams. It had taken Frank since 1962 to graduate from Austin A40 club racer to Grand Prix winning team chief, with plenty of tears and heartache along the way. In 1969 he first appeared on the Formula 1 scene, entering a private Brabham for his close friend, brewery heir Piers Courage. However, when Piers was killed the following summer in one of his cars, a de Tomaso, it was a major body blow from which the team's fortunes took years to recover.

Frank would be the first to admit that his efforts in the early 1970s were precarious, to say the least. My journalist colleague, Denis Jenkinson, once said to him, 'Frank, you could be king of Formula 2 rather than messing about at the back of the Grand Prix grids. Why don't you do that?'

Frank replied, 'Because I want to be like Ken Tyrrell.' At the time, Ken's team was right up at the sharp end of the Formula 1 business. What goes around, comes around, as they say, and time would come when Ken Tyrrell would dearly have liked to be as successful as Frank Williams...

On another occasion I was mildly critical in print of his team's efforts during the 1974 season. My remarks received a bristling response through the post. 'Just in case you might think the

Joy-day for Jabouille. On the winner's rostrum at Dijon after winning the 1979 French Grand Prix in the formidable new ground-effect Renault.

contrary,' ran the letter, 'I'm not in Formula 1 just to ponce round the pit lane wearing fancy sweaters. I'm serious about this business...' He certainly sounded like it.

Yet it was not until 1978 that Williams finally began to look like a truly serious Grand Prix team, having landed Saudi Arabian sponsorship and the driving talents of Alan Jones, the latter at a time when nobody else really wanted him.

'He was part of what might be called the founding triumvirate of Team Williams,' enthused Frank in 1989. 'Along with Patrick Head and the Saudis (Williams attracted considerable backing from a variety of Saudi Arabian companies during the early 1980s) he won us our first Grand Prix, our first World Championship. Yes, he was a role model for what we thought a Grand Prix driver should be like. He gave 100 per cent of himself inside the cockpit and was outstandingly concise when it came

Ground-effect pacemaker. Alan Jones keeps his superb Williams FW07 ahead of Gilles Villeneuve's Ferrari 312T4 during the opening stages of the 1979 Dutch Grand Prix at Zandvoort, with Jabouille's Renault trailing in third place. At this stage in the game the Cosworth-engined Williams was still a match for the French turbocars.

to describing how the car was behaving. Subsequently, Keke Rosberg and Nigel Mansell demonstrated some of those same qualities, but our relationship with Jonesey was quite special.'

Alan grew up the son of the hard-driving, hard-spending post-war Australian racing hero Stan Jones, a tough nut who lived life in the fast lane, burning the candle at both ends. He imbued his son with qualities of determination that bordered on the stubborn. Ferociously committed, Alan Jones matured into a Grand Prix driver of great speed and ability during his time with Williams, a spell which would lead him to the World Championship crown in 1980.

Just what a down-to-earth, no-nonsense individual Jones actually was came back to me quite dramatically a decade later when I was sitting at a press conference just prior to the Australian Grand Prix at Adelaide. Ayrton Senna was pouring his heart out to the members of the Fourth Estate about how unjustly he'd been treated over his Japanese Grand Prix disqualification, when I noticed Jones at my shoulder frowning in disbelief.

'Jeez,' he whispered, nodding at the misty-eyed Ayrton, 'I knew motor racing was dangerous, but I'd never believed one of the hazards you press guys risked was being bored to death!' A down-to-earth lad, our Alan, not given over-much to sentiment. That said, I can't help thinking that his remarks about Ayrton might have been coloured by his intense antipathy towards another Brazilian, Nelson Piquet, during his motor racing heyday. Back in 1980, one of the standard team jokes at Williams was that Jones got up an hour early every day during the season – so that he could dislike Nelson Piquet that much longer...

Williams designer Patrick Head clearly assimilated all the lessons provided by Chapman's Lotus 79. The previous year Head opted for a conventional, flat-bottomed chassis in the Williams FW06 which proved good enough to establish the team as a possible contender. Now Head pencilled the car which would effectively rule Grand Prix racing for the next three years.

The Williams FW07 was, admittedly, late off the drawing board. It did not make its race debut until round five of the Championship struggle. By that time the tally of race victories stood at Ligier, 2; Ferrari, 2.

Yes, this was to be Ferrari's year, although you would have been hard-pressed to find many people who would bet that way at the start of the season. While Reutemann went off to Lotus, the Italian team amazed everybody in the Formula 1 business by signing South African Jody Scheckter to partner Villeneuve for 1979. Surely, this was not going to work...

Jody had been one of the spectacular new Formula 1 talents of the early 1970s. However, there had been a time when everybody feared for him, concluding his speed was tempered by no sense of prudence whatsoever. Certainly, this viewpoint had been strengthened in the summer of 1973 when, at the wheel of a McLaren M23, he triggered a first lap multiple collision which brought the British Grand Prix to a halt, wiping out almost half the field. Yet, as the decade wore on, Scheckter steadily matured and, perhaps, was perceived as losing the fine cutting edge of his ambition.

After three years with Tyrrell, followed by two with Wolf, Scheckter sat down and thought through his best potential opportunities for 1979. He came to the conclusion that Ferrari offered him the most, even allowing for the fact that he would have to take on the incumbent Villeneuve in a direct head-to-head. Jody rightly judged that his experience would likely give him a marginal edge over Villeneuve's youthful exuberance. Moreover, Scheckter's ego was well under control, unusually for a Grand Prix driver. He could accept the fact that Villeneuve was the quicker driver. He had to.

Jody came face-to-face with that reality in front of his home crowd, in the South African Grand Prix, the third round of the title battle. Having struggled through the first two races of the year using the outmoded 312T3, Ferrari designer Mauro Forghieri unveiled his definitive challenger for 1979 when pre-race testing began at the high-altitude circuit near Johannesburg.

The Ferrari 312T4 represented a game attempt at marrying ground-effect aerodynamics to a flat-12 cylinder engine, a challenge long ago dropped by Gordon Murray who had persuaded Alfa Romeo to produce a V12 engine in time for the start of the season in order for him to produce a true ground-effect challenger. The irony was that the 'compromise' Ferrari design, with its excellent Michelin radials, punchy engine and two front-line drivers, proved sufficiently competitive over a broad range of circuits to carry Scheckter to the World Championship.

The debut of the Brabham BT48 at Buenos Aires had been lurid, to say the least. Gordon Murray had attempted to take the ground-effect concept one step further by attempting to generate all the car's downforce by means of the side pods. Nose wings were no longer part of the equation, and the conventional rear wing was originally replaced by nothing more than a full-width, adjustable tail flap. It turned out to be an absolute, 22 carat nightmare.

Murray said: 'In some ways, I suppose you could say that I rather overestimated what the opposition might produce after we'd all spent a season watching the Lotus 79 run away with everything. I anticipated that everybody else would take a giant step forward, so I figured that Brabham should take an even bigger stride in an attempt to leapfrog ahead of the fresh opposition. So we built the BT48 and took it to Buenos Aires, only for everybody else to turn up with imitations of the Lotus 79 which, really, represented not very much in terms of real progress . . .'

Thus Murray found himself and the Brabham team operating miles away from base, with a brand new sliding skirt ground-effect car, powered by a totally new and untested engine. It was not a recipe for a happy time . . .

'The trouble was, we didn't understand centres of pressure,' Gordon continued. The centre of pressure is the point along the underside of the aerodynamic side pod at which maximum downforce is developed, ideally as close to the centre of the car

Villeneuve in extremis. Mauro Forghieri's ground-effect Ferrari 312T4 was not in the same class as the Williams – certainly not in this precarious condition as the late lamented Gilles attempts to salvage something – anything – from his 1979 Dutch Grand Prix tyre failure.

as possible. 'We arrived in Argentina with the low-mounted rear wing, springs which were far too soft and skirts which tended to stick up over any bumps... Any dynamic input of any sort – acceleration, braking or cornering – unsettled the whole car, causing the centre of pressure to rocket backwards and forwards along the car two or three feet in either direction.'

Much the same problem would be encountered by Team Lotus, for Colin Chapman's design team was thinking along broadly similar lines for the type 79's successor. The Lotus 80, unveiled just before the Brands Hatch Race of Champions, featured a rear wing which amounted to no more than a full-width tail flap, as well as a complex system of full-length skirts following the contours of the monocoque from the nose box back to a point aft of the rear wheels. Controlling the aerodynamic downforce proved a similarly unmanageable nightmare and, by mid-season, Lotus had reverted to its now-obsolete type 79s while Chapman settled down for a lengthy spell of second thoughts.

Back at Buenos Aires, practice had not been long underway before Niki Lauda returned thoughtfully to the pit lane, reporting that it felt as though the BT48 was attempting to take off on the straight, this unsettling quality only partially rectified by the fitting of a conventional rear wing at the end of the first day's qualifying. It would take until Kyalami for the Brabham-Alfa to score its first Championship point, Lauda leading Nelson Piquet

---

Forghieri's Challenge for Ferrari

'Everybody tended to write us off for 1979, even though our flat-bottomed 312T3 had won five races in 1978. The overwhelming feeling in the pit lane was that the narrow crankcase of a V8 was absolutely indispensable to the design of a ground-effect chassis. But, although it wasn't the fastest car on every circuit, I think we proved with the T4 that we could compete in the ground-effect stakes.'

That was Mauro Forghieri's recollection of the 1979 season, the year in which Ferrari won against the odds. As technical director of the most famous Grand Prix team in the business, Mauro had by this time been working in Maranello's racing department for seventeen years. He had stayed the course remarkably well in what was traditionally regarded as one of the most highly political engineering positions in the Formula 1 business. Yet he would be the first to admit that Ferrari won in 1979 largely because of its better state of readiness early in the year.

'We didn't have our new car ready in time for the first two races,' he concedes, 'but we had put wins under our belt at Kyalami and Long Beach before the new Williams FW07 came along. We also had mechanical reliability on our side, so by the time Regazzoni won in the new Williams at Silverstone we had four victories to our credit.'

Forghieri also acknowledges the performances of Jody Scheckter and Gilles Villeneuve as a hugely significant bonus. 'They set each other off superbly; they were both highly motivated, but in different ways. They both wanted to win and each thought he had worked out the best way to achieve that. In fact, they were both proved correct...'

past the chequered flag by only a length. It was the day Niki realised that new boy Nelson would be a tough nut to crack...

Not only did the 1979 Kyalami race also mark the debut of the Ferrari T4, it proved to be the Grand Prix at which Renault team manager Jean Sage should have walked down the starting grid wearing that kimono he had purchased in Tokyo sixteen months earlier. For this was the race at which Jabouille, now partnered in a two-car Renault line-up with Rene Arnoux, qualified the French turbo car on pole position for the first time. At the end of the opening lap, Jabouille's little yellow machine simply streaked past the Ferraris to take the lead going into the Crowthorne right-hander at the end of the Kyalami circuit's long start/finish straight. It was certainly an eye-opening moment...

Unfortunately, the race was stopped after two laps owing to a downpour, after which the restart saw Villeneuve and Scheckter make the event their own personal property. Only a late pit stop for tyres deprived Scheckter of a home victory, his French Canadian team-mate beating him past the chequered flag by just over three seconds.

Scheckter would have to suffer a repeat of this apparent ignominy again at Long Beach, where Villeneuve beat him commandingly for a second time. Not until Zolder would Jody win for the first time that season, a race which would see Villeneuve's championship aspirations suffer a mathematically devastating blow when he lost third place, out of fuel, on the very last lap.

To strengthen his Championship hand, Scheckter followed that up with a superb triumph at Monaco. On the eve of that race, Carlos Reutemann told me: 'If Jody wins here tomorrow, for sure Ferrari will put all its efforts behind him to win the Championship.' Carlos, seasoned to the political ways of Maranello, was right on the button with his assessment.

Off-track, the relationship between Scheckter and Villeneuve was unusually warm and cordial. Both Monaco-based, their widely contrasting characters paradoxically produced a strong personal bond. Professionally, they enjoyed working together. Off duty, they would quarrel like warring schoolboys with the ferocity that can only be sustained between true friends. Moreover, each had a high regard for the other's ability behind the wheel, to the point where they could relax and didn't have to be forever competing away from their cars.

Renault, meanwhile, had done a great deal of work to the V6 turbo engine over the winter and this was duly installed in an elegant ground-effect chassis produced by the design team steered by Michel Tetu. Built round a shapely aluminium monocoque, it was distinguished by top-louvred side pods and an elegant rear wing mounted atop strikingly scalloped end plates. The car made its competition debut at Jarama, but it was not until Monaco, the sixth round of the Championship, that the new French machines appeared with the heavily revised engines which were destined to make such a significant improvement to their competitive form.

In order to improve the lazy throttle response, Bernard Dudot and his team changed the single Garrett turbo for a revised system, whereby a smaller turbo, supplied by KKK, was fitted to each bank of cylinders. Hand in hand with this development, the new car was fitted with a water intercooler designed to reduce the temperature of the air entering the engine under pressure. Exhaustive tests revealed these changes to provide not only better throttle response, but enhanced piston durability, a big problem in a tiny engine where heat dissipation is a major challenge.

The team faced problems with the intercoolers cracking at Monaco, where Regazzoni stormed to a close second place behind Scheckter to give the new Williams FW07 its best placing yet, but a month's break followed before the French Grand Prix at Dijon-Prenois. Renault was aiming high by this point, having tested exhaustively at the challenging circuit, close to the heart of Beaujolais country, and figured they were in good shape.

The die was effectively cast during a tyre test session held at Dijon-Prenois shortly before the French race. Wolf designer Harvey Postlethwaite recalls monitoring a speed trap on the main straight, when suddenly a Renault tripped it running almost 20mph faster than anything else on the track.

'I remember it vividly,' he laughed over ten years later. 'Up to that point the Renault had been pretty much of a laughing stock, spending most of the time setting fire to itself. Then here we were watching the Cosworth V8 cars droning up the hill towards the pits at Dijon, dragging themselves along at about 130mph, when suddenly the Renault goes by and registers almost 160mph. I thought, "that can't be right". Then it did it again.

'In retrospect, I suppose it's all too easy to say that we should have all rushed out and got turbos from anywhere we could, but you tend to forget the state of the art at the time. Even the biggest teams only had between thirty and forty staff, and most of us had hardly mastered the business of installing DFVs, never mind taking on turbo programmes. In any event, where were we going to get them from even if we'd wanted them?'

Gilles Villeneuve's Ferrari T4 burst into the lead at the start, and it took Jabouille forty-six of the race's eighty laps before he finally forced through to the front. Thereafter the Michelin-shod Renault stormed imperiously to a commanding victory. Behind,

Jacques Laffite, seen leading team-mate Patrick Depailler en route to victory in the Argentine Grand Prix at Buenos Aires, made the most of it while he could.

Villeneuve, his tyres in tatters, became embroiled in a ferocious brake-locking, wheel-banging joust with René Arnoux during the dying moments of the race.

Some seasoned observers reckoned it was an insane demonstration of utterly undisciplined driving, others saw it merely as free expression on the part of two completely committed racers. Gilles just held off René to the flag, the two men leaping from the cockpit into each other's arms with delight. Such mutual outpourings of fraternal pleasure would become less a feature of the Formula 1 landscape in the decade that followed...

Cynics suggested that Renault might have got away with running a 2 litre on home ground, but such a calumny is unworthy. The low ambient temperature on race day helped the turbo's cause enormously, and, even though Renault would not win again that summer, both Jabouille and Arnoux kept sufficiently in play close to the front of the field to prove that the Dijon success may have been slightly lucky, but it was by no means a fluke.

By the time Jabouille made his way on to the Dijon winner's rostrum, Formula 1 had been deprived of one of the decade's more colourful characters. The Monaco Grand Prix had marked

Narrowing the Turbo Gap

Back in the summer of 1977, when frustrated Renault mechanics used to extinguish turbo fires on their 'yellow peril' with the aid of a broom, many of the French team's rivals simply roared with laughter at the way in which this new organisation went about its motor racing. They were dismissed out of hand and suggestions that developments in sophisticated metallurgy would make this technical route the only one to follow were viewed with a similar degree of contempt.

Even so, there were a few who cried out in the wilderness. Cosworth co-founder, Keith Duckworth, was the one who warned perhaps more vociferously than anybody else about the implications of an explosion of turbo technology, while Bernie Ecclestone and Max Mosley were also able to read the long-term trends, but tended to keep their reservations to themselves as much as possible.

It was not really news that their colleagues in the FOCA ranks particularly wanted to hear!

the last race outing for James Hunt, the Englishman having decided to quit abruptly mid-season, not yet 32-years-old.

Almost three years had passed since Hunt's celebrated World Championship success, a period which had seen a steady decline in the Wellington-educated driver's fortunes. Despite a trio of wins in 1977, McLaren had fallen from the high wire pretty spectacularly by the end of that season and 1978 had turned out to be an embarrassing debacle for them. Hunt's motivation was also called into question by many critics, but, determined to have one more decent season before hanging up his helmet for good, he switched to Walter Wolf Racing at the start of 1979.

This alliance reunited him with Harvey Postlethwaite, the talented designer who had been one of the technical cornerstones of James's much-hyped alliance with Lord Alexander Hesketh's team in his pre-McLaren days. In 1978, Harvey had been one of the first designers to understand the significance of Chapman's ground-effect development, rushing a new skirted Wolf design into action in the middle of the season for Jody Scheckter's use. Now Jody had defected to Ferrari, Harvey was to take his ground-effect thinking a stage further with the WR7 design which James would campaign from the start of 1979.

It would seem that James quit the sport because he no longer considered the danger to be worth it. He also appreciated that the onset of ground-effect technology made the designer's contribution to the driver/chassis equation by far the most significant element, a feeling he made public at the time. The strong implication behind his remarks was that Postlethwaite had produced a dud. Harvey was absolutely fit to be tied at the time; I well recall a lengthy telephone conversation with him that left me with the distinct impression that if he never spoke to James again, then it would be too soon. But, although taking very much a second place to his mounting personal apprehension, James's assessment of the diminishing contribution of the driver was quite a valid point. Not that his relationship with Postlethwaite would ever be worth much thereafter, Harvey always subsequently detecting a nervous edge of criticism in any of James's remarks about him.

Significantly, perhaps, when the chance of driving one of the Ligier JS11s arose after Patrick Depailler was injured in a mid-season hang-gliding accident, Hunt initially showed interest in reversing his retirement decision. Not for long though; James knew one could be hurt behind the wheel of any Grand Prix car. Meanwhile, over in the Brabham camp, Niki Lauda was reaching a similar conclusion, although for subtly different reasons which would not be made public for another few months.

Meanwhile, the next race on the agenda was the British Grand Prix at Silverstone, a circuit on which one might reasonably have expected turbo power simply to flatten the opposition. Not so. Silverstone was to be the preserve of the sensational ground-effect Williams FW07s, a race in which Alan Jones and Clay Regazzoni would be the class of the field, providing the long-awaited breakthrough for Frank's ambitious organisation.

Jabouille joined Jones on the front row, but Silverstone was to be Williams territory from the start. Those of us who had attended the pre-race tyre test sessions had returned from Stowe corner with the hairs on the back of our necks standing ramrod straight having witnessed Jones's sensational quick laps. The stocky, muscular Australian seemed to wear his FW07 as an extension of his driving suit, the whole driver/car combination exuding an awesome confidence. One look at Jones with his helmet on was sufficient to send rivals running for cover. He radiated power, control and simmering agression. Strapped into the cockpit, sight of him in a rear-view mirror would have much the same intimidating effect as that produced by Ayrton Senna a decade later. You messed with Alan Jones at your peril . . .

Alan qualified six-tenths of a second ahead of Jabouille to take pole position, muscled into the lead midway round the opening lap and stormed away into the distance. For sixteen laps Jabouille hung on to second place, but Regazzoni wasn't to be denied. From Lap 17 to 38 Frank's two cars held the opposition at bay, running in 1-2 formation. Then a thin pencil of smoke from the rear of Jones's FW07 heralded his retirement with a cracked water pump. Regazzoni was handed the Williams team's maiden Grand Prix victory on a plate.

Clay was almost forty, already nine years into a career that had seen him score his own personal Grand Prix win back in 1970. Then he won the Italian Grand Prix at Monza, only his fifth

Formula 1 outing, in the wake of Jochen Rindt's tragic fatal accident in practice. The genial Swiss with the shaggy moustache seemed like a survivor from another age as he stood aloft on the winner's rostrum. And he toasted his victory in orange juice, diplomatically waving away the traditional champagne in deference to the Williams team's Saudi Arabian sponsors. This protocol would be adhered to rigidly by both Williams team drivers throughout 1979.

Silverstone also marked a glimmer of hope from the McLaren ranks for the first time in over a year, the team taking the first step towards climbing out of the monumental hole dug for McLaren's reputation by the conspicious failure of their first foray into ground-effect construction, the M28.

After Ronnie Peterson's sad death the previous autumn, former Brabham driver John Watson was recruited to lead the team alongside Frenchman Patrick Tambay. A gentle Ulsterman from Hollywood, on the banks of Belfast Lough, Watson was one of most naturally stylish drivers of his era, although with only a single race win to his credit by the end of 1978. He'd got on well with Lauda – and would do so again as his McLaren team-mate in 1982 and 1983 – but had known his days were probably numbered in the Brabham team since the French Grand Prix that summer. 'I was on pole, and Bernie came to me to ask, should I find myself running first, would I be prepared to let Niki through?' he recalls. 'I think he got the impression I wouldn't . . .' In the event, it was all academic as the Lotus 79s took the race by its throat from the word go.

By the end of the 1978 season, McLaren's new ground-effect car was ready for preliminary testing. At first glance, it looked a tidy proposition – if a trifle large.

For McLaren designer Gordon Coppuck, the man who had pencilled the championship-winning M23s, this was the beginning of the end for his Formula 1 career. The mild-mannered and popular engineer had fallen into a fundamental trap on two crucial counts when it came to producing the M28. Firstly, he reached the conclusion – one which, admittedly, seemed quite valid at the time – that the bigger the side pod area, the more downforce would be generated.

The M28 was thus built with a vast acreage of underbody, the effect of which was to cause so much aerodynamic drag that the car was hopelessly short on straight-line speed. Also, Coppuck had built the fuel tanks across the full width of the car, like the now-superseded Lotus 78, a snag which left him almost no room for manoeuvre in terms of revising the underbody profile of the side pod.

The result was an enduring nightmare for the first few races of

the year, after which McLaren's managing director, Teddy Mayer – often an abrasively outspoken customer – told Coppuck, effectively, to copy the Williams FW07 concept and rush through a new car, with a single central tank, in time for the British Grand Prix. The result of these frantic endeavours was the McLaren M29 which John Watson demonstrated to be no mean tool, displacing Scheckter's Ferrari on the last lap of the British Grand Prix to earn a fourth place on the car's maiden outing.

Arnoux finished second for Renault at Silverstone, and while Jabouille sustained the impetus of Renault's challenge by qualifying superbly on pole position for the German Grand Prix at Hockenheim, a stupid spin into a sand trap whilst running second to Jones's Williams on the eighth lap took the pressure off the Australian. Despite a deflating rear tyre, he cantered comfortably home to win from team-mate Regazzoni.

All the while, Scheckter had been quietly amassing World Championship points and went into the eleventh round of the Championship, at the Osterreichring, with a 7 point advantage over Ligier's Jacques Laffite. Jones won his second victory of the season, but Villeneuve finished second and now moved into second place in the title chase 6 points behind Scheckter, the South African battling Laffite all the way to the last lap only to be overtaken by the French driver for third place a few corners from home.

The Gérard Ducarouge-designed ground-effect Ligier JS11s set fresh standards for a short time during the early races of 1979.

Further back down the field, the veracity of James Hunt's early-season observations seemed to be confirmed by the drastic disappointment experienced by Carlos Reutemann. On this occasion the Argentinian appeared to have all but given up, trailing around at the back of the field in his Lotus 79. Yet Lotus engineer Nigel Bennett would later confirm that this apparent off-day had 'absolutely nothing to do with Carlos'. Team Lotus had apparently broken its golden rule against making changes to a car's set-up which had not previously been thoroughly tested. With the Lotus 79's form fading fast, they made an adjustment which had absolutely the opposite effect to that intended, relegating Reutemann to the status of an apparently hopeless also-ran.

Villeneuve's extraordinary fighting spirit went on public display once again at Zandvoort, the dune-lined seaside circuit which regularly played host to the Dutch Grand Prix. While Arnoux put Renault's name up in lights again with a fine pole position, the French turbo V6 was only 0.2sec faster than Jones's Williams FW07 and, from the start, the race developed into a superb battle between the Australian and Villeneuve's Ferrari.

Arnoux was eliminated in a first corner collision with Regazzoni's Williams, so while Jabouille held third place in the other Renault for twenty-five laps before clutch failure intervened, the turbos never got a look in on the two-car battle for the lead. Jones led for ten laps before Villeneuve muscled ahead, the French Canadian leading until Lap 47 when a deflating rear tyre pitched him into a spectacular spin across Jones's bows on one of the fastest sections of the course.

Alan went hard on to the brakes to miss the Ferrari, but by the time Villeneuve had recovered, the Williams was long gone over the horizon. That didn't stop Gilles from mounting as determined a counter-attack as he could manage. Two laps later that over-taxed, deflating tyre finally flew apart as he hurtled past the pits. Miraculously, he managed to keep the wayward Ferrari running in a more-or-less straight line, skittering to a crippled halt in the sand on the outside of the fast right-hander beyond the pits.

Momentarily, it seemed as though his race was over. Yet he manhandled his three-wheeled Ferrari into some semblance· of hobbled action yet again, dragging it round to the pits on its progressively disintegrating suspension and under belly. It was another demonstration of his unflinching determination and sheer zeal for motor racing.

This sort of overwhelming passion was a philosophy at the opposite end of the scale from the pragmatic approach displayed by twice World Champion Niki Lauda. While Villeneuve had been up at the front of the title chase, battling it out with

Scheckter, the Williams and Ligier teams, Lauda had suffered a traumatic season with the Brabham-Alfa Romeo. Making some sort of sense of the chassis was a task they at least partly accomplished, but the variation in performance between one Alfa V12 and another was an anomaly calculated to drive Niki up the wall.

In fact, the Italian Grand Prix was the last occasion on which the Alfa V12 was used in a Championship race. Niki finished fourth on a day when Jody Scheckter sealed his Championship crown by winning from the front for Ferrari and, a week later, the Austrian took the Brabham BT48 to a somewhat fortuitous victory in the non-title race at Imola, a scene-setter for the 1980 Italian Grand Prix which would be held at that circuit. Brabham by this time had decided to switch back to Cosworth DFV power, the British team working all hours of the day and night for several weeks to produce three new cars in time for the Canadian Grand Prix at Montreal.

By that stage, however, Lauda had become increasingly bored with motor racing as a whole. His fledgeling airline, LaudaAir, was on the verge of taking an option on a DC-10 (an extremely risky business decision, as things turned out) and aviation matters in general were increasingly occupying his mind. Mid-way through first practice at Montreal, he came into the pits and beckoned Bernie Ecclestone to the cockpit of his car. Its over, said Niki, I want to quit. He was, he said, fed up with driving round in circles. Ecclestone, a racer himself, understood. Within a few minutes Lauda had left the circuit, and motor racing, apparently for good.

The last two races of the season produced no real surprises. Jones held off Villeneuve to win in Montreal, a sensational battle between two men who were emerging as the outstanding talents of their generation. At Watkins Glen, in the rain-soaked United States Grand Prix, Villeneuve was the victor after Jones lost an inadequately secured wheel just after a tyre stop. It was a momentous win for Gilles to round off an even more splendid performance in practice at one point during which, he had been no less than 12sec per lap faster than the next quickest car. In torrential rain...

The Renaults continued to be fast, but fragile. So what was new? Nobody else looked like joining the turbo bandwagon as 1980 beckoned.

Or so it seemed.

THE TURBO YEARS' RESULTS 1979

Winner's average speed

January 21, ARGENTINE GRAND PRIX, Buenos Aires

1	Jacques Laffite	Ligier-Cosworth JS11	(122.78mph)
2	Carlos Reutemann	Lotus-Cosworth 79	
3	John Watson	McLaren-Cosworth M28	
4	Patrick Depailler	Ligier-Cosworth JS11	
5	Mario Andretti	Lotus-Cosworth 79	
6	Emerson Fittipaldi	Fittipaldi-Cosworth F5A	

February 4, BRAZILIAN GRAND PRIX, Interlagos

1	Jacques Laffite	Ligier-Cosworth JS11	(117.23mph)
2	Patrick Depailler	Ligier-Cosworth JS11	
3	Carlos Reutemann	Lotus-Cosworth 79	
4	Didier Pironi	Tyrrell-Cosworth 009	
5	Gilles Villeneuve	Ferrari 312T3	
6	Jody Scheckter	Ferrari 312T3	

March 3, SOUTH AFRICAN GRAND PRIX, Kyalami

1	Gilles Villeneuve	Ferrari 312T4	(117.19mph)
2	Jody Scheckter	Ferrari 312T4	
3	J-P Jarier	Tyrrell-Cosworth 009	
4	Mario Andretti	Lotus-Cosworth 79	
5	Carlos Reutemann	Lotus-Cosworth 79	
6	Niki Lauda	Brabham-Alfa Romeo BT48	

April 8, UNITED STATES GRAND PRIX, Long Beach

1	Gilles Villeneuve	Ferrari 312T4	(87.81mph)
2	Jody Scheckter	Ferrari 312T4	
3	Alan Jones	Williams-Cosworth FW06	
4	Mario Andretti	Lotus-Cosworth 79	
5	Patrick Depailler	Ligier-Cosworth JS11	
6	J-P Jarier	Tyrrell-Cosworth 009	

April 29, SPANISH GRAND PRIX, Jarama

1	Patrick Depailler	Ligier-Cosworth JS11	(95.97mph)
2	Carlos Reutemann	Lotus-Cosworth 79	
3	Mario Andretti	Lotus-Cosworth 80	
4	Jody Scheckter	Ferrari 312T4	
5	J-P Jarier	Tyrrell-Cosworth 009	
6	Didier Pironi	Tyrrell-Cosworth 009	

May 13, BELGIAN GRAND PRIX, Zolder

1	Jody Scheckter	Ferrari 312T4	(111.24mph)
2	Jacques Laffite	Ligier-Cosworth JS11	
3	Didier Pironi	Tyrrell-Cosworth 009	
4	Carlos Reutemann	Lotus-Cosworth 79	
5	Riccardo Patrese	Arrows-Cosworth A1	
6	John Watson	McLaren-Cosworth M28	

May 27, MONACO GRAND PRIX, Monte Carlo
1 Jody Scheckter   Ferrari 312T4   (81.34mph)
2 Clay Regazzoni   Williams-Cosworth FW07
3 Carlos Reutemann   Lotus-Cosworth 79
4 John Watson   McLaren-Cosworth M28
5 Patrick Depailler   Ligier-Cosworth JS11
6 Riccardo Patrese   Arrows-Cosworth A1

July 1, FRENCH GRAND PRIX, Dijon-Prenois
1 J-P Jabouille   Renault RS10 turbo   (118.88mph)
2 Gilles Villeneuve   Ferrari 312T4
3 René Arnoux   Renault RS10 turbo
4 Alan Jones   Williams-Cosworth FW07
5 J-P Jarier   Tyrrell-Cosworth 009
6 Clay Regazzoni   Williams-Cosworth FW07

July 14, BRITISH GRAND PRIX, Silverstone
1 Clay Regazzoni   Williams-Cosworth FW07   (138.80mph)
2 René Arnoux   Renault RS10 turbo
3 J-P Jarier   Tyrrell-Cosworth 009
4 John Watson   McLaren-Cosworth M29
5 Jody Scheckter   Ferrari 312T4
6 Jacky Ickx   Ligier-Cosworth JS11

July 29, GERMAN GRAND PRIX, Hockenheim
1 Alan Jones   Williams-Cosworth FW07   (134.27mph)
2 Clay Regazzoni   Williams-Cosworth FW07
3 Jacques Laffite   Ligier-Cosworth JS11
4 Jody Scheckter   Ferrari 312T4
5 John Watson   McLaren-Cosworth M29
6 Jochen Mass   Arrows-Cosworth A1

August 12, AUSTRIAN GRAND PRIX, Osterreichring
1 Alan Jones   Williams-Cosworth FW07   (136.52mph)
2 Gilles Villeneuve   Ferrari 312T4
3 Jacques Laffite   Ligier-Cosworth JS11
4 Jody Scheckter   Ferrari 312T4
5 Clay Regazzoni   Williams-Cosworth FW07
6 René Arnoux   Renault TS10 turbo

August 26, DUTCH GRAND PRIX, Zandvoort
1 Alan Jones   Williams-Cosworth FW07   (116.62mph)
2 Jody Scheckter   Ferrari 312T4
3 Jacques Laffite   Ligier-Cosworth JS11
4 Nelson Piquet   Brabham-Alfa Romeo BT48
5 Jacky Ickx   Ligier-Cosworth JS11
6 Jochen Mass   Arrows-Cosworth A2

September 9, ITALIAN GRAND PRIX, Monza
1 Jody Scheckter   Ferrari 312T4   (131.85mph)
2 Gilles Villeneuve   Ferrari 312T4
3 Clay Regazzoni   Williams-Cosworth FW07
4 Niki Lauda   Brabham-Alfa Romeo BT48
5 Mario Andretti   Lotus-Cosworth 79
6 J-P Jarier   Tyrrell-Cosworth 009

September 30, CANADIAN GRAND PRIX, Montreal

1	Alan Jones	Williams-Cosworth FW07	(105.96mph)
2	Gilles Villeneuve	Ferrari 312T4	
3	Clay Regazzoni	Williams-Cosworth FW07	
4	Jody Scheckter	Ferrari 312T4	
5	Didier Pironi	Tyrrell-Cosworth 009	
6	John Watson	McLaren-Cosworth M28	

October 7, UNITED STATES GRAND PRIX, Watkins Glen

1	Gilles Villeneuve	Ferrari 312T3	(106.46mph)
2	René Arnoux	Renault RS10 turbo	
3	Didier Pironi	Tyrrell-Cosworth 009	
4	Elio de Angelis	Shadow-Cosworth DN9	
5	Hans Stuck	ATS-Cosworth D3	
6	John Watson	McLaren-Cosworth M29	

DRIVERS' WORLD CHAMPIONSHIP

Posn	Driver	Points
1	Jody Scheckter	51
2	Gilles Villeneuve	47
3	Alan Jones	40
4	Jacques Laffite	36
5	Clay Regazzoni	29
6	Carlos Reutemann	20
	Patrick Depailler	
8	René Arnoux	17
9	John Watson	15
10	Mario Andretti	14
	Jean-Pierre Jarier	
	Didier Pironi	
13	Jean-Pierre Jabouille	9
14	Niki Lauda	4
15	Elio de Angelis	3
	Jacky Ickx	
	Jochen Mass	
	Nelson Piquet	
19	Riccardo Patrese	2
	Hans Stuck	
21	Emerson Fittipaldi	1

CONSTRUCTORS' CHAMPIONSHIP

Posn	Constructor	Points
1	Ferrari	113
2	Williams	75
3	Ligier	61
4	Lotus	39
5	Tyrrell	28
6	Renault	26
7	McLaren	15
8	Brabham	7
9	Arrows	5
10	Shadow	3
11	ATS	2
12	Fittipaldi	1

1980

Alan Jones's failure to win the 1979 World Championship was due at least in part to the late arrival on the scene of the Williams FW07. Thus, when the 1980 season opened in Buenos Aires on 13 January, the Argentine Grand Prix, for Jones and his entrants, was largely a question of sustaining the momentum of the previous year, a challenge they rose to with admirable effect. The superb Patrick Head-designed Williams chassis had now been modified to 'B' specification – producing even more aerodynamic downforce than before – allowing the rugged Australian to qualify comfortably on pole position, ahead of 1979 pacesetter Jacques Laffite's Ligier.

Gone from the Williams team, however, was Clay Regazzoni. The genial, easy-going Swiss who had scored that memorable maiden victory for the team at Silverstone the previous summer, was not really in the same class as Jones. With the Williams star now very much in the ascendant, it was decided to sign on another front-line driver to maximise the team's winning potential. The answer to this challenge came in the form of Carlos Reutemann.

This complex Argentinian gentleman was never to realise his full potential behind the wheel of a Grand Prix car and, to this day, he remains one of the most remarkable conundrums of his time. Moody, perfectionist, yet sometimes unpredictable and capable of being de-motivated by outside influences, fundamentally, Carlos was blessed with an enormous talent.

Propelled into Formula 1 in the early 1970s on the crest of the same South American wave that produced Emerson and Wilson Fittipaldi, and the late Carlos Pace, Reutemann had been the mainstay of the Brabham team's efforts from 1972 to mid-1976. Then he fell out with Bernie Ecclestone and bought his way out of his contract in the middle of the season, signing up with Ferrari the following year.

In 1977 he joined Niki Lauda in the Maranello line-up and, for some reason I've never fully understood, the normally pragmatic Austrian driver took against him in a big way. I can only think that Niki regarded Reutemann as symbolic of the forces within Ferrari who considered him to be washed up and finished after his fiery accident in the German Grand Prix the previous summer. When asked whether he regarded Reutemann as a team-mate or a rival, Niki once replied, devastatingly, 'neither...'

Reutemann only won a single race for Ferrari in 1977, but his talent blossomed the following year after Niki moved to Brabham. Carlos won four Grands Prix and at one point seemed as though he might have a tilt at the World Championship. Always something of a loner, in 1979 he switched to Lotus, running alongside Mario Andretti. But he caught the Lotus 79 a year too late and no success came his way. He then signed a two-year contract with Williams for 1980 and 1981.

Coming on to Jones's patch was never going to be easy. Alan, bright, tough and intelligent, represented the established focal point of the Williams team's efforts. And while Regazzoni had been happy to bowl merrily along, playing second fiddle,

By the start of 1980, Team Lotus had opted for a conventional machine while Chapman developed the 'twin-chassis' concept off-stage. This is new boy Elio de Angelis with the Lotus type 81 at Long Beach, California.

Reutemann was clearly not out of the same mould. A switch to Williams, a shot at the wheel of the FW07B, represented Reutemann's best chance of winning the World Championship. But to realise that personal ambition he would have to overcome Jones's simply towering self-confidence, a task he never quite managed.

It is not really accurate to say that Jones went on to the defensive, as such. He simply got his head down and asserted his authority by being faster than Reutemann. Four years earlier, if you'd have suggested Jones was a World Championship contender, chances are you'd have been laughed out of court. Even in 1977, when he hauled the overweight Shadow DN8 to a fortuitous victory in the Austrian Grand Prix, few people regarded him as anything more than a determined journeyman. But now he had the right car beneath him. . .

In Buenos Aires, Jones started as he meant to continue. In sweltering temperatures, and with the track surface crumbling like a meringue, he seized the lead at the start and began pulling commandingly clear of his pursuers. On Lap 17 it seemed as though he might be in trouble, diving into the pits to have a way-ward plastic bag removed from his radiator intakes. He resumed fourth, storming through to take the lead again by Lap 30. He won by 23sec from Nelson Piquet's Brabham with Keke Rosberg's Fittipaldi a dogged third. Reutemann's FW07B overheated and blew its engine. The Renault turbos were disappointingly midfield contenders on this occasion, both Arnoux and Jabouille posted as early retirements once the race began.

Elsewhere in the field, there had been some interesting driver changes. With Lauda now retired, Nelson Piquet had found himself promoted to the status of Brabham team leader, a role which the young Brazilian would assume with considerable gusto and aplomb. Patrick Depailler, now winning an excruciatingly painful recovery to physical fitness following that hang-gliding accident the previous summer, had joined Bruno Giacomelli in the works Alfa Romeo line-up. His position at Ligier, filled temporarily by fading Formula 1 star Jacky Ickx in the second half of 1979, was now taken by the ice-cold, ruthlessly determined Didier Pironi.

Reutemann's berth at Lotus was now filled by 20-year-old Elio de Angelis, partnering Mario Andretti, while Ferrari still had Scheckter and Villeneuve on hand. Jody's car now carried the prestigious number 1, traditionally allocated to the reigning World Champion.

Sadly, Maranello's uprated version of the 1979 car proved dramatically uncompetitive. Retaining the flat-12 engine with modified cylinder heads, the challenge of producing a really worthwhile ground-effect chassis now overwhelmed the Italian team. True, the 312T5 was quicker than its immediate predecessor, but the opposition had registered an even bigger improvement. Villeneuve briefly ran second at Buenos Aires before a front suspension breakage sent him spearing into the catch fencing at high speed. He was lucky to walk away unharmed.

A fortnight later, the Brazilian Grand Prix took place at Sao Paulo's spectacular Interlagos circuit, a bumpy 4.89 mile track situated within the sprawling outer suburbs of this huge industrial city. At one point, concern amongst the drivers about the deteriorating state of the track surface made it look as though the race might be in jeopardy at one point. Many influential members of the Grand Prix Drivers' Association wanted to boycott the event, but when it came to a vote on the subject the necessary 60 per cent majority in favour of such a move could not be reached.

This second round of the World Championship was to provide everybody with a stunning reminder of the potential threat posed by the Renault turbo. Jean-Pierre Jabouille may not go down in Grand Prix history as a great racer, but his talents as a test and development driver undoubtedly continued to play an indispensable role in the early success of the Renault Formula 1 team. Despite that success in the French Grand Prix the previous summer, throughout much of the 1979 season he'd only bumped along with the team's technical director François Castaing, the man who had originally designed the French V6 engine in its 2 litre guise at the start of the decade. For 1980, Castaing had moved to another division within the company and Jabouille now found himself working with Bernard Dudot and Michel Tetu. The three men got on splendidly, and it showed.

With Goodyear deciding not to supply its contracted teams with super-sticky qualifying tyres – which, in its view, proved nothing – Michelin, for the time being at least, continued to provide such short-life rubber for Renault and Ferrari. It helped Jabouille to squeeze into pole position at Interlagos, a mere 0.2sec faster than Pironi's Ligier, and although Villeneuve exploded through from the second row at the start to lead the opening lap, Renault's team leader moved confidently ahead on the second lap. Pironi and Laffite chased hard for Ligier, but by Lap 14 it was René Arnoux who had moved into second place, making it a Renault 1-2 for the time being.

However, unbeknown even to his pit crew in these days before radio communication between car and engineers, Jabouille had been keeping his fingers firmly crossed ever since the fourth lap when he had noticed his engine's turbo boost pressure begin to fluctuate. This was symptomatic of imminent turbo failure and his fears were duly confirmed with twenty-four of the race's forty laps completed. The turbo failed completely, his boost pressure all but died and he coasted into the pits for good.

This failure left Arnoux in command, but the other Renault was now coming under increasing pressure from Elio de Angelis. The new Lotus recruit was driving a tremendous race on only his second outing for Colin Chapman's team, more than making up for the disappointment occasioned by Andretti's second lap spin into retirement. But the Lotus 81's Goodyear tyres were well worn as the race moved into its closing stages, so Elio had to settle for second place, just over 20sec adrift. Had the other Renault wilted, then de Angelis stood to emerge the youngest ever Grand Prix winner...

Jones trailed home a disappointing third, one of the few days on which Frank Williams mildly admonished him for driving less than his best. So much fuel was pumped out of the FW07B once the race was over that Jones used to refer to that outing as

Man of the future. On his Grand Prix debut in the 1980 Argentine Grand Prix at Buenos Aires, a youthful Alain Prost heads his McLaren M29 towards sixth place and the first of many World Championship points.

The turbo stakes were raised when Ferrari entered the game with the fast, but crudely engineered 126CK, which was seen briefly in practice for the 1980 Italian Grand Prix at Imola in the hands of Gilles Villeneuve.

'my Mobil economy run' whenever the subject was raised. Reutemann's second outing with Williams was even more dispiriting than his first; his car broke a driveshaft on the second lap.

Further back down the field, a young Frenchman by the name of Alain Prost was carving something of a niche for himself. Winner of the 1979 Monaco Formula 3 classic, Prost had been recruited to partner John Watson in the McLaren line-up after a test session at Paul Ricard which had seen managing director Teddy Mayer almost sprinting for his briefcase to grab a draft contract for the new lad to sign. At Buenos Aires he had qualified the M29 an amazing twelfth, finishing sixth to take a Championship point on his maiden outing. At Rio, he qualified thirteenth and finished fifth. By contrast, Watson qualified seventeenth and twenty-third respectively, failing to finish in Argentina and trailing home eleventh at Interlagos.

By the time the Grand Prix circus re-convened to contest the third round of the Championship, at Kyalami, on 1 March, the seeds of political turmoil had been sown off-stage. Ever since November 1979, increasing concern had been apparent about the dramatic increase in lap speeds produced by the latest breed of sliding skirt ground-effect car. More to the point, fear that the sudden loss of aerodynamic downforce produced when one of these skirts either stuck up, or broke, was focusing increasing attention on the desirability of ground effect in general. Yet, from the way in which FISA conducted itself over the next few months, it seemed as though they believed there was a way of 'un-inventing' ground effect, a palpably absurd stance to take.

On 13 December 1979, FISA took the decision to initiate a skirt ban in both Formula 2 and 3. Goodyear's own decision to withdraw qualifying rubber was followed, on 2 February 1980, by a FISA ruling to ban qualifying rubber officially. Then, on 22 February, FISA dropped a bombshell when Balestre announced that, as from 1 January 1981, skirts would be banned completely from Formula 1. Whilst this was a move which received a degree of approval from the drivers, the predominantly British, FOCA-aligned teams saw this as an attack on their engineering initiative, angled to favour Renault, Ferrari and Alfa Romeo – the 'grandees', as they were known.

To understand the passion which drove this dispute is to understand how two distinct groups were beginning to develop in Formula 1. The FOCA hardliners were predominantly the specialist builders, sometimes disparagingly referred to as the 'kit car constructors'. This group represented the majority of Grand Prix car constructors who used off-the-shelf Cosworth V8 engines and relied for any performance advantage on the initiative and ingenuity of their chassis designers. Renault, Ferrari and Alfa Romeo represented the 'grandees', major car companies who obviously had interest and influence which extended far beyond the spectrum of Formula 1. And FOCA frankly concluded that Balestre was steering FISA along a course calculated to favour the latter.

The turbo installation was not particularly well packaged behind the huge fuel cell necessary to satisfy its thirst over a race distance, but it would not be long before many rivals would become well acquainted with the details of its rear suspension.

Beneath the surface, however, there was a secondary consideration. FOCA was intent on fighting with every ounce of its corporate breath to defend its financial stake in the Grand Prix game. It was not going to be flattened by FISA without a fight.

Discussion and debate, designed to defuse the simmering off-track tensions, were to take place throughout the season. Meanwhile, Arnoux scored another commanding victory in the South African Grand Prix, again at Jabouille's expense, the Renault team leader this time retiring with a deflated front tyre whilst holding first place.

Second and third in South Africa were the Ligiers of Laffite and Pironi, with Reutemann finally scoring his first points of the year with a fourth place finish for Williams. Jones retired with a gearbox oil leak while running fourth just before half distance. Prost didn't take part. His McLaren had suffered a suspension breakage in qualifying which pitched him into the wall, fracturing his left wrist. This injury would cause him to miss the ensuing Long Beach Grand Prix in California, where Englishman Stephen South deputised for him alongside Watson.

The 1980 Long Beach race lingers in the memory for two reasons. Firstly, it marked the occasion of Nelson Piquet's first Grand Prix victory. The Brazilian started from pole position in the compact Gordon Murray-designed Brabham BT49 and led throughout, never to be challenged all the way to the chequered flag. Sadly, it was also to be the last Grand Prix outing for Clay Regazzoni.

Having enjoyed his time with Williams, Clay now found himself obliged to take a step down the ladder of Formula 1 fortune when his contract with Frank's team was not renewed at the end of 1979. He signed up with Morris Nunn's tiny Ensign team, reviving a previous association. He had driven for Ensign in 1977 after being turned out of Ferrari, and got on well with Nunn and his crew. Rejoining them was no great drama for the mild-mannered Clay. 'You misunderstand why I race in Formula 1,' he once replied to an inquiring journalist. 'I don't always have to be a potential winner. Just driving in Formula 1, being part of the scene, is enough for me. . .'

Although only qualifying on the back row of the grid, Clay plugged on doggedly at Long Beach and, with fifty of the race's eighty laps complete, he was up to fourth place, seemingly set to earn Ensign a healthy dollop of Championship points. Tragically, approaching the right-hand hairpin at the end of Shoreline Drive, the Ensign's brake pedal broke and Clay went careering straight on down the escape road, cannoning into Ricardo Zunino's Brabham which had been parked there ever since its first lap retirement after a minor collision.

Regazzoni was fortunate to escape with his life, but he would be paralysed from the waist down and thereafter confined to a wheelchair. The accident provoked one of those spontaneous reactions from FISA which would become so characteristic of Balestre in the years that followed. Whilst the FISA president was seen as taking a positive line when he announced that an investigation into driver safety in general would be initiated, he badly compromised himself by suggesting that certain designers were compromising constructional safety in the interests of enhanced car performance.

He linked these comments specifically with the Regazzoni accident and the incidents which had befallen Prost and the Swiss driver Marc Surer, who broke both his ankles when his ATS crashed in practice at Kyalami. McLaren predictably went on to the defensive, accusing Balestre of making 'ill-considered and

Gilles Villeneuve in practice at Imola 1980.

possibly libellous' statements in connection with Prost's shunt. The whole episode was eventually smoothed over, but it had served merely to fuel the growing unease between the constructors and those entrusted with the control of the sport.

After Long Beach, Arnoux and Piquet shared the Drivers' Championship points lead just as Renault and Brabham were equal in the battle for Constructors' points. Neither Renault had scored any points at Long Beach, but Arnoux scraped home a lapped fourth in the Belgian Grand Prix at Zolder to open out a two point advantage. By this stage Alan Jones had ousted Piquet from second place by virtue of a splendid second place at Zolder, chasing winner Didier Pironi's Ligier for all he was worth.

Renault's continuing level of mechanical unreliability prevented either Jabouille or Arnoux from a scoring finish at Monaco, a race which was inherited by Reutemann after Jones and Pironi, who raced ahead, had battled for the lead until both retired. Jones suffered a differential failure while Pironi lost control and glanced a guard rail as he struggled to hold the Ligier in gear.

Towards the end of the race a rain shower coated the track with a treacherous, glistening veneer, but Reutemann kept command to take his first victory at the wheel of a Williams. After the race there was more chaos as the second-place Laffite berated Balestre for not having stopped the race, while Arnoux was apoplectic with rage at the way in which Patrese's Arrows had bundled his Renault off the track during their personal battle over a lowly tenth place.

At Monaco, a sequence of events occurred which seemed trivial when regarded in isolation. At the start of the season it had been agreed that a mandatory drivers' briefing would take place at every race, but at Zolder and Monaco, a handful of drivers were told not to attend, being advised that FOCA would take care of their penalties.

Inevitably, the drivers were fined and, when the money was not forthcoming, Balestre indicated that unless those drivers actually paid their fines, their licences would be suspended prior to the the Spanish Grand Prix at Jarama on 1 June. Having effectively manipulated their way into a major confrontation with the sport's governing body, the FOCA brigade now decided this was the issue on which to stand and fight. They announced that, unless the fines were quashed, the FOCA teams would not take part in the Spanish race.

What happened next may have seemed valid enough at the time, but, with the benefit of an historical perspective, it amounted to an abuse of power and influence, both by FISA and FOCA. It really did not seem to matter one iota that the Spanish organisers' race was being ruined.

Jones and Williams: a Partnership that Clicked

Frank Williams probably admired Alan Jones because, deep down, he too was a racer. The man who created one of Britain's most successful Formula I teams ever, tried his hand at Formula 3 during the mid-1960s. He wasn't hopeless, but friends agree that description comes pretty close. Wisely, he channelled that burning competitive instinct into running a team.

Alan Jones was like Frank in more ways than one might imagine. His commitment to his chosen profession was absolutely the equal of Frank's and the fact that they had both encountered considerable hardship as they clawed their way to the top had hardened the cutting edge of their resolve. Moreover, he formed a fine working relationship with Patrick Head, giving the Williams designer enough information about a car's behaviour without embroidering it with extraneous comments. Alan lucidly described how the chassis was behaving, tossing the ball firmly into Patrick's court to come up with any technical solutions that may have been needed.

Jones's determination was phenomenal. He might not have always been the best qualifier – though often he was with the superb Williams FW07 – but he would give every race his best shot with considerable ferocity. Even off-duty, a tennis game would assume the same degree of intense importance as any Grand Prix. In or out of a car, Alan had to be a winner.

His relationship with the team personnel reflected a rare degree of mutual respect flavoured with genuine friendship. It wasn't the sort of respect mechanics had for Lauda or Senna, it ran deeper than that. Many of the men who worked on the Williams team in 1979 and 1980 had come up the hard way – all the way – with Frank. That sort of experience produced a special kind of bond, of which Alan Jones was an inextricable part.

There followed a complex dispute whereby the organising club, whose sporting powers had been delegated to the Spanish Automobile Federation, sought to revoke that delegation and reassume those sporting powers. FISA regarded this as a totally invalid move, but withdrew their officials from the meeting when the Spanish club announced that the race would not be administered under FISA regulations. FOCA fully supported – and indeed helped initiate – this course of action, optimistically relying on the prospect that the FIA would back the Spanish club's move rather than supporting FISA. That was a predictably forlorn hope. Ludicrous, even.

Ferrari, Renault and Alfa Romeo abstained from participating in what was demonstrably an illegal race. They really had no choice in the matter of course, for taking part in an event which did not have the blessing of the sport's official governing body would almost certainly have compromised their activities in other areas of the sport. Not for the first time was Grand Prix racing holding itself up to ridicule in the full glare of the public spotlight.

The race itself was well worth waiting for, Championship status or not. As one of the prime FOCA runners, the Williams team had become suffused with an increasing amount of gung-ho patriotism which some pit lane regulars found a trifle tiresome. Beating the stuffing out of anything French became something of

Patrick Depailler preparing for action in his Alfa V12, early during the 1980 season. Having fought back to fitness following a hang-gliding accident the previous summer, this popular Frenchman died in a testing accident at Hockenheim just prior to the German Grand Prix.

a symbolic preoccupation for Frank, the team and, particularly, Alan Jones. And if there were no Renaults around, a Ligier would do instead.

Just before the start, Jones's Williams showed signs of overheating, so the Australian went to the line fingers firmly crossed. Reutemann rocketed into an immediate lead, pursued by Jones only until he missed a gear change and dropped back to sixth, allowing Laffite to take up the chase in one of those dreaded Ligiers.

Unfortunately Jacques managed to take both himself and Reutemann off when his out-of-control Ligier T-boned the Argentinian after breaking a steering arm a few yards earlier against Spanish tailender Emilio de Villota who was, ironically enough, himself driving an ex-works Williams fielded by a private team. But Jones nursed his overheating FW07B to a fine victory, although his efforts attracted no Championship points at the end

of the day. At the end of the month he produced a repeat performance to tuck up both Ligier and Renault on home ground, winning the French Grand Prix at Paul Ricard in stupendous style. That hoisted him to the head of the Championship points table for the first time since Rio.

Renault was by now a spent force as far as challenging for the World Championship was concerned, a spate of valve breakages throughout the summer helping to fritter away the team's early advantage. But at least the French team could console itself that it was doing better than Ferrari whose 3 litre flat-12 machine was busy going nowhere, even in the hands of the inspired Gilles Villeneuve. Mid-season, after the British Grand Prix at Brands Hatch, Jody Scheckter announced that he would be retiring from the cockpit at the end of the season. It was a decision that had been in the back of his mind for some time since winning the 1979 Championship, but the pathetic performance of the T5 made his decision irrevocable.

In that break between the Spanish and French Grands Prix, Ferrari took the opportunity to signal their impending arrival on to the turbo scene as the second constructor to climb aboard the forced induction bandwagon. It had become increasingly clear to Maranello that the Ferrari racing department was working in an ever-tightening technical straitjacket, not only with regard to the problems involved in packaging the 3 litre flat-12 within an effective ground-effect chassis, but in respect of the potential which could feasibly be extracted from a naturally-aspirated 3 litre, 12 cylinder engine.

With approximately 525bhp regarded as the most that a 3 litre could deliver, the first generation turbo brigade was aiming for around 650bhp. That seemed a breathtaking power output at the start of the decade, yet within six years the ever accelerating pace of development would see some manufacturers approaching twice that figure.

Ferrari opted for a wide, 120 degree four-cam V6 with a bore and stroke of 81 x 48.4mm producing a total capacity of 1496.43cc. Installed in a chassis which was little more than a travelling test bed, the new turbo Ferrari was designated 126C (Competizione) and featured Maranello's customary multi-tubular spaceframe, overlaid with stressed alloy panelling — a method of construction increasingly regarded as unsophisticated and primitive by the standards of the day.

The wide-angle V6 had its inlet camshafts on the outside of the vee, exhaust on the inside, allowing very short pipes from each bank to duct into the turbines and compressors mounted behind the larger, and very high, fuel cell. Villeneuve, typically, could hardly wait to see the new Ferrari which appeared in public at

Imola on Saturday, 13 September, during second qualifying for the Italian Grand Prix. Italy's prestige motor race was this year forsaking its traditional home at Monza, as a trailer for establishing a San Marino Grand Prix at that circuit in years to come.

Interestingly, even though the chassis was primitive in the extreme, Villeneuve managed a lap time 0.6sec faster than in the 312T5 he would race – and crash – in the following day's race. But the Ferrari turbo's best time was still 1.6sec slower than René Arnoux's pole position best in the Renault RE25. Even at this early stage, the signs were promising.

Over the ensuing winter, Ferrari pursued two parallel engine development programmes. One was a relatively conventional exhaust-driven forced-induction system, using turbochargers manufactured by Kuhlne, Kopp and Kausch, a specialist concern based in the German town of Eperspach. The alternative system was the 'Comprex' pressure wave supercharging concept developed by Brown-Boveri, the Swiss corporation whose experience with developing gas turbine power units for marine and railway applications stretched back over four decades.

The Comprex system involved a direct drive supercharger, belt-driven from the rear of a camshaft, working in conjunction with the exhaust gases providing pressure waves to compress the incoming air as it entered the inlet manifold. It had the advantages of instant throttle response – and made a simply glorious noise – but there were installation problems for the supercharger sat high in the vee between the two banks of Ferrari cylinders, upsetting the weight distribution of the car and interfering with the, admittedly rather crude, aerodynamics. Despite a great deal of cooperation from Brown-Boveri, with whom Ferrari signed a contract guaranteeing the exclusive use of the Comprex system for racing purposes through until the end of 1981, Maranello eventually concluded that the KKK turbocharged system was the route to pursue.

Meanwhile, back on the World Championship trail, the Grand Prix fraternity was to be touched by disaster shortly before the German Grand Prix. Testing his Alfa Romeo at Hockenheim in preparation for that event, Patrick Depailler fell victim to a major chassis breakage at high speed. The French driver was killed instantly when his machine charged the barrier at the very fast Ostkurve. What made the tragedy ironic and totally unforgivable was the fact that the catch fencing, a feature of most contemporary race tracks supposedly installed to offer competitors added protection, was rolled up and stowed behind the guard rail at the time of the accident. It had not been erected yet. By the time practice for the race got underway, it had. Cruelly, the stable door had been closed too late...

Alan Jones came to Germany with another blistering victory, this time in the British Grand Prix at Brands Hatch, under his belt. But while the Australian qualified his Williams on pole position at Hockenheim, it was Jabouille's Renault which led from the start until just beyond half distance when an easy victory slipped through the French team's fingers yet again, this time due to a valve spring breakage. Arnoux was sidelined from third place by an identical problem occurring within a lap of his team-mate's demise, the legacy of sustained revving at 10,200rpm, so Jones was apparently presented with victory on a plate.

Unfortunately, a late race puncture intervened to send the Australian scuttling into the pit lane, so Jacques Laffite emerged a lucky winner for Ligier, only taking the lead with five laps to go. Reutemann and Jones finished second and third for Williams, so the British team was almost home and dry in the Constructors' Championship battle.

The Hockenheim paddock at Grand Prix time inevitably fills up with a large contingent from the German motor industry, so if BMW personnel were even thicker on the ground than usual at the 1980 race, the uninformed observer could be forgiven for not raising an eyebrow. After all, throughout 1979 and 1980 they supported the M1 Procar series, in which a field of their delectable central-engined coupes provided the means for a handful of Formula 1 drivers to do battle with some of their less celebrated rivals during the course of European Grand Prix weekends.

However, there was a lot more to it than that. The BMW board had finally decided it would sanction the manufacture of a Formula 1 engine. Having done that, it cast around for a partner to furnish the necessary chassis as the Munich-based car company had absolutely no intention of building the complete car.

In fact, BMW had been considering such a project for a couple of years. Towards the end of 1979, with Niki Lauda signalling that he had had his fill of grappling with Alfa Romeo engines, they had attempted to put together a prestige package with McLaren, revolving round the Austrian twice World Champion. McLaren's American operation, based at Livonia, near Detroit, had been fielding a team of 2.1 litre turbocharged saloons in the US domestic IMSA championship, so the link was firmly established. So a deal was hatched up whereby Lauda would drive a Marlboro-backed McLaren-BMW turbo.

The entire project had been agreed in principle, only requiring the green light from BMW's board. But BMW's competitions manager, Jochen Neerpasch, misjudged the mood in senior management circles. Major car manufacturers can be notoriously

Didier Pironi, seen here during testing at Paul Ricard, took Depailler's place at Ligier in 1980. The cool, calculating Frenchman would beat Jones to victory in the Belgian Grand Prix.

Max Mosley: Seeking the Solution to Formula 1's Problems

On the night prior to the 1980 Spanish Grand Prix, Max Mosley spent much of the evening drafting FOCA's side of the argument concerning the furore with FISA over the race's legitimacy. He wasn't satisfied so, at four o'clock on race morning, he was up again re-writing the draft. He was the Costas Gratsos to Ecclestone's Aristotle Onassis, the indispensable right-hand, a legal eagle whose mental dexterity help FOCA's cause stay afloat for longer than it might have done without him.

Although Mosley was no longer involved with a specific team like Ecclestone, he had amassed plenty of valuable experience as one of the founder directors of March Engineering. But he relinquished that role at the end of 1977, preferring to concentrate on legal consultancy work, an increasing amount of which involved the business of FOCA.

The youngest son of British fascist leader Sir Oswald Mosley, Max studied law at Oxford before being called to the bar in 1963. He specialised in the complex area of patent law before becoming seduced by the world of motor racing. Conveniently, the increasing political nature of front-line Formula 1 provided a tailor-made outlet for his talents.

Max's eloquence whilst arguing the toss with FISA inevitably earned him the soubriquet 'Silver Tongue'. But for all that saturnine gloss, to this day he passionately believes in the merits of FOCA's stand against FISA in the early 1980s.

'FISA may have appeared to have the force of legality behind them as the sport's rulers,' he reflects, 'but the way they framed the regulations left the FOCA teams no choice but to fight. Whatever others might think, they were – and still are – the backbone of the Formula 1 business. They had to fight and they had to present a front of solidarity.

'As Bernie was fond of saying at the time, "If we don't all hang together, we'll all hang separately..."'

jumpy when it comes to sanctioning expenditure on ambitious motor racing programmes, regarding them with understandable caution as a double-edged sword.

Where the directors needed romancing into the idea, where some diplomatic massaging would have reaped dividends, Neerpasch presented them with what amounted to a *fait accompli*. At the last minute, they shied away. BMW insiders have since told me that the board of directors really wanted to sanction the project, yet they felt that Neerpasch could not get away with backing them into a corner. They rejected the proposal.

In the wake of this rejection, Neerpasch began making alternative plans, as his assistant, Dieter Stappert, increasingly became aware. Eventually, Neerpasch confided that he had accepted an offer to join the Talbot combine in order to establish a new competitions department. What he failed to tell Stappert, who opted to stay on as his successor at BMW, was that part of the deal involved the German company developing their stillborn Formula 1 engine on behalf of Talbot.

When this information was imparted to Stappert, he remonstrated energetically with the BMW directors, pointing out that such a move was nothing short of outrageous. Happily, they did not take such a trenchant line with him as they had earlier done with Neerpasch. A few weeks of high-pressure negotiations followed and, on 24 April 1980, BMW finally made public the decision that Formula 1 was on their agenda.

BMW was not new to motor racing by any stretch of the imagination. Countless victories in saloon car races throughout the world, as well as a firm record of achievement in Formula 2 throughout the 1970s lay behind them. Under the technical stewardship of the beaming Paul Rosche, since 1975 general manager of BMW Motorsport and one of the company's most talented racing engineers for many years before that, the Formula 1 project got underway.

But Formula 1 was not merely a question of demonstrating BMW's technical excellence. From a promotional standpoint, it was of crucial importance that the Grand Prix power unit should be based on a production car engine.

With enormous accumulated experience on their wide range of 4 cylinder engines, there was never any real doubt that BMW's Formula 1 challenge would be a 4 cylinder turbo. With a bore and stroke of 89.2 x 60mm, the 1499cc BMW started out based round unmodified, although lightened, production car blocks.

Opposition for Jones. Carlos Reutemann testing the Williams FW07B, wearing Jones's race number 27, after switching from Team Lotus at the end of 1979.

The company's engineers discovered that high mileage blocks performed best, the ageing reducing the stresses within the metal.

On a 6.7:1 compression ratio, the BMW M12/13 unit (the thirteenth variation based round the M12 4 cylinder engine which harked back to the mid-1960s) initially developed 557bhp at 9,500rpm using a single KKK turbocharger. But the engine would not be seen in public action until the summer of 1981 (when Nelson Piquet briefly used it during qualifying for the British Grand Prix at Silverstone) and would not race until the 1982 South African Grand Prix.

Returning to the summer of 1980, Piquet found himself in the position of making a late bid for the World Championship. After Hockenheim, the Championship battle moved to Austria where Jabouille notched up Renault's third victory of the season, albeit by less than a second from Jones's Williams.

Despite Jabouille's success, Renault emerged from the Austrian race in a dejected mood, for René Arnoux went into the tenth round of the Championship battle anxious to sustain an outside chance of becoming the first turbo-powered World Champion. Joint fifth in the points table, he needed a win to succour his prospects. He started from pole position, more than a second faster than his team-mate, the French turbo's performance advantage enhanced by the 2,000ft altitude of this superb 3.69 mile circuit in the heart of the Styrian countryside.

Following those Hockenheim failures, the Renault engines had been fitted with stiffer valve springs and the team was in a confident mood, calculating that Osterreichring would involve consistent revving at 10,600rpm, 400rpm in excess of the 'danger zone' identified during the German race. But although Arnoux qualified over a second faster than his team-mate, only more disappointment awaited him come the race.

It was absolutely characteristic of the mood prevailing at the time, that any upsurge in turbo performance was greeted with disparaging cries of 'screwdriver tuning' and 'special tyres' from the rival normally-aspirated brigade. So it proved at Osterreichring, but it was Renault's race strategy which let them down in the race.

Rightly identifying Jones's Williams as potentially the most dangerous opposition, the French team opted to run Jabouille's car on softer race tyres. Jean-Pierre, whose Championship hopes were by this stage non-existent, was to be used in the role of a hare, hopefully drawing Jones into a high speed battle from the outset. Arnoux, running harder tyres, would aim to last the distance with no trouble. Either way, both Renaults went to the startline brimful of fuel for this event which, at 199.368 miles, was right on the outside edge of the 200 mile maximum permissible for World Championship Grands Prix.

Jones muscled through from the second row of the grid to lead for the first couple of laps – but then Arnoux went whistling by the Williams, followed, a lap later, by Jabouille. But the harder of the two Michelin race compounds would not, ironically, stand the pace. At the end of Lap 21, Arnoux came trailing into the pits for fresh rubber. He resumed tenth, came storming back to seventh by Lap 30, then found himself obliged to change tyres yet again.

This drama left Jabouille with the task of conserving his softer tyres as best he could, a task which he judged superbly to beat Jones by a minuscule margin. But with Arnoux now out of the Championship running, the issue as to who took the title boiled down to a two-horse race between Jones and Piquet.

As a footnote to the 1980 Austrian Grand Prix, the man who lined up last on the starting grid should not be overlooked without a mention. In the final flickering moments of qualifying, young Nigel Mansell squeezed Team Lotus's third type 81 into the race. Looking back, it was a momentous turning point in the career of the young Midlander who had been recruited the previous autumn as Team Lotus's official test driver. Such a role was widely predicted as a passport to oblivion, and if Mansell had failed to make the cut in Austria it is possible that the ruthless Chapman would have ticked him off his list for good.

Tyre problems undermined his efforts, but a delighted Jabouille survived to beat Alan Jones to the chequered flag.

By the summer of 1980, only Renault's unreliability stood between the French team and consistent success. This shot of Arnoux leading Jabouille, two laps into the Austrian Grand Prix, records René's last chance to keep in play for the Championship.

Mansell failed to finish, gamely going to the line with fuel leaking into the cockpit even before the start. In mounting discomfort he flogged round near the tail of the field before engine failure granted him merciful release from the painful burns. But Nigel now had his shoulder firmly wedged in the Grand Prix door. Seven years later he would be back at the Osterreichring, on the winner's rostrum.

Jones, meanwhile, went into the 1980 Dutch Grand Prix at Zandvoort with an 11 point lead over his Brazilian rival, but he came out of it only 2 points ahead. Despite the fact that Arnoux and Jabouille planted their Renaults firmly on the front row of the grid, Jones ran round the outside of them at the start to take an immediate lead. At the end of the opening lap he was already two seconds ahead. Then he made an elementary error...

Coming out of the tight hairpin behind the paddock, Alan glanced in his mirror to see how the opposition was doing, allowing the Williams FW07B momentarily to ride over the kerb on the exit to the corner. As he turned into the next corner, the full implications of his mistake became apparent. Instead of that glued-to-the-road feeling, the Williams began to understeer as its front tyres lost their grip. No downforce! In that brief excursion from the tarmac he had destroyed the delicate sliding skirt on the right-hand side pod of his car, that crucial, absurd, frustrating aerodynamic appendage, the functioning of which could spell the difference between success and failure. Cursing himself, he aimed for the pits at the end of the opening lap.

Arnoux led for a single lap and then Laffite's Ligier briefly went ahead. But from Lap 13 onwards, Nelson Piquet's Brabham took command and stormed away to beat Arnoux by 13sec. With three races to go, the title battle was now wide open.

Renault sustained its qualifying advantage in preparation for the one-off Italian Grand Prix at Imola, but by Lap 4 Piquet had again burst through into a lead he would never lose. Jones spent the first half of the race trying to scramble past Jabouille's second place Renault, after which he and team-mate Reutemann ran strongly home to finish 2-3 behind the victorious Brabham.

Prior to the penultimate round of the Championship, at Montreal, Jones walked the entire distance from the paddock to the starting grid wearing his helmet, balaclava and gauntlet gloves. His dark green overalls, like battle fatigues, heightened the image of a commando just about to go into action. By contrast, Piquet looked like a jockey being lifted on to his horse. Although Nelson was on pole position, few people bet against Jones.

At the start, Alan's Williams got the jump on Piquet going into the first right-hander, the Australian grabbing the racing line into the first corner. The two cars banged wheels, Piquet got pushed sideways. Further back, Keke Rosberg went hard on to his Fittipaldi's brakes, spun on his cold tyres and triggered off a multiple pile-up. The race was stopped.

The Williams crew repaired Jones's car, but Piquet's had sustained a bent steering arm which obliged him to take the spare for the restart. Nelson snatched the lead on the second lap, pulling steadily ahead until Lap 24 when the Brabham's engine abruptly expired. His Championship prospects now dead, he could only watch as Jones reeled off the remaining laps to take motor racing's most prestigious award. Sadly, this success came on a day when Jean-Pierre Jabouille crashed his Renault, due to suspension failure, and sustained a serious leg fracture which would mark the beginning of the end for his Formula 1 career.

A week later, Jones would round off his Championship season by winning the United States Grand Prix at Watkins Glen. It was eight years since he had won the British Formula 3 Championship to mark him as a man with a future. Eight years since his father's body had returned to its native Australia with one of Alan's Formula 3 victory garlands stowed inside the coffin.

Stan Jones would undoubtedly have been proud of his lad's achievements. By any standards, Alan was a chip off the old block.

THE TURBO YEARS' RESULTS 1980

Winner's average speed

January 13, ARGENTINE GRAND PRIX, Buenos Aires
1	Alan Jones	Williams-Cosworth FW07	(113.98mph)
2	Nelson Piquet	Brabham-Cosworth BT49	
3	Keke Rosberg	Fittipaldi-Cosworth F7	
4	Derek Daly	Tyrrell-Cosworth 009	
5	Bruno Giacomelli	Alfa Romeo 179	
6	Alain Prost	McLaren-Cosworth M29B	

January 27, BRAZILIAN GRAND PRIX, Interlagos
1	René Arnoux	Renault RE20 turbo	(117.40mph)
2	Elio de Angelis	Lotus-Cosworth 81	
3	Alan Jones	Williams-Cosworth FW07	
4	Didier Pironi	Ligier-Cosworth JS11	
5	Alain Prost	McLaren-Cosworth M29B	
6	Riccardo Patrese	Arrows-Cosworth A3	

March 1, SOUTH AFRICAN GRAND PRIX, Kyalami
1	René Arnoux	Renault RE20 turbo	(123.19mph)
2	Jacques Laffite	Ligier-Cosworth JS11	
3	Didier Pironi	Ligier-Cosworth JS11	
4	Nelson Piquet	Brabham-Cosworth BT49	
5	Carlos Reutemann	Williams-Cosworth FW07	
6	Jochen Mass	Arrows-Cosworth A3	

March 30, UNITED STATES GRAND PRIX WEST, Long Beach
1	Nelson Piquet	Brabham-Cosworth BT49	(88.47mph)
2	Riccardo Patrese	Arrows-Cosworth A3	
3	Emerson Fittipaldi	Fittipaldi-Cosworth F7	
4	John Watson	McLaren-Cosworth M29	
5	Jody Scheckter	Ferrari 312T5	
6	Didier Pironi	Ligier-Cosworth JS11	

May 4, BELGIAN GRAND PRIX, Zolder
1	Didier Pironi	Ligier-Cosworth JS11	(115.82mph)
2	Alain Prost	Williams-Cosworth FW07B	
3	Carlos Reutemann	Williams-Cosworth FW07B	
4	René Arnoux	Renault RE20 turbo	
5	J-P Jarier	Tyrrell-Cosworth 010	
6	Gilles Villeneuve	Ferrari 312T5	

May 18, MONACO GRAND PRIX, Monte Carlo
1	Carlos Reutemann	Williams-Cosworth FW07B	(81.20mph)
2	Jacques Laffite	Ligier-Cosworth JS11	
3	Nelson Piquet	Brabham-Cosworth BT49	
4	Jochen Mass	Arrows-Cosworth A3	
5	Gilles Villeneuve	Ferrari 312T5	
6	Jochen Mass	Arrows-Cosworth A3	

June 1, SPANISH GRAND PRIX, Jarama (race stripped of Championship status)

1	Alan Jones	Williams-Cosworth FW07B	(95.69mph)
2	Jochen Mass	Arrows-Cosworth A3	
3	Elio de Angelis	Lotus-Cosworth 81	
4	J-P Jarier	Tyrrell-Cosworth 010	
5	Emerson Fittipaldi	Fittipaldi-Cosworth F7	
6	Patrick Gaillard	Ensign-Cosworth N180	

June 29, FRENCH GRAND PRIX, Paul Ricard

1	Alan Jones	Williams-Cosworth FW07B	(126.65mph)
2	Didier Pironi	Ligier-Cosworth JS11	
3	Jacques Laffite	Ligier-Cosworth JS11	
4	Nelson Piquet	Brabham-Cosworth BT49	
5	René Arnoux	Renault RE20 turbo	
6	Carlos Reutemann	Williams-Cosworth FW07B	

July 13, BRITISH GRAND PRIX, Brands Hatch

1	Alan Jones	Williams-Cosworth FW07B	(125.69mph)
2	Nelson Piquet	Brabham-Cosworth BT49	
3	Carlos Reutemann	Williams-Cosworth FW07B	
4	Derek Daly	Tyrrell-Cosworth 010	
5	J-P Jarier	Tyrrell-Cosworth 010	
6	Alain Prost	McLaren-Cosworth M29	

August 10, GERMAN GRAND PRIX, Hockenheim

1	Jacques Laffite	Ligier-Cosworth JS11	(137.26mph)
2	Carlos Reutemann	Williams-Cosworth FW07B	
3	Alan Jones	Williams-Cosworth FW07B	
4	Nelson Piquet	Brabham-Cosworth BT49	
5	Bruno Giacomelli	Alfa Romeo 179	
6	Gilles Villeneuve	Ferrari 312T5	

August 17, AUSTRIAN GRAND PRIX, Osterreichring

1	J-P Jabouille	Renault RE20 turbo	(138.69mph)
2	Alan Jones	Williams-Cosworth FW07B	
3	Carlos Reutemann	Williams-Cosworth FW07B	
4	Jacques Laffite	Ligier-Cosworth JS11	
5	Nelson Piquet	Brabham-Cosworth BT49	
6	Elio de Angelis	Lotus-Cosworth 81	

August 21, DUTCH GRAND PRIX, Zandvoort

1	Nelson Piquet	Brabham-Cosworth BT49	(116.19mph)
2	René Arnoux	Renault RE20 turbo	
3	Jacques Laffite	Ligier-Cosworth JS11	
4	Carlos Reutemann	Williams-Cosworth FW07B	
5	J-P Jarier	Tyrrell-Cosworth 010	
6	Alain Prost	McLaren-Cosworth M30	

September 14, ITALIAN GRAND PRIX, Imola

1	Nelson Piquet	Brabham-Cosworth BT49	(113.98mph)
2	Alan Jones	Williams-Cosworth FW07B	
3	Carlos Reutemann	Williams-Cosworth FW07B	
4	Elio de Angelis	Lotus-Cosworth 81	
5	Keke Rosberg	Fittipaldi-Cosworth F8	
6	Didier Pironi	Ligier-Cosworth JS11	

September 28, CANADIAN GRAND PRIX, Montreal
1	Alan Jones	Williams-Cosworth FW07B	(110.00mph)
2	Carlos Reutemann	Williams-Cosworth FW07B	
3	Didier Pironi	Ligier-Cosworth JS11	
4	John Watson	McLaren-Cosworth M29	
5	Gilles Villeneuve	Ferrari 312T5	
6	Hector Rebaque	Brabham-Cosworth BT49	

October 5, UNITED STATES GRAND PRIX, Watkins Glen
1	Alan Jones	Williams-Cosworth FW07B	(126.37mph)
2	Carlos Reutemann	Williams-Cosworth FW07B	
3	Didier Pironi	Ligier-Cosworth JS11	
4	Elio de Angelis	Lotus-Cosworth 81	
5	Jacques Laffite	Ligier-Cosworth JS11	
6	Mario Andretti	Lotus-Cosworth 81	

DRIVERS' WORLD CHAMPIONSHIP

Posn	Driver	Points
1	Alan Jones	67
2	Nelson Piquet	54
3	Carlos Reutemann	42
4	Jacques Laffite	34
5	Didier Pironi	32
6	René Arnoux	29
7	Elio de Angelis	13
8	Jean-Pierre Jabouille	9
9	Riccardo Patrese	7
10	Derek Daly	6
	Jean-Pierre Jarier	
	Keke Rosberg	
	Gilles Villeneuve	
	John Watson	
15	Emerson Fittipaldi	5
	Alain Prost	
17	Bruno Giacomelli	4
	Jochen Mass	
19	Jody Scheckter	2
20	Mario Andretti	1
	Hector Rebaque	

CONSTRUCTORS' CHAMPIONSHIP

Posn	Constructor	Points
1	Williams	120
2	Ligier	66
3	Brabham	55
4	Renault	38
5	Lotus	14
6	Tyrrell	12
7	Arrows	11
	Fittipaldi	
	McLaren	
10	Ferrari	8
11	Alfa Romeo	4

1981

While Jones and Piquet had been enlivening the second half of the 1980 Championship season with their battle for the title, the simmering cauldron of dissent between FISA and FOCA finally bubbled over with considerable rancour and bitterness.

Balestre continued to interfere with the commercial aspect of Formula 1, effectively attempting to intervene in contracts between FOCA and the race promoters, and made clear his avowed intention of forcing through the ban on aerodynamic side skirts for the 1981 season.

In pursuing this latter course of action, the FISA president would by-pass the regulation requiring two years' notice of any fundamental change in technical regulations by invoking the overriding requirements of safety. By the end of 1980, the FOCA-aligned teams had virtually decided to go it alone with their own eighteen-race Championship, run to rules published by the 'World Federation of Motorsport', an organisation which, in reality, existed only on paper. On the face of it, this was utter madness which had no chance of credibility or survival. FOCA and its members would have become instant pariahs, outcasts within the international motor sporting community.

It was indicative of how far FOCA considered it had been pushed that the Constructors' Association seriously contemplated a pirate series, running to the existed 'skirted' regulations. Grand Prix racing now faced a situation where FISA had three two-car teams behind it, but held the loyalty of the national clubs under whose sanction the races took place. However, FOCA held a theoretically strong hand, its members fielding most of the cars and the organisation locked into many commercial contracts with the individual race promoters. The truth was, neither could do without the other.

The skirt ban was widely perceived as aiding the turbo brigade purely on the basis that neither Ferrari nor Renault could make a ground-effect chassis which was as competitive as a Williams, a Brabham, a Lotus or whatever. Truth was, while Maranello's chassis technology was trailing badly, Renault professed horror at the prospect of the loss of sliding skirts. They had spent a year making their own ground-effect machine work quite effectively and appreciated that ground effect enabled you to have more of the power working for more of the time.

As Harvey Postlethwaite later remarked: 'I could never understand why ground-effect was regarded by many British teams as some sort of trade-off for turbocharged engines. From the moment the turbos arrived, it was only a matter of time before somebody installed one in a ground-effect chassis that worked properly.' Although some British teams were sceptical, Renault believed they had already done just that.

Interestingly, although the FOCA constructors were up in arms, the drivers relished the idea of a return to skirt-less cars, although they did have some misgivings about retaining ground-effect underbody profiles without skirts.

Alan Jones summed it up nicely towards the end of his Championship year: 'I curse the day when skirts were invented because I believe that the cars have now developed to the point where they are quite simply too fast. I liked sliding a car around and I'm sure the spectators enjoyed watching it; and I don't believe that anybody watching can really tell the difference between a car lapping Silverstone in 1min 12sec and 1min 18sec.

'On the other hand, I just don't see how skirts can be banned if we're going to retain aerodynamic underbodies. We'll get a situation where the cars are generating considerable ground effect at 180mph and almost none at all at 80mph. On a bumpy circuit that's going to be a lethal nightmare.

Sign of things to come. From left to right: *Ron Dennis, John Watson and John Barnard were in on the ground floor when McLaren International was founded at the start of 1981. Barnard's new carbon-fibre composite McLaren MP4 (*opposite) *would be driven by Watson and Andrea de Cesaris throughout that season.*

'What I would really like to see are flat-bottomed cars without skirts, like the old Williams FW06. But until flat undersides become compulsory, we must keep skirts to keep the chassis behaviour consistent . . .' In the event, the worst of both worlds, as envisaged by the new World Champion, would become the norm for 1981. Jones's utopian concept of a return to flat-bottomed racers would not be realised until 1983. And by then, he had been in retirement for over a season.

At the same time, Ferrari continued to echo the message that a ban on skirts would be a Good Thing, although the motivating factor here was unashamed self-interest. Quite simply, their flat-12-engined 312T5 had advertised to the world just how hopeless Maranello actually was when it came to sliding-skirt aerodynamic technology. Get rid of the skirts, reasoned Ferrari, and our flat-12 engine might suddenly find itself receiving a fresh lease of life . . .

While the politics raged behind the scenes, one major team had become the subject of a major internal re-structuring. McLaren Racing now became McLaren International after an amalgamation with the Project 4 organisation, founded by Ron

Brave new effort. Brian Henton and Derek Warwick pose during a Goodwood test session with the prototype Toleman TG181 which brought Brian Hart's 415T 4 cylinder, single turbo engine into the Grand Prix fray at the start of 1981.

Dennis and his partner Creighton Brown. It was a shotgun marriage instigated by McLaren's long-time sponsor Philip Morris, whose Marlboro brand livery Emerson Fittipaldi and James Hunt had carried to the World Championship in 1974 and 1976 respectively. Ever since the advent of ground-effect technology, and the dismal failure of the M28, McLaren's star faded fast. Now the team's prospects would be re-invigorated to startling long-term effect.

Ron Dennis, then 33 years old, was destined to raise the standard of the Formula 1 game in the decade that followed. Motor racing, particularly at Grand Prix level, is brimful of talented individuals, so Dennis had no monopoly on this score. But this former Cooper and Brabham mechanic was a visionary in the sense that he displayed a unique talent for looking further ahead, taking a longer term view, than any of his rivals. While most people were thinking in terms of next season, Dennis was working on a strategy to cover his team's options for the next three or four years.

In retrospect, his track record in the junior formulae signalled the direction in which he was to proceed. His Formula 1 apprenticeship had been served in the late 1960s, when Formula 1 mechanics grubbed round gravel-strewn paddocks, finishing the day oily and streaked with grease. This was absolute anathema to the meticulous newcomer who had been attracted to Formula 1 not through any romantic, youthful passion for racing cars as such, but more by the notion of engineering excellence. Ron pursued painstaking excellence and attention to detail with such zeal in the ensuing years to the point where paddock jokes about his preoccupation became legendary. Once they're poking fun at you in this business, you know you've made it. . .

After a stint with Brabham, which saw him rise to the position of chief mechanic by the end of 1969, Ron and his friend Neil Trundle founded a Formula 2 team called Rondel Racing. Using hired Brabham chassis and a leased transporter, Rondel soon gained a reputation for smarter-than-average turnout and shrewd attention to detail. It was a cachet that would stay with Ron's Formula 2 operations throughout the 1970s, by which time he was keen to make the move into Formula 1 with his own team.

The 'amalgamation' with McLaren was, to all intents and purposes, a takeover by Dennis and his newly recruited colleague John Barnard, then a promising designer who had served his motor racing apprenticeship in the company of Patrick Head with the Huntingdon-based Lola company during the early 1970s. Barnard had also spent a spell with McLaren during the M23's heyday, working alongside Gordon Coppuck, but his most recent achievement had been the design of the striking Chaparral 2K which had led the 1979 Indy 500 in the hands of Al Unser before succumbing to gearbox trouble.

Towards the end of November 1979, a chance telephone call lit the blue touch paper of a partnership which would blaze a trail to three consecutive World Championships. Barnard's old pal Patrick Head, had pointed Ron Dennis in John's direction when the Project 4 boss was shopping round, ostensibly for somebody to design his team a new Formula 2 car. The two men met, talked – and Barnard discovered that Dennis was really after a Formula 1 design.

Early in 1980, Dennis and Brown assessed what would be involved in moving up into Formula 1. The investment was clearly going to be enormous, but their close relationship with Marlboro put them in pole position when the time came to casting round for a partner to save the McLaren operation. From this moment onwards, Barnard stepped up his investigation into the feasibility of manufacturing a complete chassis out of carbon-fibre composite, an exciting new aerospace material which was still in its infancy as far as Grand Prix racing was concerned.

Carbon fibre was to become to chassis technology what the turbo was to engine development. Blended together during the mid-1980s, they would produce the fastest, strongest and safest Grand Prix cars ever seen. However, as with the turbocharged engine, the business of learning how to use carbon fibre to best effect was a frustratingly long path, strewn with endless, unexpected pitfalls.

Back on the hyperactive political Formula 1 scene, throughout the summer of 1980 a succession of proposals and counter-proposals were pushed back and forth across the negotiating table as FOCA and FISA jockeyed for position. Eventually it was suggested that lap speeds might be controlled by insisting on treaded tyres, rather than slicks, in conjunction with the existing sliding skirt regulations.

On the basis of the events of that summer, many Formula 1 insiders reached the conclusion that Balestre was prevaricating when he assured FOCA that the FISA Technical Commission would examine these proposals, his move prompted by short-term expediency to ensure the French Grand Prix took place without falling a victim to a FOCA boycott. When Michelin announced there was no way in which it could countenance tyre performance restrictions formulated round the 'mandatory' re-introduction of treaded tyres, Balestre used this as a pretext to jettison the entire FOCA 'compromise' package.

Into the winter of 1980/81, the battle continued with race organisers hovering on the edge of an abyss, not really knowing which way to jump. Did they go with FISA, and have no cars? Or side with FOCA, and step outside the accepted envelope of legality?

Eventually, the scheduled start of the season took place. FOCA took a gamble and ran their own race, to sliding skirt regulations, at Kyalami on 7 February. Just as at Jarama the previous year, the 'grandees' – Ferrari, Renault and Alfa Romeo – stayed away. Carlos Reutemann's Williams FW07B won from Nelson Piquet's Brabham BT49 and the Lotus 81 of Elio de Angelis.

In the team's motorhome immediately after the race, Frank Williams briskly remarked, 'Now we've got to make certain we get the 9 points for this win.' Reutemann shot him a thoughtful sideways glance, then muttered prophetically, 'No way I think I get those 9 points.' As with Jones's success in the previous year's Spanish Grand Prix, Williams had just won another illegal race.

Just as it seemed to Balestre that he was about to win what seemed, to the outside a world, an esoteric and bewilderingly inconsequential battle, Renault and Fiat found their nerve

Opposite: Storm clouds of controversy surrounded the imaginative 'twin chassis' Lotus 88, built round a carbon-fibre/Kevlar monocoque and unveiled early in 1981. Elio de Angelis is seen practising Chapman's new challenger at Rio, and in the pit lane at Long Beach, before the car was excluded from both meetings.

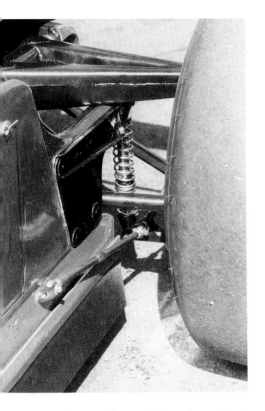

Above and opposite: The 'secondary' aerodynamic chassis on the type 88 was supported by these additional coil springs front and rear, while the main chassis structure containing the driver was catered for by the bigger inboard springs activated by the large fabricated rocker arms.

beginning to waver. The second race on the calendar was at Long Beach, California and the United States market was an absolutely crucial area of expansion for Renault, in particular. In a nutshell, Renault could not afford to let participation at Long Beach slip away. In essence, the need to compete in this first race of the season applied pressure on all parties to reach a speedy settlement of this damaging dispute.

Only ten days before the Californian race the alleged outbreak of peace between FISA and FOCA was formally announced. There had been an initiative during January in which representatives of all the Formula 1 teams had met beneath the umbrella of Enzo Ferrari's hospitality at Maranello to draw up details of what might best be described as an Armistice between the warring parties. In the run-up to the American race this gelled into what became known as the Concorde Agreement. In a nutshell, it acknowledged FISA's right to make the rules, and FOCA's to control the financial structure of the sport. In other words, who made how much money and when.

So everybody raced at Long Beach, the cars all apparently conforming with FISA's newly instigated requirement that there should be 6cm ground clearance beneath the cars, supposedly at all times. Goodyear had by this time withdrawn from the Formula 1 game, albeit temporarily, fed up with all the political in-fighting, uncertainty and rancour. As a result, Michelin agreed to provide their radial rubber for the entire field.

It is absolutely characteristic of the combative nature of any sport that rules are there to be all-but broken. Just as the contemporary breed of ultra-aggressive professional tennis player feels it is imcumbent on him to query any line call, the Grand Prix designer reads any regulation apparently intended to restrict car performance – and then attempts to work out a method of circumventing its effect. So it was in 1981. The results would have done credit to Roland Emmett.

A few days before the Long Beach race, I took the opportunity to drive out into the desert close to the giant Edwards Air Force base and, whilst exploring that awesome expanse of uninhabited California, dropped in at the tiny club racing track at Willow Springs. What should I find but Nelson Piquet and Brabham designer Gordon Murray fussing over a lone BT49C kitted out with an experimental hydro-pneumatic suspension lowering system.

In Formula 1 terms, this development was calculated to be pure dynamite, not only conferring an instant performance advantage on the Brabham but threatening to open a rift within the FOCA ranks at a time when they were theoretically supposed to be presenting a united front against FISA's erratic onslaught.

Murray's system utilised a system which allowed the car to rise on its springs to pass the 6cm rule when stationary, or running at low speeds in the pits, but as speed built up the aerodynamic downforce would press the car down closer to the track, enabling it to achieve a significant degree of ground effect.

The system did not work properly during practice at Long Beach, so Piquet's BT49C – as the 1981 Brabham was designated – ran to a comfortable third place in conventionally sprung trim. Alan Jones carved his way past Carlos Reutemann's sister car to open the season on a suitably high note for a reigning World Champion, the Williams team-mates now using 'C' specification versions of the FW07 which was now into its third Formula 1 season and showing no dulling of its competitive edge.

Reutemann had lost the lead at Long Beach due to a slight error of judgement, the hard-charging Jones inserting his car through a tiny gap opened by the Argentinian. But Frank Williams made it clear that the terms of the contracts with his two drivers placed an obligation on Reutemann to defer to his Australian team leader if he found himself leading a Williams 1-2 by less than seven seconds. In the rain-soaked second round of the World Championship, at Rio de Janeiro, Carlos felt himself unable to fulfil that commitment...

The rain poured down throughout the Brazilian Grand Prix but, despite this, Nelson Piquet and the Brabham team took the insane gamble of starting from pole position on dry weather slick tyres, feeling that the odd flickering shaft of sunlight on the distant horizon signalled an imminent end to the monsoon. It didn't, and their extraordinarily wayward decision simply had the effect of wiping out Piquet's chances in front of his adoring home crowd.

Reutemann ran at the front for the entire distance, shadowed by Jones who, naively, was waiting for Carlos to let him through. Alan controlled his public simmering fury with great tact and diplomacy after the race, whilst at the same time making a mental note that Reutemann wasn't to be trusted any more than anybody else out on the circuit. He was beginning to see Niki Lauda's viewpoint on the enigmatic Argentinian driver.

Another few lines of Grand Prix history, meanwhile, had been written at Long Beach. On its maiden outing, the KKK-turbocharged Ferrari 126C burst through from the third row of the starting grid in the hands of Gilles Villeneuve to lead the race for a few hundred yards, the gutsy French Canadian ace immediately running wide at the first hairpin and dropping to fourth place at the end of the opening lap. Driveshaft failure was eventually to cause Gilles's retirement while running sixth, but his newly recruited team-mate Didier Pironi convincingly

Once the type 88 had been banned, Team Lotus fell back on this hurriedly developed type 87, (opposite), based round the same carbon-fibre/Kevlar chassis. From the cockpit of what was essentially a 'single chassis' type 88, new boy Nigel Mansell puts on a brave face outside Team Lotus's headquarters, Ketteringham Hall, Norfolk.

demonstrated the Ferrari V6 engine's potential during a spirited dice with Mario Andretti's Alfa Romeo.

The deluge of technical controversy which was destined to stretch well into the following year now rapidly gained momentum to the point where the 1981 season rocketed by in a blur of pit lane controversy. Mentally, one recalled the races not so much by performances on the circuit, more by what was happening in the scrutineering bay or the stewards' office. The Argentine Grand Prix at Buenos Aires was one such event which bought two messy disputes to a head.

For Colin Chapman, the two years since the eclipse of his epochal Lotus 79 had been challenging in the extreme. In the commercial world, Group Lotus, the publicly quoted company which was the road car manufacturing arm of his empire, found itself bogged down in ever more controversy surrounding its involvement with the ill-starred DeLorean sports car project. The efforts of American entrepreneur John DeLorean to set up a sports car manufacturing company in Ulster had attracted an enormous amount of financial support from Britain's Labour government.

Even so, most dispassionate observers quickly concluded that there was no realistic commercial future for the striking two-seater coupé, distinguished by its gull-wing doors and little else. The whole affair snowballed into a political *cause-célèbre*, ploughing relentlessly on towards a disastrous conclusion when the whole company went bust, much to nobody's surprise.

Lotus had been commissioned to re-engineer the original DeLorean design and, in the wake of the company's failure, Chapman would, after his death, become restrospectively implicated in a plot to defraud that company of many millions of pounds, a large proportion of which had originally been provided by the Government in the form of grants. With his Grand Prix team in disarray, it is almost impossible to imagine the psychological pressure under which Chapman operated during that fraught time, a level of stress which almost certainly contributed to his fatal heart attack in December 1982, at the early age of 54.

Yet, in many ways, Formula 1 had been Chapman's therapy. It was an opportunity for the engineer within him to take the initiative, but the final straw which sapped much of his remaining enthusiasm for Grand Prix racing came when FISA outlawed his strikingly imaginative Lotus 88 after the first few races of the 1981 season.

Gilles Villeneuve's Ferrari 126CK in the early stages of the 1981 Monaco Grand Prix in which he would score a memorable first victory for Maranello's turbocar.

During the summer of 1979, the failure of the aerodynamically complex Lotus 80 set Chapman thinking in terms of separating the aerodynamic and and suspension loads. The result of these deliberations was a novel 'twin chassis' design in which the aerodynamic loadings were absorbed by an outer 'chassis', linked to the bottom of the uprights by small coil spring/dampers, while the driver remained in a central monocoque, the conventional rocker arm suspension of which absorbed the dynamic loadings produced by braking, cornering and acceleration.

There were two very fundamental advantages produced by Chapman's concept. The aerodynamic behaviour of the car was theoretically stabilised, while the driver no longer had to be battered by the need to run ultra-stiff conventional suspension, thereby minimising the fatigue factor. The concept was first tested in skirted form during November 1980, under the designation type 86 and built round an aluminium honeycomb monocoque. But even after those two tests, the type 86 ran into trouble with the rule-makers, at the moment when Balestre was at the absolute height of his 'no skirts' crusade.

As news of the Lotus 86 began to leak out within the Grand Prix world, FISA issued one of its famous 'rule clarifications', another increasingly questionable method by which the sport's governing body would seek to subtly change regulations which had, hitherto, seemed set in stone. FISA reminded participants that 'any specific part of the car influencing its aerodynamic performance . . . must remain immobile in relation to the sprung part of the car.'

On the face of it, the new Lotus was in trouble, even though Chapman was re-working the concept to suit the new 'skirtless' regulations for the 1981 season. Moreover, the new 'second generation' twin-chassis challenger, designated type 88, was intended to set a fresh trend in chassis design with its carbon fibre/Kevlar chassis construction.

Familiar sight. Alain Prost helps marshals to extinguish a turbo fire on his Renault RE20 during practice for the 1981 British Grand Prix at Silverstone.

Alan Jones on Retirement

Immediately after trailing home fifth in the 1981 Austrian Grand Prix, Alan Jones dropped a firm hint as to what might be in his mind for the future when he threatened to retire 'unless something is done about the regulations which have produced the absurd breed of car which we have to drive today.'

He was right. These stiffly-sprung machines with virtually zero suspension movement were punishing the drivers as never before. Jones felt these were no longer racing cars which responded to skill and finesse; they were bucking broncos in which you hung on doggedly until fatigue or mechanical problems caught you out.

However, the decision to quit – finally communicated to Frank Williams around the time of the Italian Grand Prix at Monza – was well advanced in his own mind. It wasn't just the ultra-stiff suspension. Jones could see the way the technical wind was blowing and realised that a turbo would be necessary for the future. As things turned out, Frank's deal with Honda was still over two years away. 'It was only Renault's incompetence, rather than our brilliance, which enabled us to win the Championship in 1980,' he concluded.

The man who moved Frank Williams to remark, 'I haven't been as excited about any driver since Ronnie Peterson' after watching from the pit wall at Long Beach in 1979 as Alan battled his way to third place behind the Ferraris of Villeneuve and Scheckter, would subsequently realise that he had quit Formula 1 too soon.

Fleetingly, he would be back in 1983; more seriously, with the Haas Lola team, in 1985. But by then money would be the overriding motivation in Jones's personal equation.

Coincidentally, the Formula 1 world would see a confluence of carbon-fibre technology unveiled at the start of the 1981 season with the arrival on the scene of John Barnard's all carbon-fibre McLaren MP4 a couple of days before Chapman's Kevlar-enhanced carbon-fibre Lotus 88. The Lotus boss used the occasion to have a joke at McLaren's expense; 'I'm sorry to tell them that carbon-fibre alone is out of date. . .'

Those pioneering days of carbon-fibre technology were watched with heart-in-mouth concern by some more conservative members of the Formula 1 design establishment. What was to become the manufacturing cornerstone of Grand Prix chassis technology as the turbo era unfolded was initially regarded by many engineers with a degree of caution which bordered on suspicion.

Carbon fibre had its roots in the aerospace industry from the time in the early 1960s when the British, US and Japanese governments funded complex research programmes investigating the prospects for developing new ultra-light, extremely stiff material which could be used for highly demanding aerospace applications.

The man in the street may have heard muffled mentions of carbon fibre, in connection with the development of Rolls-Royce aero engines during their troubles in the early 1970s which ended with the company going into receivership. Rolls-Royce used carbon fibre in the manufacture of compressor fans in its RB2-11 jet engine and, a few years later, the material began to be employed in Formula 1 applications.

Wing supports were one of the first areas to attract the use of carbon fibre, but when Rolf Stommelen's Hill GH1 became airborne and crashed heavily, killing four onlookers, whilst leading the 1975 Spanish Grand Prix at Barcelona, the mere mention of carbon fibre produced an understandable bout of jitters. The Hill's rear wing support had been manufactured from this material and it became increasingly clear that not sufficient was known about its behaviour under sustained loadings.

The carbon-fibre manufacturing process involves heat treating a special acrylic fibre to produce filaments of almost pure carbon. Tightly packed bundles of these filaments are then saturated with a small amount of resin, before being oven cured at around 120°C, transforming it into the stiff, light material which laymen would identify as carbon-fibre sheet.

However, unlike the manufacture of glass-fibre panels, a

Moving in for the kill. John Watson's Cosworth-engined McLaren MP4 hustles René Arnoux's ailing Renault RE20 just prior to grabbing the lead of the 1981 British Grand Prix and scoring the first win for McLaren International.

Nelson Piquet tests the prototype Brabham-BMW turbo during practice for the 1981 British Grand Prix. It would not make its race debut until the following year's South African race.

methodology familiar to the motor racing community for over two decades, the direction in which carbon fibre was 'laid up' became a matter of crucial importance for Grand Prix car chassis. For best effect, the carbon fibres had to be laid in the optimum direction for absorbing the various chassis loadings. A designer had to make very specific choices about how to lay up the fibres in specific directions and, with a lack of accumulated experience within Formula 1 on which to draw, many designers watched and waited as the trail-blazers pressed ahead.

In fact, Brabham designer Gordon Murray had been amongst the pioneers when it came to using carbon-fibre on some panels within the the Cosworth-powered BT49s. But the team lost a couple of cars in major accidents over the ensuing season, prompting the somewhat conservative Murray, whose overriding consideration was driver safety, to ease back.

Eventually, Murray persuaded Bernie Ecclestone that it would be a good idea to destroy a complete car in the sort of crash test that was normally reserved for pre-production prototype road cars. Capitalising on their fledgeling alliance with BMW, this exercise was duly carried out in the German company's Munich test centre, an investment which garnered a huge harvest of data relating to the behaviour of carbon fibre in severe impacts.

Over at the revitalised McLaren factory, John Barnard had pursued his theory to fruition thanks to a programme of collaboration with Hercules Aerospace, a company based in Salt Lake City which operated at the sharp end of missile and rocket motor technology. The MP4, built from moulded sections of carbon fibre manufactured in only five large pre-fabricated sections, was unveiled in London before making a hesitant debut at Long Beach, only in practice. Beautifully aerodynamic, with body panels fitting like a glove, the new McLaren displayed a splendidly high standard of detail finish. 'I've promised Marlboro that we will win one Grand Prix this season,' Ron Dennis told me confidently in California. Going into the turbo era, I remember thinking that seemed like an increasingly tall order for a Cosworth DFV-engined car. Never underestimate the power of positive thought...

Lotus's offering involved strengthening the basic carbon fibre with Kevlar, a new material also developed for the aerospace industry by Du Pont Chemicals in the USA. Its anti-tear qualities were correctly judged as ideal to complement the proven strength of carbon fibre; in fact, carbon fibre/Kevlar cloth was now available, pre-impregnated with the requisite epoxy resin. Lotus evolved a system whereby two layers of carbon/Kevlar cloth sandwiched a core of Nomex honeycomb material, impregnated with resin, folded round the appropriate internal bulkheads and then cured within a pressurised oven.

The introduction of carbon fibre into the manufacture of monocoque effectively killed three birds with one well-aimed stone. The cars were stronger, safer and more rigid, the last-named point becoming an increasingly demanding priority to meet bearing in mind that the ground-effect trend led to monocoques becoming as slim as possible, with central fuel cells, in order to leave the maximum possible space for aerodynamic side pods. In general, if one halves the cross-sectional area of a chassis, its torsional stiffness is reduced by between four and eight fold.

However, whilst there could be no faulting the logic behind the technical development of these cars, the Lotus 88 would inevitably fall foul of the rule-makers. Colin Chapman's breezy air of confidence, coupled with his belief that Formula 1 was all about pushing back the frontiers of technical development, would fail him on this crucial occasion. Formula 1 in the early 1980s showed all the signs of being stifled by a maze of over-complex rules.

The man who had broken new ground with the monocoque Lotus 25 and the side-radiator type 72, now found himself frustratingly hemmed in. It was only three years since the Lotus 79 had burst on to the Grand Prix scene, yet the mood had changed dramatically. If ground effect had been developed and harnessed for the first time in 1981, many teams feel there is little doubt that FISA would have found some pretext on which to outlaw the concept in about five minutes flat.

Immediately after the Lotus 88's unveiling in London, it was flown to California for the Long Beach race. It duly passed scrutineering and was allowed to practice in the hands of Elio de Angelis, accompanied by the ugly sight of the FOCA pack in full cry. Faced with many objections from rival teams, the stewards back-tracked and excluded the Lotus 88 at the end of the first day. Chapman duly appealed, and was told that he would be permitted to run the car for the rest of the meeting on the strict understanding that, if he lost the appeal, any points that it might score would be forfeit.

The Lotus 88 was then black-flagged off the circuit on Saturday morning when the race stewards announced that they had seached the FISA rules further and discovered that it was not permitted for a car to run whilst under protests, even though an appeal had been lodged. This regulation was widely regarded as extremely unfair, yet no subsequent attempt was made to wipe it from the rule book, and it would resurface unpleasantly some eight years later to prevent Nigel Mansell from participating in the 1989 Spanish Grand Prix even though an appeal against such exclusion had been lodged.

First win. Prost's Renault RE30 triumphed in the 1981 French Grand Prix at Dijon-Prenois, but mechanical unreliability kept the French team away from the World Championship title yet again.

The US national motor sporting authority (ACCUS) subsequently decreed the Lotus 88 to be in conformity with the regulations. FISA replied that this judgement applied only as far as the USA was concerned. The car was taken to Rio, only to be black flagged from Brazilian Grand Prix practice. In Buenos Aires, it was turned down at scrutineering for the Argentine Grand Prix.

Chapman stormed away from Argentina, leaving a press statement to be distributed in his wake. Amongst other things, it tore into FISA: '...we have witnessed the changes which have taken place in Grand Prix racing, and unfortunately seen what was fair competition between sportsmen degenerate into power struggles and political manoeuvrings between manipulators and money men attempting to take more out of the sport than they put into it ... if one does not clean it up, Formula 1 will end in a quagmire of plagiarism, chicanery and petty rule interpretation forced by lobbies manipulated by people for whom the word sport has no meaning.'

FISA's inability to police its own technical regulations resulted in the 1981 6cm ground clearance regulations. The handle on the right of this Brabham BT49C's cockpit controls the hydraulic suspension jacking system which will enable the car to conform with the ground clearance rules when checked, but snuggle down close to the track surface when out on the circuit.

Cynics might look back on Chapman as something of a visionary, but this spontaneous shot from the hip was just the sort of thing to bring Balestre catapulting from his cage in a right old lather. The FISA president, who could never resist passing a microphone without bellowing into it, ranted that Chapman's remarks had discredited the World Championship and that Team Lotus would now be subjected to a $100,000 fine.

This was rip-roaring stuff, but if anybody believed that the storm surrounding Grand Prix racing had abated with Chapman's departure, they could not have been further from the truth. The next item on the agenda turned out to be a storm of indignation surrounding the Brabham BT49C's suspension lowering system. Nelson Piquet romped away with the Argentine Grand Prix, beating Carlos Reutemann's Williams FW07C into second place.

That in itself wasn't so bad, but when Hector Rebaque breezed past Argentina's hero to run second in the other Brabham entry everybody smelt a rat. Only a broken rotor arm forestalled a Brabham 1-2 and, predictably, everybody was up in arms about the winning car's specification.

Of course, as Patrick Head was to reflect, there was really nothing illegal about the clever suspension lowering system. But what clearly was illegal was the fact that the BT49C's skirts were touching the ground, even if the basic concept relied on their operating on a cushion of air just above it.

The way in which the skirts tucked inwards at speed ensured that the wear was on the lower outer edge, not the bottom, which in itself enabled Gordon Murray and his engineers to go through the pantomime of showing round the skirts and saying 'look, there's no wear on the bottom of the skirt' with a clear conscience.

In any event, the whole fiasco of the 6cm ground clearance rule was thrown into accurate perspective as the utter farce it really was when FISA decided it couldn't police these foolish regulations, threw its hands up in corporate despair and allowed manually-operated suspension jacking devices to be installed.

This amounted to a complete acceptance that the cars were running illegally out on the circuit, but as long as the driver operated his cockpit control before coming into the pit lane, thereby lifting his skirts whilst in the scrutineering bay, all was deemed acceptable. The 6cm ground clearance requirement was quite simply a bad rule which deserved to be scrapped.

By this stage in the current chapter, you might be wondering what had happened to the turbo brigade in the first three races of the season. The answer is, not much. Prior to Argentina, it had been a thin time for Renault, but new recruit Prost chased Piquet home in second place, a rather eclipsed Arnoux trailing in fifth.

Past, present and future McLaren drivers confer during practice for the 1981 Dutch Grand Prix. If John Watson (in cockpit) had suggested that retired twice World Champion Niki Lauda (centre) had a go, little did he know that the Austrian would take him at his word. James Hunt (left), who won the title for the team in 1976, harbours no such ambitions.

McLaren's Restoration

Bruce McLaren was born in Auckland, New Zealand, on 30 August 1937. He died on Tuesday, 2 June 1970 when one of his own team's Can-Am sports cars crashed during a private test session at the Goodwood circuit, near Chichester, in Sussex. During his 32 years, he not only became one of the world's most accomplished Grand Prix drivers, but founded a racing team which would keep his name to the forefront of his chosen sport throughout the two decades following his death.

Appropriately, Bruce himself won McLaren's first Grand Prix victory, the 1968 Belgian event. Thereafter the team would score victories, courtesy of Denny Hulme, Peter Revson, Emerson Fittipaldi, Jochen Mass, James Hunt, John Watson, Niki Lauda, Alain Prost and Ayrton Senna.

Yet McLaren's own relaxed 'management by committee' approach, in which Bruce involved co-directors Teddy Mayer, Tyler Alexander and Phil Kerr, survived his death. Ironically, it contributed to the team's decline in the late 1970s, but not before Emerson Fittipaldi (1974) and James Hunt (1976) bagged a couple of World Championships. It would take the clear-thinking leadership qualities of Ron Dennis and the design department autocracy of John Barnard to get the show back on the rails.

It was also supremely appropriate that the first victory for the new order was scored by John Watson. In 1976, when the Ulsterman triumphed in the Austrian Grand Prix driving a Penske, it seemed as though his career was destined to take off like Hunt's. But two years apiece with Brabham and the old McLaren regime did little for Watson's morale, the novice Prost outclassing him in 1980 when it seemed as though the technique of driving ground-effect machines eluded him.

Armed with the new carbon-fibre MP4 in 1981, happily it all clicked into place once again for the popular Watson and he scored a memorable victory in front of his home crowd at Silverstone.

Chez Ferrari, despite all the tyre-smoking brio, Gilles Villeneuve had yet to score the Ferrari turbo's first Championship point.

However, the Italian team saw the dawn break over the bright new future at Imola in the inaugural San Marino Grand Prix. Villeneuve qualified on pole position, he and Pironi sharing the lead between them for forty-six of the race's sixty laps. Only an ill-timed sequence of tyre stops on a track surface which was sometimes wet, sometimes dry, stood between Villeneuve and a likely victory. He finished seventh, two places behind Pironi. But it had been a day of driving acrobatics for the two Ferrari men, their chassis clearly not in the same street as those crafted by the specialist British teams.

Villeneuve was not to be in with a chance of the Championship in 1981, but Ferrari's turbo learning-curve proved far steeper than Renault's. In its fourth season grappling with that forced-induction V6, the French 'national racing team' had started to look like an increasingly high-priced lemon, beset with mechanical unreliability.

Symptomatic of the rut into which they had dropped was Arnoux's failure to qualify his sleek new Renault RE30 which made its debut in the Belgian Grand Prix at Zolder. Adding insult to injury, Prost was out with clutch trouble as early as Lap 2. The Renault teams lack of organisational cohesion would always

Lauda back in action. After two years away from the cockpit, Niki tried this McLaren MP4 under conditions of great secrecy at Donington Park late in 1981. It convinced him that a comeback was a great idea . . .

handicap its efforts, to a greater or lesser extent, right through to its demise at the end of 1985.

By contrast, when Ferrari got a sniff of success, it galvanised the famous Italian *équipe* to push even harder. How Villeneuve ever manhandled his great scarlet truck round to take second place on the starting grid at Monaco defied belief. Piquet, winner at San Marino, just squeezed him out from pole position. But Nelson's fastest lap time was set at the wheel of a special lightweight 'qualifying car', another increasingly well-practised subterfuge indulged in by the Brabham team to retain a performance edge during those two crucial days of preparation for a Grand Prix.

Villeneuve scored a stupendous victory through the streets of the famous Mediterranean principality, but only after Jones had flustered Piquet into sliding into the barriers, much to the Australian's intense amusement. During the preceding Belgian Grand Prix, Piquet had flown off the road after making contact with Jones's Williams, after which he voiced some ill-considered threatening noises on the subject of retaliation. Jones, built like a block of flats, muttered words to the effect that there wasn't enough time to worry about the Piquets of this world. The matter went no further.

Carlos Reutemann was an enigmatic personality, combining great natural flair with a deeply introspective temperament. He should have won the 1981 World Championship, yet the manner in which he allowed it to slip from his grasp almost suggested he was happier without it.

Below: *Carlos Reutemann crests the rise out of Casino Square during practice for the 1981 Monaco Grand Prix. The previous year he had emerged a lucky winner, but this race would see him eliminated in an early collision with Mansell's Lotus.*

Ferocious battle for the lead of the 1981 Belgian Grand Prix at Zolder with the Williams FW07Cs of Reutemann and Jones sandwiching Piquet's Brabham BT49C. Carlos won after both his rivals crashed out of the battle.

Jones then lost the Monaco race lead to Villeneuve when he stopped to investigate a fuel pick-up problem, something of a Williams Achilles Heel throughout the summer of 1981. It cropped up again to rob him of victory in the German Grand Prix at Hockenheim, although these disappointments could be set against his driving error at Zolder when he fell off the road trying to give Reutemann a driving lesson he would not forget.

Villeneuve's capacity for improvisation behind the wheel produced yet another memorable Ferrari victory at Madrid's twisty Jarama circuit during the Spanish Grand Prix. It was a classic triumph of a powerful, ill-handling chassis over a quartet of less powerful, but good-handling cars. Once ahead, the Ferrari turbo just bottled them up through the corners and squirted away down the straights. The slightest error would have seen Jacques Laffite's Ligier, John Watson's McLaren, Carlos Reutemann's Williams and Elio de Angelis's Lotus slip through, but no such bonus was forthcoming.

This was another race which Jones threw away. Having erupted into an initial lead, his prospects of an easy victory vaporised in the wake of a time-consuming spin. But if Ferrari was doing well, Renault was not. It was beginning to look as though the French team was simply discarding the World

Championship for theatrical effect. It hardly seemed possible that, given their turbo experience, on the one hand they could seem so promising, yet on the other still be so technically unreliable.

However, the French Grand Prix at Dijon provided the French team with a happy second anniversary of Jabouille's maiden turbo victory. Alain Prost scored the first in what was to become an avalanche of victories over ensuing seasons, although he was immeasurably aided by a torrential rain shower which resulted in the race being flagged to a halt after fifty-nine of its scheduled eighty laps.

At that point, Nelson Piquet's Brabham BT49C had been running ahead of Prost's Renault RE30, but the French car switched to soft compound Michelin rubber for the remaining twenty-two laps to emerge winner on aggregate. The Brabham team, along with Williams, had recently switched back to Goodyear rubber as the Akron company returned to the Formula 1 fray, but the American firm had no correspondingly soft tyre compound available for Piquet to use in these unusual circumstances. In the end, Prost won by just over two seconds from John Watson's McLaren MP4, Piquet trailing in third place ahead of turbo men Arnoux and Pironi.

Heavy traffic on the opening lap of the 1981 United States Grand Prix West at Long Beach with Reutemann's Williams leaning into the first right-hand hairpin in pursuit of Riccardo Patrese's disappearing pole position Arrows. Didier Pironi's Ferrari 126CK turbo (no. 28) is right behind Jones's Williams, looking for a gap inside Nelson Piquet's Brabham BT49.

Another turbo victory denied. Jacques Laffite's Ligier-Matra slips inside René Arnoux's fading Renault to take the lead in the 1981 Austrian Grand Prix at Osterreichring.

The British Grand Prix weekend opened with Team Lotus firing a desperate final salvo in the battle to keep the twin-chassis concept alive, presenting a further revised version, designated 88B, to the scrutineers who duly accepted its legality. But the British Grand Prix organisers were overruled by FISA under threat of having the race's Championship status withdrawn. The stewards duly trawled the rule book, decided that they would have to defer to the sport's governing body, and Chapman's final foray into the realms of Formula 1 technical ingenuity was buried for ever.

Arnoux and Prost buttoned up the front row for Renault, then proceeded to snatch defeat from the jaws of victory yet again, running in 1-2 formation in the early stages only to succumb to engine failure. That opened the way for Ron Dennis's prediction to be realised, John Watson storming home to an emotional victory for the carbon-fibre McLaren MP4/4. Didier Pironi's Ferrari went out with tyre failure, a few laps after Villeneuve had triggered a multiple accident at the Woodcote chicane, eliminating Alan Jones's Williams and the McLaren of Andrea de Cesaris. How Watson managed to creep through this chaos without becoming involved himself was to remain one of the mysteries of the 1981 season.

Carlos Reutemann was now ensconced in a 17 point lead at the head of the World Championship table thanks to victories at Rio and Zolder, allied to a string of consistent top six results. Yet this genial man took my breath away that evening at Silverstone by betting me £25 that he would not win the title. It was almost as if he felt embarrassed by the possibility of becoming World Champion, overawed by the prospect of achieving something which, privately, he seemed to doubt he was worthy of. It made me feel extremely uncomfortable.

Yet, amazingly, Reutemann's prophecy came true. The balance of the season would see his advantage gradually frittered away to the stage where he went into the final race at Las Vegas with only 1 point in hand over Nelson Piquet. Even so, on the eve of that incongruous scramble round the parking lot of the Caesars Palace casino in America's gambling capital, it still seemed he would be able to pull it off.

Reutemann started from pole position in that final race of the year, yet immediately seemed to capitulate the moment the start was given. Alan Jones bounded off into the distance, leading all the way to flag on what was billed as his last-ever Formula 1 race. Fed up with the spine-jarring ride produced by FISA's absurd ground-clearance regulations, he had earlier announced his retirement, ostensibly to a life of cattle farming in his native Australia.

Prost finished second for Renault, too late to salvage any title prospects, while Piquet, dehydrated in the fearful heat and almost passing out in the cockpit of his Brabham, struggled home fifth. It was enough to steal the title from under Reutemann's nose, the Argentinian driver fading to eighth at the end.

Jones leads Villeneuve and Reutemann during the opening stages of the 1981 Spanish Grand Prix. Soon after, the Australian would spin off, handing the lead – and eventual victory – to the Ferrari turbo.

Reutemann's engineer on the Williams team was Neil Oatley, a mild-mannered, pleasant character and a passionate fan of his chosen sport. In 1989, as a member of the Honda Marlboro McLaren design team, he would produce the McLaren MP4/5 which carried Alain Prost to his third World Championship. To this day, he does not know what came over Reutemann that day in the blazing Nevada sunshine.

'Carlos's mental commitment out of the cockpit was certainly the closest I've ever seen to Ayrton Senna's,' Oatley told me. 'He could be a phenomenally quick driver, absolutely brilliant when the conditions were right. But I never really understood what happened to him that day at Las Vegas. His car was slightly stiffer sprung than Jones's, but that wasn't a really significant difference. It was as if he had convinced himself he wasn't good enough to win.

'It didn't take a lot to de-tune him. At Monza the same year, he had been blindingly quick during qualifying, splitting the Renaults on what was a power circuit,and qualifying on the front row. But there was a slight rain shower before the start which certainly out-psyched him . . .'

That account of events is undeniable. Running third on Lap 15, Reutemann suddenly dropped to eighth in a single lap when a few more raindrops brushed the circuit. He finished a distant third behind Prost's winning Renault and Alan Jones, the Australian driving his Williams with a broken finger sustained in a brawl following a traffic accident in West London.

Early in 1990, Reutemann talked to me about those two apparent mysteries of his career, Las Vegas and Monza, 1981. 'I used much stiffer springs than Jones and was very happy with the car,' he recalled. 'Fantastic! I was easily quickest in first qualifying, so I said, please, just don't touch the car at all before the race. Then in untimed practice on the second day, I tapped a rear wheel of Piquet's Brabham. The impact bent a rocker arm on my car and, after it was replaced, it never handled properly again.

'I switched to another car which just didn't suit me; different driving position, different handling, different feel to the gearchange. On race day I didn't have the chance to choose the tyres individually, something to which I usually attached great importance. The tyres I used caused a handling imbalance and there were slight brake problems.

'It was just hopeless . . .'

THE TURBO YEARS' RESULTS 1981

Winner's average speed

February 7, SOUTH AFRICAN GRAND PRIX, Kyalami (later excluded from Championship – run under 1980 skirted regulations)
1	Carlos Reutemann	Williams-Cosworth FW07B
2	Nelson Piquet	Brabham-Cosworth BT49B
3	Elio de Angelis	Lotus-Cosworth 81
4	Keke Rosberg	Fittipaldi-Cosworth F8C
5	John Watson	McLaren-Cosworth M29C
6	Riccardo Patrese	Arrows-Cosworth A3

(112.31mph)

March 15, UNITED STATES GRAND PRIX WEST, Long Beach
1	Alan Jones	Williams-Cosworth FW07C
2	Carlos Reutemann	Williams-Cosworth FW07C
3	Nelson Piquet	Brabham-Cosworth BT49C
4	Mario Andretti	Alfa Romeo 179
5	Eddie Cheever	Tyrrell-Cosworth 010
6	Patrick Tambay	Theodore-Cosworth TR3

(87.60mph)

March 29, BRAZILIAN GRAND PRIX, Rio
1	Carlos Reutemann	Williams-Cosworth FW07C
2	Alan Jones	Williams-Cosworth FW07C
3	Riccardo Patrese	Arrows-Cosworth A3
4	Marc Surer	Ensign-Cosworth N180
5	Elio de Angelis	Lotus-Cosworth 81
6	Jacques Laffite	Ligier-Matra JS17

(96.59mph)

April 12, ARGENTINE GRAND PRIX, Buenos Aires
1	Nelson Piquet	Brabham-Cosworth BT49C
2	Carlos Reutemann	Williams-Cosworth FW07C
3	Alain Prost	Renault RE20B turbo
4	Alan Jones	Williams-Cosworth FW07C
5	René Arnoux	Renault RE20B turbo
6	Elio de Angelis	Lotus-Cosworth 81

(124.67mph)

May 3, SAN MARINO GRAND PRIX, Imola
1	Nelson Piquet	Brabham-Cosworth BT49C
2	Riccardo Patrese	Arrows-Cosworth A3
3	Carlos Reutemann	Williams-Cosworth FW07C
4	Hector Rebaque	Brabham-Cosworth BT49C
5	Didier Pironi	Ferrari 126C turbo
6	Andrea de Cesaris	McLaren-Cosworth M29F

(101.20mph)

May 17, BELGIAN GRAND PRIX, Zolder
1	Carlos Reutemann	Williams-Cosworth FW07C
2	Jacques Laffite	Ligier-Matra JS17
3	Nigel Mansell	Lotus-Cosworth 81
4	Gilles Villeneuve	Ferrari 126C turbo
5	Elio de Angelis	Lotus-Cosworth 81
6	Eddie Cheever	Tyrrell-Cosworth 010

(112.12mph)

May 31, MONACO GRAND PRIX, Monte Carlo
1	Gilles Villeneuve	Ferrari 126C turbo	(82.04mph)
2	Alan Jones	Williams-Cosworth FW07C	
3	Jacques Laffite	Ligier-Matra JS17	
4	Didier Pironi	Ferrari 126C turbo	
5	Eddie Cheever	Tyrrell-Cosworth 010	
6	Marc Surer	Ensign N180	

June 21, SPANISH GRAND PRIX, Jarama
1	Gilles Villeneuve	Ferrari 126C turbo	(92.68mph)
2	Jacques Laffite	Ligier-Matra JS17	
3	John Watson	McLaren-Cosworth MP4	
4	Carlos Reutemann	Williams-Cosworth FW07C	
5	Elio de Angelis	Lotus-Cosworth 87	
6	Nigel Mansell	Lotus-Cosworth 87	

July 5, FRENCH GRAND PRIX, Dijon-Prenois
1	Alain Prost	Renault RE20B turbo	(118.30mph)
2	John Watson	McLaren-Cosworth MP4	
3	Nelson Piquet	Brabham-Cosworth BT49C	
4	René Arnoux	Renault RE20B turbo	
5	Didier Pironi	Ferrari 126C turbo	
6	Elio de Angelis	Lotus-Cosworth 87	

July 18, BRITISH GRAND PRIX, Silverstone
1	John Watson	McLaren-Cosworth MP4	(137.64mph)
2	Carlos Reutemann	Williams-Cosworth FW07C	
3	Jacques Laffite	Ligier-Matra JS17	
4	Eddie Cheever	Tyrrell-Cosworth 010	
5	Hector Rebaque	Brabham-Cosworth BT49C	
6	Slim Borgudd	ATS-Cosworth D5	

August 8, GERMAN GRAND PRIX, Hockenheim
1	Nelson Piquet	Brabham-Cosworth BT49C	(132.53mph)
2	Alain Prost	Renault RE30 turbo	
3	Jacques Laffite	Ligier-Matra JS17	
4	Hector Rebaque	Brabham-Cosworth BT49C	
5	Eddie Cheever	Tyrrell-Cosworth 011	
6	John Watson	McLaren-Cosworth MP4	

August 16, AUSTRIAN GRAND PRIX, Osterreichring
1	Jacques Laffite	Ligier-Matra JS17	(134.03mph)
2	René Arnoux	Renault RE30 turbo	
3	Nelson Piquet	Brabham-Cosworth BT49C	
4	Alan Jones	Williams-Cosworth FW07C	
5	Carlos Reutemann	Williams-Cosworth FW07C	
6	John Watson	McLaren-Cosworth MP4	

August 30, DUTCH GRAND PRIX, Zandvoort
1	Alain Prost	Renault RE30 turbo	(113.71mph)
2	Nelson Piquet	Brabham-Cosworth BT49C	
3	Alan Jones	Williams-Cosworth FW07C	
4	Hector Rebaque	Brabham-Cosworth BT49C	
5	Elio de Angelis	Lotus-Cosworth 81	
6	Eliseo Salazar	Ensign-Cosworth N180	

September 13, ITALIAN GRAND PRIX, Monza
1 Alain Prost   Renault RE30 turbo   (129.89mph)
2 Alan Jones   Williams-Cosworth FW07C
3 Carlos Reutemann   Williams-Cosworth FW07C
4 Elio de Angelis   Lotus-Cosworth 81
5 Didier Pironi   Ferrari 126C turbo
6 Nelson Piquet   Brabham-Cosworth BT49C

September 27, CANADIAN GRAND PRIX, Montreal
1 Jacques Laffite   Ligier-Matra JS17   (85.25mph)
2 John Watson   McLaren-Cosworth MP4
3 Gilles Villeneuve   Ferrari 126C turbo
4 Bruno Giacomelli   Alfa Romeo 179
5 Nelson Piquet   Brabham-Cosworth BT49C
6 Elio de Angelis   Lotus-Cosworth 81

October 17, CAESARS PALACE GRAND PRIX, Las Vegas
1 Alan Jones   Williams-Cosworth FW07C   (97.90mph)
2 Alain Prost   Renault RE30 turbo
3 Bruno Giacomelli   Alfa Romeo 179
4 Nigel Mansell   Lotus-Cosworth 87
5 Nelson Piquet   Brabham-Cosworth BT49C
6 Jacques Laffite   Ligier-Matra JS17

DRIVERS' WORLD CHAMPIONSHIP

Posn	Driver	Points
1	Nelson Piquet	50
2	Carlos Reutemann	49
3	Alan Jones	46
4	Jacques Laffite	44
5	Alain Prost	43
6	John Watson	27
7	Gilles Villeneuve	25
8	Elio de Angelis	14
9	René Arnoux	11
	Hector Rebaque	
11	Eddie Cheever	10
	Riccardo Patrese	
13	Didier Pironi	9
14	Nigel Mansell	8
15	Bruno Giacomelli	7
16	Marc Surer	4
17	Mario Andretti	3
18	Slim Borgudd	1
	Andrea de Cesaris	
	Patrick Tambay	
	Eliseo Salazar	

CONSTRUCTORS' CHAMPIONSHIP

Posn	Constructor	Points
1	Williams	95
2	Brabham	61
3	Renault	54
4	Ligier	44
5	Ferrari	34
6	McLaren	28
7	Lotus	22
8	Alfa Romeo	10
	Arrows	
	Tyrrell	
11	Ensign	5
12	ATS	1
	Theodore	

1982

It would be an illusion to think that the life of a Formula 1 team revolves solely round the noisy, frenetic hubbub of a Grand Prix weekend. The race itself remains merely the icing on the cake, mirroring how well the jobs of design, engineering, testing and development have been done by any individual team. The race is Formula 1 putting on its most glamorous public face. Few members of the public realise what is involved in the drudge of mid-winter test sessions and the off-stage frustrations as a new Grand Prix car is coaxed into competitive life.

The Circuit Paul Ricard has become the traditional home of the French Grand Prix in recent times. Situated in scrubland above the Mediterranean resort of Bandol, it can be as parched as a furnace in early July and the fans have carefully to weigh up the competing attractions of the beach before sweltering in queues of traffic to gain access to the track. But swelter they do. Five months later, there would be no queues, yet a pre-Christmas visit to the paddock would reveal ranks of transporters, just as on Grand Prix weekend.

During the winter of 1981/82, for two weeks, Paul Ricard played host to the Brabham-BMW team. With the Mistral, that piercing wind which lends its name to the circuit's long back straight, blowing with a vengeance, it was a raw, bitter and depressing place to be. Yet the team was sowing the seed corn of a World Championship success, however unlikely that may have seemed at the time.

To be frank, Dieter Stappert was now worrying as to whether BMW's 4 cylinder turbo really did have much of a long-term future. During this test, the German engines were popping like fire crackers, seldom running long enough for the Brabham BT50 test car to accumulate any serious mileage. Yet Stappert recalls being highly impressed with Nelson Piquet's singleminded approach to the business of developing this new project.

In addition to the BMW turbo test car, one of the Cosworth-engined Brabham BT49Cs had been brought down to the southern French track for the team's new number two driver, Riccardo Patrese, to try out. Patrese, confident and ebullient following his transfer from Arrows, was revelling in the feel of his new machine, reeling off a succession of lap records to the accompaniment of salivating approval from a supportive Italian press corps.

Yet Piquet never made a move towards the Cosworth-engined car. In his view, there was no point. The team's future success depended on sorting out the BMW engine, so why waste time with yesterday's machine? Here he was, the newly-crowned World Champion, standing patiently in the pit garage, watching as the BMW and Bosch technicians fiddled anxiously with their new baby. It was a telling index of his determination.

Listening to the off-season gossip, considering the new cars that were in the pipeline and watching various new faces crop up in fresh places, the lay observer might have been forgiven for thinking that Formula 1 had passed through the eye of the political storm into more tranquil waters. But that would have been an unfortunately naive interpretation of the situation. There was plenty more acrimony, unpleasantness and uncertainty destined to make the Grand Prix world shudder before the Turbo Era became established beyond doubt.

On the political front, in the wake of the the turmoil surrounding the Lotus 88, Basil Tye, managing director of the RAC's Motor Sports Association (RACMSA), decided to challenge Jean-Marie Balestre in the elections for the FISA presidency held in October 1981. It proved to be about as worthwhile a project as Sir Anthony Meyer's attempts to unseat the Sitting Tenant of Number Ten Downing Street in the Tory Party leadership elections of 1989. Tye, a great enthusiast who perhaps misjudged the temperature of the water as far as taking on Balestre was concerned, was roundly trounced by Balestre who added insult to injury by strongly admonishing the Englishman for having the temerity to try!

Whilst it remains debatable whether or not the FOCA-aligned teams were playing a straight bat throughout their wearing battles with the sport's governing body, I always felt that the RAC, as custodian of the sport in Britain, was relying far too much on the French sense of fair play in its dealings with FISA. This gentlemanly feeling could not have been better reflected when, at the height of all this drama, I found myself talking to Sir Clive Bossom, chairman of RACMSA, on a flight back from the Monaco Grand Prix.

Sir Clive is one of those nice old buffers who I have always imagined to be found dozing in a leather-lined House of Commons library. Chatting about the FISA/FOCA conflict, he suddenly said: 'I think the time is coming where we may have to say "Jean-Mary (sic), we think it is perhaps better that you stand down . . ."' I forebore from asking whether he would ever dare suggesting a similar strategy to Margaret Thatcher. Oh that life in the Formula 1 jungle were so straightforward!

You had to hand it to FOCA, though. The well-connected Max Mosley managed to get Jonathan Aitken, Tory MP for Thanet, to stand up in Parliament as early as 1980 to make an impassioned plea on behalf of the British Grand Prix teams threatened with extinction by these unreasonable ogres in Paris. Referring to Bernie Ecclestone and his colleagues as 'robust entrepreneurs' it was good theatrical stuff. I have always made a mental note to treat anything I hear emanating from the House of Commons with some scepticism ever since. Aitken already knew something about Formula 1 from another angle; one of his 'day jobs' included working for Albilad, the trading company of the Saudi Royal Family. Albilad was also one of the Williams team sponsors.

Technically, it looked as though the rules had been improved with the abandonment of the suspension jacking systems which had made Formula 1 look so absurd throughout the previous summer. Now flexible – not sliding – skirts were permitted, a course of action which may have looked moderately promising for those designers with a grasp of ground-effect aerodynamics. However, these regulations spawned a breed of Grand Prix machine which, if anything, depended on even stiffer suspension than in 1981 in order to stablise its under-car aerodynamics. The result was a fearful pounding for the drivers who complained unceasingly, and with justification, of back ache, muscular pains and pulled muscles. The minimum weight limit was also reduced by 5kg to 585kg, a move seen as a crumb of comfort to the non-turbo specialists with the capability, for now at least, of building a lighter overall package.

On the driver front, of course, there were several key changes. Undoubtedly the most highly publicised was the return to the cockpit of Niki Lauda following a two season retirement during which his airline had fallen on financially unfortunate times. For some months, Niki had begun to realise that he missed the spice of personal competition and, throughout 1981, we began to notice his presence increasingly at European races. His connections with Marlboro made him an ideal candidate for McLaren, his signing proving a considerable personal coup for the ambitious Ron Dennis who also announced his long-term plans for a brand-new turbo Formula 1 engine manufactured exclusively for the team by Porsche.

Meanwhile, over at Williams, an unfortunate sequence of events had left the team facing a minor crisis. Not only was Alan Jones throwing in the towel, but Carlos Reutemann also told Frank he was retiring in the wake of that disappointment at Las Vegas, where he failed to grasp the Championship. This posed a

All kitted up and ready to go. Alain Prost helped raised Renault's game in the turbo stakes, but mechanical problems denied him a shot at the Championship in 1981, 1982 and 1983.

real problem for the front-line British team which, having established itself as a World Championship contender, now faced the challenge of training up new blood.

Reutemann would change his mind, thankfully, and return to do the first two races of the season. He finished second at Kyalami then crashed at Rio after a tangle with Arnoux's Renault. At that point, this complex man decided, yes, he did want to retire after all, and unobtrusively slipped away from the Grand Prix scene only two months before Britain was flung into the Falklands conflict with Argentina. There is no reason to suppose for a moment that Reutemann had any prior knowledge of how events would subsequently unfold, even though it is clear that it would have been extremely embarrassing for Britain's leading Grand Prix team to have continued employing an Argentinian during those turbulent months.

However, back in November 1981, Williams hit a seam of gold when Finnish driver Keijo Rosberg was signed up to replace Jones. Keke, as he was universally known, was to mature into one of the great characters of the Formula 1 decade, for in addition to being one of the most committed, determined and blindingly fast drivers of his era, he was an extrovert entrepreneur of rare genius.

If Rosberg had come on the scene a generation or so earlier, he would have dealt in 'war surplus', driven a white Jaguar Mark 5 and worn co-respondent's shoes – the sort of guy who would have been able to get his hands on nylons during the height of the Blitz. His chain smoking drove the ultra-fit Frank Williams up the wall. Keke was flashy, confident and full of beans. Sauntering about the Grand Prix paddocks as if he owned the place, he loved to keep up with the latest tittle-tattle and would never shy away from giving his opinions on controversial matters.

I never quite believed that the Williams team came fully to understand this cocky character who was 33 years old when he got his break in a test session at Paul Ricard. Yet there was no mistaking the fact that he was an exciting driver. Although Keke would occasionally remark, 'The biggest problem with Frank Williams is that he's never forgiven me for not being Alan Jones,' the fact remained that he was a Williams-sort-of-driver. The kind of guy who took a car by the scruff of its neck, an instinctive racer.

Ironically, after a year in which the technical regulations had been at the centre of just about every controversy going, the 1982 season opened with a major furore surrounding the drivers. Niki Lauda celebrated his return by loading a potentially sensitive gun, then getting others to fire it. Whilst going through his paperwork prior to the start of the season, the meticulous

Austrian read the small print on his 1982 FISA super-licence. What he understood did not please him in the slightest.

The licence, so it seemed, was being issued to drivers in conjunction with a specifically nominated team, leading Lauda to conclude that some sort of restrictive cartel was in action and raising the possibility that the teams might start controlling who-goes-where. In retrospect, it was a slightly paranoid response which could have been delivered to FISA when they received their licence application forms two months earlier were it not for the fact that only Lauda seemed to notice these implications.

Whatever the motivation, the season kicked off on a less-than-promising note with no practice on the first day at Kyalami, the drivers barricading themselves into a Johannesburg hotel room while negotiations continued. Eventually the strike was broken by some sort of compromise arrangement which did not prevent FISA imposing fines on all who had transgressed. That was understandable, but hardly conciliatory.

For Piquet, however, a special slice of humiliation awaited him when he returned to the Kyalami pit lane. Bernie Ecclestone was absolutely furious that the drivers should attempt collectively to disrupt the show, a message imparted to Piquet when he found that all three Brabham-BMWs were now carrying Riccardo Patrese's race number two. Bernie also insisted that Nelson should have a medical check-up after this night-long farce locked into the hotel, raising the tension further. Nelson qualified second to Arnoux's Renault only to botch the start, so it was hardly surprising that he flew into a sand trap — and out of the race — as early as Lap 4. Prost won, despite a stop to change a punctured tyre, from Reutemann and Rene Arnoux with Lauda an impressive fourth on his comeback drive.

The Brabham-BMWs clearly promised to be formidable weapons once developed to a competitive pitch, for Gordon Murray's chassis technology was of high quality, notwithstanding his reservations over the use of carbon fibre. Renault would continue the season using 'B' versions of the RE30, the French team eschewing carbon fibre in all but the side pods of these aluminium alloy chassis. Over at Ferrari, however, big changes had been afoot since Harvey Postlethwaite arrived on the design staff during the summer of 1981, providing Maranello with instant access to contemporary British thinking on the question of chassis design.

During the first year with the turbo 126CK, Ferrari quickly came to understand that there was no way in which its traditional panelled tube-frame chassis could provide the long-term solution to coping with the mechanical and aerodynamic loadings which were envisaged in the next few seasons of the

turbo era. Thus Postlethwaite was recruited and given a free hand to raise the standards of Ferrari's chassis technology to an appropriate level.

At the time he received an approach from Ferrari, the halcyon days of Wolf Racing were far behind Harvey. After James Hunt's retirement in mid-1979, Keke Rosberg, then a hard-charging new boy, was recruited to take his place. But the keen edge of Walter Wolf's Formula 1 ambition had dulled by now and, at the end of the season, the team merged with Fittipaldi Automotive, the team owned by Brazilian brothers Emerson and Wilson Fittipaldi. What followed was a gradual downward spiral into oblivion. . .

Thankfully, Ferrari gave Postlethwaite the opportunity to step off the sinking Fittipaldi ship before it finally disappeared below the waves. Assessing the situation on his arrival at Maranello, he concluded that he would really like to build a carbon-fibre

Villeneuve leads Pironi at Imola – Didier would win against team orders, much to Gilles's thinly suppressed fury.

Nelson Piquet takes the weight off his feet after collapsing with heat exhaustion after winning the 1982 Brazilian Grand Prix. However, he and second place man Keke Rosberg (left) were in for a nasty shock when they were disqualified in the 'water bottle controversy' and third man Prost (right) was awarded victory.

composite chassis immediately for 1982. But although he felt he had the necessary knowledge, he knew that the team was a long way behind in terms of the required technology. Therefore, having persuaded Enzo Ferrari that a switch to carbon fibre should be made only when the facilities were available in-house at Maranello, he set about producing a stop-gap chassis built from alloy/Nomex honeycomb sandwich sheeting.

Since Ferrari had not even the capability to carry out resin bonding work, Postlethwaite had to secure supplies of bonded honeycomb sheeting from the Belgian Hexcel company. The method of manufacture adopted for the 'C2' version of the 126 line was very similar to that which he had employed on the Wolf WR7 driven by Hunt and Rosberg. The sheeting was folded round internal carbon-fibre bulkheads, then glued together to form an extremely light and rigid structure.

The suspension and running gear were broadly similar to those used on the 1981 car, Ferrari starting the season with rocker arm activation of the spring/damper units, a system also retained by Renault and McLaren. But Williams, and later Ferrari, would eventually follow Brabham's lead in employing the lighter pull-rod systems which conferred valuable aerodynamic advantages in addition to helping in the endless search for weight reduction.

Of course, Postlethwaite's efforts merely set about the task of bringing Ferrari's chassis up on to a par with its engine development, the Italian team still set in the fundamental, age-old belief that a chassis was merely something that suspended four wheels and prevented the driver's backside from scraping along the road. During 1981 and into 1982, Ferrari really got into top gear when it came to getting the best out of contemporary turbo technology.

One of the earliest problems experienced by all the turbo teams was this vexed question of 'throttle lag' – caused by the turbines slowing down too much when the driver's foot was off the throttle, producing a delay in response when he went back on to that pedal. To keep the turbines spinning, irrespective of engine speed or the amount of exhaust gas reaching the turbines, Ferrari linked the compressor manifold to the exhaust manifold by means of a valve which, when the throttles closed, opened to pass compressed air into the turbines. Once back on the throttle again, this valve closed and stopped the combustion taking place within the turbines. Renault's answer to the same conundrum had been to squirt a jet of fuel into the turbo, an expedient which also kept the turbines spinning when the driver was off the throttle.

Whilst the Ferrari system had proved extremely effective during 1981, it imposed enormous strains and stresses on the turbine blades and bearings, so the concept was revised for 1982. Much the same result was achieved by extensive experimentation with the ratio between turbine and compressor, along with a bigger turbo boost control valve and detail work on porting, ignition and valve gear.

Of course, the ever-increasing temperatures developed within the combustion chamber of a turbocharged engine was a potential trouble area, so a system of water injection was developed by the team's fuel supplier, Agip, and first raced on the cars mid-season at Detroit. Following a principal similar to that used to cool jet engines, the Agip engineers developed a highly complex system whereby a globule of water could be encapsulated within a globule of petrol, lowering the temperature of the fuel as it entered the combustion chamber. At the point of combustion, the water turned to steam, effectively 'exploding' the surrounding petrol, offering improved atomization and better mixture control within the combustion chamber.

By the end of the 1982 season, Ferrari emerged with the Constructors' Championship with three race wins to the team's credit. Hard up against Renault, Brabham-BMW and the agile Cosworth-propelled runners from Williams, McLaren and Lotus, the bare facts suggest this was quite an achievement. But the trouble with hard facts is they reveal nothing of the human element. In 1982, that aspect would be tragic and troubling in the extreme for the famous Italian team.

The new 126C2s gave Gilles Villeneuve and Didier Pironi a better chance of running at the front than they had been afforded in 1981. Yet the relationship between these two was to deteriorate catastrophically, indirectly contributing to the death of Villeneuve in practice for the Belgian Grand Prix at Zolder.

The complex sequence of events leading up to this tragedy have their roots in what many people regarded at the time as a deliberate misinterpretation of the regulations by the FOCA-aligned teams in an effort to stem the turbo tide and extend the Cosworth engine's Indian summer. However, although the designers' efforts to play King Canute did not pay off, they left a legacy of bitterness hanging in the air like November fog. It took a long time to clear...

For me, this contorted tale started in February 1982, when a group of press men were invited to Ketteringham Hall, Team Lotus's base at Hethel, for the unveiling of the Cosworth-engined type 91. This was an undramatic, nicely styled and conventional machine, but nothing which seemed likely to frighten the turbo brigade. During the course of conversation with Colin Chapman, I recall drawing his attention to what looked like a crushed plastic bag, tucked away in one of the side pods.

It was explained to me that this was the receptacle in which water would be carried to cool the brakes. Jets of water were to be sprayed into the brake ducts, reducing the temperature of the cooling air. Like a blind man stumbling through a field of land mines, I idly remarked that this looked to me like a clever way of running underweight, of carrying disposable ballast ...

I don't know what made me say that, but the effect on Colin Chapman was electrifying. In a second, he was transformed from a relaxed mood of urbanity to a highly agitated frame of mind, lecturing me loudly that this was the trouble with bloody journalists, that they didn't understand the rules, the technicalities and so-on. In retrospect, it was clever stuff. He threw me off the trail. I mean, who the hell was going to tell Colin Chapman that he didn't understand the regulations? Not me, for sure ...

In retrospect, I wish I'd had more faith in my own judgement. What Chapman, and indeed all his FOCA colleagues had in mind was a clever scam. They had chosen to drive a coach and four through the meaning of the regulations, seeking to legitimise their attempts to race illegally beneath the prevailing weight limit by bending their interpretation of the regulations.

The rule they were seeking to circumvent defined 'weight' as 'the weight of the car in running order with its normal quantity of lubricants and coolants, but without any fuel or driver on board'. In the past, it had been permissible to top up oil tanks prior to post-race scrutineering, so now the idea was to jettison

---

Keke Rosberg: Taking the Battle to the Turbos

To become the last world champion at the wheel of a naturally-aspirated car before the heyday of the turbo, Keke Rosberg drove his heart out through 1982. Although he only won a single Grand Prix, this was an unusual year in which no other driver triumphed in more than two races.

'Sure, it was frustrating not to have a turbo,' shrugs Rosberg, 'but there was no point in complaining about it. Anyway, I think I proved, when I put the FW08 on pole position for the British Grand Prix at Brands Hatch, that a Cosworth car could be competitive on all but the fastest circuits.'

Even so, Keke's opposite-lock brio bugged the hell out of Williams's sometimes pugnacious chief designer Patrick Head. Many times we would hear Patrick saying, 'I've told him that if he only tidied up his driving style, he would be even quicker than he is!' Rosberg airily dismissed this criticism with a shrug and a puff on his cigarette. 'I drive that way because that's how I like it and it seems to work pretty well.'

On one occasion, Frank Williams made the mistake of attributing Keke's occasional first lap moments to a lack of physical stamina. 'That's bullshit,' responded the Finn, admonishing his boss. 'We were starting the races with low tyre pressures so that they came up to precisely the correct temperature when they warmed up. It was necessary to manhandle the car on the opening lap because it was extremely twitchy until the tyres warmed up.'

Keke was proud of the fact that he always raced flat-out to the bitter end of his races. Waspishly alluding to the Brazilian Grand Prix, where he finished second to a totally exhausted Nelson Piquet, he chuckled, 'Anyway, I'm not the one who faints after a race ..."

most of this water ballast early in the race, in the vague general direction of the brakes, run underweight to the finish, and then top-up the water tank to ensure that the car topped the 580kg mark before the scrutineers checked it at the end of the event.

The FOCA teams found their idea put to the test at the second round of the Championship, the Brazilian Grand Prix at Rio. After Gilles Villeneuve's Ferrari C2 was harried into a mistake and crashed out of the lead, Nelson Piquet, driving a Brabham BT49D-Cosworth rather than the temperamental BMW turbo machine on this occasion, went through to win after a great battle with Keke Rosberg's Williams FW07C. Prost was third and, in the scrutineering bay, the latest controversy duly engulfed the Grand Prix fraternity . . .

While the stewards of the meeting were quite happy to let the whole thing pass, Renault formally registered a protest. This was rejected by the stewards but, perhaps predictably, upheld by an FIA Court of Appeal. Twenty-nine days after crossing the line at Rio, Prost moved from third to first place in the Brazilian Grand Prix, extending his Championship advantage to 11 points after only two races.

Before the FIA produced its verdict, the United States Grand Prix West took place at Long Beach, producing Niki Lauda's first victory of the season in the McLaren MP4B from Keke Rosberg's Williams and the Ferrari of Villeneuve. Unfortunately Gilles was subsequently disqualified for an aerofoil dimensional infringement, a not-totally-unexpected course of events after Ferrari chief engineer Mauro Forghieri produced a twin-plane rear aerofoil with both sections neatly staggered, one ahead of the other.

This, in effect, gave Ferrari a full-width rear wing which exceeded the permissible 110cm maximum. Forghieri tried to argue that there was nothing which said that the coachwork had to be measured from the centre-line of the cars. The stewards rejected this spurious contention, although many felt that Forghieri was simply attempting to emphasise just how loosely written was the rule book.

The action then moved on to Imola, in part, at least. Outraged by the FIA Court of Appeal's stance on the subject of 'brake cooling', most of the FOCA-aligned teams chose to boycott this event, claiming that they 'could not design new cars for the new regulations in time'. Tyrrell turned up, unwilling to throw away a three-race sponsorship deal, trumpeting like a rogue elephant about the validity of FOCA's standpoint, despite his presence. He also wasted no time in sticking a spoke into the wheel by lodging a protest against Renault, Ferrari and Toleman, the latter having financed the development of Brian Hart's compact 4 cylinder 415T turbo engine. The motive behind this protest was, in part, to placate his furious FOCA colleagues, many of whom would never forgive him for breaking ranks and attending this race.

Tyrrell's contention was that 'turbines' were forbidden in the technical regulations. The stewards rightly sent him away with a flea in his ear, pointing out that the word 'turbine' referred to turbine engines as such and not the turbines used within an exhaust-driven forced-induction engine. FOCA had earlier expressed the view that a turbocharger amounted to a secondary engine, a stance which some at FISA privately accepted, but it was five years too late for arguing out such esoteric points.

Although at the time it was difficult to see FOCA's viewpoint, the benefit of hindsight enables one to see more clearly their concern about the erratic manner in which the rules were being applied. Of course, that does not mean that they were right. But they were trying to show that, since 'topping-up' was not mentioned in the technical regulations, so it could be allowed.

As one of their number pointed out, turbocharging was not specifically mentioned in the technical regulations either, but it had crept into the Formula 1 equation on the back of a theoretical equivalency rule dreamed up to suit a completely different set of circumstances from those which prevailed in the early 1980s. And anyway, they continued; the rule permitted 'supercharged' engines, not 'turbocharged' nor even 'forced induction'. In FOCA's view, supercharging was not turbocharging.

Of course, the race fans at Imola could not have cared less about this political dispute. They were just happy that two Ferraris were racing and duly packed into the circuit in just the same numbers as they would have done if a full field was on hand. It was a salutary warning never to underestimate the pulling power of Ferrari on the team's home ground.

Although Prost's Renault was an early casualty with engine trouble, the race developed into a splendid three-way battle between Arnoux and the two Ferraris. René did the lion's share of the leading until, with only sixteen laps to go, his RE30B also succumbed to a major engine malfunction. Into the lead surged Villeneuve, with Pironi in his wheel tracks . . .

From the outset the Ferrari duo had been worried about fuel consumption, so Gilles now eased back considerably. The time-honoured routine for Ferrari drivers under such circumstances had been that, whoever should be ahead at the moment the cars assumed 1-2 formation at the head of the field should take the race. It was a policy which had worked well amongst honourable drivers in the past. Aside from that, it was a safe and sound policy intended to prevent team-mates and rivals from time-wasting internecine battles which could result in both men losing the race at the end of the day.

Gilles was desperately trying to slow the pace of their private battle, in response to signals from the pit wall. But Pironi seemed resolutely determined to make a race of it, and to hell with the consequences for his car's fuel consumption. On the penultimate lap, after swapping places several times, Pironi allowed Villeneuve through into the lead. Gilles just thought he was being honest, but in fact it was duplicity which prompted that piece of tactical good manners.

With Villeneuve taking things easily, changing up 1,000rpm early, Pironi caught him unawares on the last lap, blasting through to win. Gilles felt cheated. 'I'd have been mad at myself if I'd just plain been beaten,' he fumed, 'but second place because he steals the race from me, that's something else.'

I am tempted to think that the ice-cold Pironi knew exactly what sort of response this move would elicit from Villeneuve. In the two weeks remaining to the Belgian Grand Prix Gilles was distracted, preoccupied about the way in which he had been wronged by a man whom he, wrongly as things had transpired, regarded as a friend. He vowed never to speak to Pironi again.

Even Enzo Ferrari made sympathetic noises in Villeneuve's direction, perhaps designed to counter team co-ordinator Marco Piccinini's assertion, in the immediate aftermath of Pironi's victory, that there were no team orders in effect. During practice for the Belgian race, spurred on no doubt by the fact that Pironi had just lapped quicker than him, Villeneuve took one risk too many as he tried to dive inside the March 821 driven by slow-

René Arnoux's Renault RE30B storms away from the field in the opening stages of the 1982 French Grand Prix at Paul Ricard. Prost unwisely trusted Arnoux to conform with his pre-race agreement, with the result that Alain ended up a disillusioned second...

coach Jochen Mass. The dawdling German driver moved the wrong way and the irreparable happened in a trice.

Villeneuve's Ferrari C2 somersaulted to destruction over the rear wheel of the March and the gifted French Canadian driver died that evening in the hospital at nearby Louvain. It was an outstanding testimony to this remarkable driver that Canadian Prime Minister Pierre Trudeau despatched an air force jet to repatriate Villeneuve's body. With him died the image of the romantic Grand Prix driver cast in the Boy's Own paper mould . . .

That was the low point of an already disastrous season, made no more palatable by a leading team director accusing the writer, and a number of his colleagues, of taking back handers from Renault. In his view, nobody could even begin to espouse the FISA line if they were totally objective observers of the scene.

In the light of the recent spate of financially beneficial libel hearings in the High Court, hindsight says we should have sued. Had we done so, this charmless soul might now have been engaged in the worthy pastime of sponsoring the rest of my life. That I did not probably reflected my ambivalence towards him; I could not even take his insults seriously.

At any rate, this behaviour was only a portent of what was to come. Anybody amongst the British press corps who had taken an even vaguely pro-FISA, or pro-reason come to that, line was consigned to the outer darkness like a leper. Certain team principals who should have known better looked through us from the range of a few feet. Tempers took a long time to cool off.

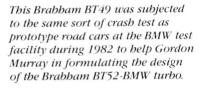

This Brabham BT49 was subjected to the same sort of crash test as prototype road cars at the BMW test facility during 1982 to help Gordon Murray in formulating the design of the Brabham BT52-BMW turbo.

After Gilles's death, Pironi emerged from his late team-mate's shadow and matured into a brilliantly accomplished and audacious performer, although increasingly he behaved as if he were bullet-proof. That is a dangerous state for a Grand Prix driver to approach, but Didier seemed to be born under a lucky star. He suffered another dreadful trauma at the start of the Canadian Grand Prix, stalling on pole position only to have Ricardo Paletti's Osella charge straight into the back of his stationary Ferrari. The young Italian newcomer suffered multiple injuries from which he later died. Pironi was shaken, but unhurt.

Later it seemed as though his troubles were behind him. Third in France, second at Brands Hatch, he followed that up by winning the Dutch Grand Prix in brilliant style. He arrived at Hockenheim, for the German Grand Prix, leading the Drivers' Championship by nine points.

A Frenchman would indeed win the German Grand Prix, but it was not Pironi. By the time Patrick Tambay, the man recruited to replace Villeneuve, took the chequered flag on 8 August, Didier Pironi's racing career was over. Surfing through a monsoon during untimed practice on Saturday morning, Pironi had run into the back of Alain Prost's Renault, the French turbo car totally concealed in the murk.

It was a virtual re-run of the Villeneuve tragedy, although Pironi was lucky, if such a label can be appropriately applied to somebody trapped in the shattered wreckage of a racing car with two badly-broken legs. Ahead lay the agony of more than thirty complex operations, but never the return to the cockpit for which Didier so fervently longed. In the summer of 1987, racing his powerboat off the Isle of Wight, he failed to ease off the throttles as he barrelled his way through the wake of a passing tanker. It was an error that proved fatal for Pironi and his two companions.

Under the circumstances, it was remarkable that Ferrari emerged with the Constructors' Championship, but it represented a just reward for dogged endeavour in the face of those fearful tragedies. For the Italian Grand Prix, Mario Andretti was lured back into a Ferrari cockpit for the first time since 1972 and helped wash away some of the unhappiness by grabbing pole position at Monza. In fact, with Arnoux winning at Monza from Tambay and Andretti, you could say that Ferrari drivers filled the first three places for, by that time, Rene had agreed to leave Renault and throw in his lot with the Prancing Horse for the following season.

Over at Renault, things were getting no better for the turbo generation's pioneers. Ironically, the one key area which endowed the RE30Bs with stupendous performance turned out

Ferrari's Season: Tragedy and Success

Success and tragedy ran hand-in-hand for Ferrari throughout 1982. Despite the death of Gilles Villeneuve at Zolder and the serious injuries sustained by Didier Pironi at Hockenheim, the famous Italian team ended the season poised on a springboard of success. From a technical standpoint, Maranello had made a considerable leap forward, thanks to the collaboration between their new designer Harvey Postlethwaite and long-time Ferrari engineer Mauro Forghieri.

Postlethwaite's calmly understated personality provided a soothing antidote to the turmoil and sadness in which the team found itself enveloped. His arrival at Maranello followed a well-beaten path. Enzo Ferrari had been a great Anglophile since the time he recruited Mike Hawthorn to his driving strength back in 1953. A decade later, John Surtees would make a huge contribution, not only winning the 1964 Championship, but also helping raise the level of Ferrari chassis technology to compete with the British. It was a process later continued by former Rootes Group engineer Mike Parkes, also an extremely competent driver.

It was not just a case of Harvey enhancing the team's immediate competitiveness, he also wrought a longer-term benefit by presiding over the technical up-grading of Ferrari's facilities. In that he met up with rather less ingrained opposition than, for example, encountered by his successor John Barnard. But Harvey wholeheartedly embraced the Italian way of life, moving his family to the Emilia Romagna region to become totally integrated with the Italian team.

He also got on like a house on fire with the Old Man. For the time being, at least...

to be the weakest link in the technical equation. At Monaco, the team introduced its own refined fuel-injection system which combined electronic control with a Bosch-Kugelfischer mechanical pump. Unfortunately, this pump had a pneumatic adjustment mechanism for its mixture cam which was replaced by a cheap and unreliable Japanese motor which proved unexpectedly susceptible to vibration and kept on failing. The cars worked well through the streets of the principality, though, but there could be no legislating for accidents.

Arnoux galloped away from the pack in the early stages, only to clip a kerb, snap into a spin and stall the engine. Unable to fire up again, a perfectly healthy machine had to be abandoned out on the circuit. Prost then crashed during the closing stages, the race apparently in the bag. To this day, he is not certain why, but almost certainly the rear suspension broke.

Prost should also have won at Detroit, Zandvoort and Osterreichring, arguably also at Paul Ricard and Las Vegas. His defeat at Arnoux's hands in the French Grand Prix raised echoes of the Pironi/Villeneuve confrontation at Imola. Lack of trust between team-mates was nothing new in Formula 1, but with increasing media interest putting the scene under an even more intense microscope throughout the past decade, such personal friction amongst the drivers went on increasingly public view. For Pironi/Villeneuve, read Arnoux/Prost, Mansell/Piquet or Prost/Senna. Once you had seen one, you'd seen them all...

However, when Renault team manager Gerard Larrousse extracted a specific promise from Arnoux that he would relinquish the lead to Prost if he found himself in that position, René readily agreed. Prost was therefore none too concerned when a damaged side skirt on his RE30B caused him to drop back considerably in second place. After all, a deal was a deal. René had given his word. Alas, when it came to it, Arnoux did not have the strength of character to go through with it. He won the French Grand Prix. Prost, fuming, was second.

In the end, Renault dropped to third place in the Constructors' standings behind Ferrari and McLaren. An over-view of their season indicates that the French national team was being overhauled on the chassis development front, even though its engines were well up to scratch on performance, if not reliability. In relative terms, Renault's turbos were at their most competitive throughout 1982. Thereafter, they trickled downhill into the history books.

Although many purist engineers screwed up their noses at the sight of an over-worked 4 cylinder turbo, the Brabham-BMW alliance was beginning to look the most promising hi-tech bet for the immediate future. The combination of Brabham's elegant, up-to-the-minute chassis work allied to BMW Motorsport's sheer determination to get things right made the future seem bright for the Anglo-German alliance.

Not that everything had been straightforward on the political front, however. In his role as FOCA president, Brabham boss Bernie Ecclestone now found himself having to develop the sort of talents required to overtake people in revolving doors. Running with the hare and hunting with the hounds hardly made a start on it!

Here was Bernie firmly in bed with a major motor manufacturer on a turbo engine deal, while at the same time trying to fight FOCA's corner as far as the anti-turbo lobby was concerned. For a while, it seemed as though his commitment to the BMW cause was wavering. Indeed, the Brabham BT50s only raced in the Belgian Grand Prix at Zolder after BMW told him to get on with the programme or forget it. The commercial implications of forgetting it would have propelled Bernie's team backwards into the second division, so the most powerful man in Formula 1 acceded to Munich's requirements.

By mid-season, however, it looked as though the boot was in severe danger of being switched to the other foot. Ecclestone and Gordon Murray, not to mention Piquet and Patrese, were getting just a touch fed-up with the BMW's seemingly endless problems with the fuel injection and electronic ignition systems. This view was enhanced when Patrese took the BT49D-Cosworth

Lotus team manager Peter Warr in his Ketteringham Hall office, photographed in early December 1982, only ten days before Colin Chapman's sudden death considerably multiplied his responsibilities.

to a lucky victory at Monaco, a race in which gearbox problems sidelined Piquet's BMW turbo-engined car.

Then came the absolute low point in the Brabham/BMW relationship, the inagural Detroit Grand Prix through the streets of the USA's Motor City. Unbelievably, Piquet failed to qualify after grappling with a truly appalling throttle response problem. It was the last thing a driver needed on a tortuous street circuit peppered with slow 90 degree corners.

Seven days separated Detroit from the Canadian Grand Prix. It was make or break time for the Anglo-German alliance. Dieter Stappert tried to head off Brabham designer Gordon Murray's inclination towards running a turbo at Montreal by putting it bluntly. 'I told Gordon, frankly, that if the team did not prepare two BMW cars, then the partnership was finished,' he recalls.

Murray agreed. Piquet had two BT50-BMWs at his disposal and qualified fourth behind the ill-starred Pironi, Arnoux and Prost in their Renaults. The delay after the Paletti accident worked in the turbo's favour. By the time the race restarted, a chill wind was blowing off the St Lawrence River. In gathering dusk, Nelson convincingly out-ran the Renault opposition to score the first Brabham-BMW victory. Second, ironically, was Patrese in the Brabham-Cosworth. The new order had beaten the old.

Of course, the battle to shed weight was always being attacked by the Brabham team which became the first to use carbon discs on a regular basis. But the BMW-engined car still needed 47 gallons to run through a race as opposed to the 38 gallons required for the Cosworth machine. Murray and his colleagues devised a new strategy. Planning to start the Brabham-BMWs with only half a fuel load, enabling them to use softer compound tyres with more grip, it was calculated that they would be able to build up a sufficiently large lead to make a refuelling stop and fit fresh tyres, yet still be in with a chance of victory.

Even at the first race this looked an over-optimistic ploy. Ten laps into the race, Piquet had only made 3sec over Niki Lauda's McLaren-Cosworth which was going through non-stop. Then Piquet's engine failed, presenting Niki with a smooth run through to his second win of the year.

Later, Patrese would come to retain the lead through one of those highly publicised pit stops during the Austrian Grand Prix only to suffer a major engine failure shortly afterwards. For the rest of the season, the Brabham-BMWs would continue their reputation for being fast and fragile.

Ferrari performed consistently enough across the season to take the Constructors' Championship thanks to the efforts of four different drivers, after Pironi's accident it was clear that the World Champion driver would come from the ranks of naturally-aspirated engine competitors. No driver would win more than two Grands Prix that season and, as it turned out, a single win would be good enough for the man who eventually won the title.

The Williams FW08 was the tool which Keke Rosberg used to do the job, the Finn barnstorming his way to the title despite a few set-backs which, if avoided, might have saved him the trouble of a down-to-the-wire battle with McLaren's John Watson in the final race of the season at Las Vegas. On that sad weekend at Zolder, Keke seemed to have the Belgian Grand Prix in the bag when he got caught out by locking rear brakes, handing victory to Watson on the penultimate lap.

Later, Rosberg would win the Swiss Grand Prix at Dijon-Prenois – only after Williams team manager Peter Collins firmly reminded the man with the chequered flag not to wave it prematurely at Prost's leading Renault which Keke only managed to haul in with just over a lap to run. He qualified brilliantly on pole position for the British Grand Prix, but vapour lock in the fuel system prevented him getting away on the parade lap and he had to start from the back of the grid. With another lap to run in Austria, he would have passed Elio de Angelis's winning Lotus. As it was, Lotus and Williams took the flag wheel to wheel.

Over at McLaren, the Super Team was very definitely in the making. In addition to Zolder, Watson won brilliantly at Detroit, which, added to Niki's two triumphs, brought the team's seasonal total to four wins. Lotus had the single victory in Austria, by which time Chapman had done a deal for the supply of Renault turbo engines for 1983, and Tyrrell at least had some consolation when the promising Michele Alboreto won the Las Vegas finale.

There was a lot of bitterness down in the ranks of the under-privileged. Several smaller teams felt that they had been deceived into supporting the early season FOCA line, particularly over the commercial pressure which had been brought to bear on them to keep in line when it came to boycotting the San Marino race. Now they saw the high-rollers – Brabham, McLaren, Williams and Lotus – all covering their options by chasing turbo deals as if their life depended on them. Which, of course, it did.

'The big teams lured us along to follow them, then left us to die,' remarked one small team owner bitterly. That is how it must have looked from the bottom of the pack, but, as would be proved time and again during the 1980s, solidarity between Formula 1 teams is built largely on quicksand.

The turbo era was now in full swing, the time for the plug-in-and-fire-up proprietary Grand Prix engine to be consigned to the history books. Nobody else would win a World Championship in a non-turbocharged car until after the turbos themselves were finally legislated out of the Grand Prix business six years later.

THE TURBO YEARS' RESULTS 1982

Winner's average speed

January 23, SOUTH AFRICAN GRAND PRIX, Kyalami
1	Alain Prost	Renault RE30B turbo	(127.86mph)
2	Carlos Reutemann	Williams-Cosworth FW07D	
3	René Arnoux	Renault RE30B turbo	
4	Niki Lauda	McLaren-Cosworth MP4	
5	Keke Rosberg	Williams-Cosworth FW07C	
6	John Watson	McLaren-Cosworth MP4	

March 21, BRAZILIAN GRAND PRIX, Rio
1	Alain Prost	Renault RE30B turbo	(112.97mph)
2	John Watson	McLaren-Cosworth MP4	
3	Nigel Mansell	Lotus-Cosworth 91	
4	Michele Alboreto	Tyrrell-Cosworth 011	
5	Manfred Winkelhock	ATS-Cosworth D5	
6	Didier Pironi	Ferrari 126C2 turbo	

April 4, UNITED STATES GRAND PRIX, Long Beach
1	Niki Lauda	McLaren-Cosworth MP4	(81.40mph)
2	Keke Rosberg	Williams-Cosworth FW07C	
3	Riccardo Patrese	Brabham-Cosworth BT49C	
4	Michele Alboreto	Tyrrell-Cosworth 011	
5	Elio de Angelis	Lotus-Cosworth 91	
6	John Watson	McLaren-Cosworth MP4	

April 25, SAN MARINO GRAND PRIX, Imola
1	Didier Pironi	Ferrari 126C2 turbo	(116.66mph)
2	Gilles Villeneuve	Ferrari 126C2 turbo	
3	Michele Alboreto	Tyrrell-Cosworth 011	
4	Jean-Pierre Jarier	Osella-Cosworth FA1	
5	Eliseo Salazar	ATS-Cosworth D5	
6	Teo Fabi	Toleman-Hart TG181 turbo	

May 3, BELGIAN GRAND PRIX, Zolder
1	John Watson	McLaren-Cosworth MP4	(116.20mph)
2	Keke Rosberg	Williams-Cosworth FW08	
3	Eddie Cheever	Ligier-Matra JS17	
4	Elio de Angelis	Lotus-Cosworth 91	
5	Nelson Piquet	Brabham-BMW BT50 turbo	
6	Chico Serra	Fittipaldi-Cosworth F8D	

May 23, MONACO GRAND PRIX, Monte Carlo
1	Riccardo Patrese	Brabham-Cosworth BT49D	(82.21mph)
2	Didier Pironi	Ferrari 126C2 turbo	
3	Andrea de Cesaris	Alfa Romeo 182	
4	Nigel Mansell	Lotus-Cosworth 91	
5	Elio de Angelis	Lotus-Cosworth 91	
6	Derek Daly	Williams-Cosworth FW08	

June 6, DETROIT GRAND PRIX, Michigan
1 John Watson   MacLaren-Cosworth MP4   (78.20mph)
2 Eddie Cheever   Ligier-Matra JS17
3 Didier Pironi   Ferrari 126C2 turbo
4 Keke Rosberg   Williams-Cosworth FW08
5 Derek Daly   Williams-Cosworth FW08
6 Jacques Laffite   Ligier-Matra JS17

June 13, CANADIAN GRAND PRIX, Montreal
1 Nelson Piquet   Brabham-BMW BT50 turbo   (107.93mph)
2 Riccardo Patrese   Brabham-Cosworth BT49D
3 John Watson   McLaren-Cosworth MP4
4 Elio de Angelis   Lotus-Cosworth 91
5 Marc Surer   Arrows-Cosworth A4
6 Andrea de Cesaris   Alfa Romeo 182

July 3, DUTCH GRAND PRIX, Zandvoort
1 Didier Pironi   Ferrari 126C2 turbo   (116.40mph)
2 Nelson Piquet   Brabham-BMW BT50 turbo
3 Keke Rosberg   Williams-Cosworth FW08
4 Niki Lauda   McLaren-Cosworth MP4
5 Derek Daly   Williams-Cosworth FW08
6 Mauro Baldi   Arrows-Cosworth A4

July 18, BRITISH GRAND PRIX, Brands Hatch
1 Niki Lauda   McLaren-Cosworth MP4   (124.70mph)
2 Didier Pironi   Ferrari 126C2 turbo
3 Patrick Tambay   Ferrari 126C2 turbo
4 Elio de Angelis   Lotus-Cosworth 91
5 Derek Daly   Williams-Cosworth FW08
6 Alain Prost   Renault RE30B turbo

July 25, FRENCH GRAND PRIX, Paul Ricard
1 René Arnoux   Renault RE30B turbo   (124.99mph)
2 Alain Prost   Renault RE30B turbo
3 Didier Pironi   Ferrari 126C2 turbo
4 Patrick Tambay   Ferrari 126C2 turbo
5 Keke Rosberg   Williams-Cosworth FW08
6 Michele Alboreto   Tyrrell-Cosworth 011

August 8, GERMAN GRAND PRIX, Hockenheim
1 Patrick Tambay   Ferrari 126C2 turbo   (130.43mph)
2 René Arnoux   Renault RE30B turbo
3 Keke Rosberg   Williams-Cosworth FW08
4 Michele Alboreto   Tyrrell-Cosworth 011
5 Bruno Giacomelli   Alfa Romeo 182
6 Marc Surer   Arrows-Cosworth A4

August 15, AUSTRIAN GRAND PRIX, Osterreichring
1 Elio de Angelis   Lotus-Cosworth 91   (138.07mph)
2 Keke Rosberg   Williams-Cosworth FW08
3 Jacques Laffite   Ligier-Matra JS19
4 Patrick Tambay   Ferrari 126C2 turbo
5 Niki Lauda   McLaren-Cosworth MP4
6 Mauro Baldi   Arrows-Cosworth A4

August 29, SWISS GRAND PRIX, Dijon-Prenois
1	Keke Rosberg	Williams-Cosworth FW08	(122.29mph)
2	Alain Prost	Renault RE30B turbo	
3	Niki Lauda	McLaren-Cosworth MP4	
4	Nelson Piquet	Brabham-BMW BT50 turbo	
5	Riccardo Patrese	Brabham-BMW BT50 turbo	
6	Elio de Angelis	Lotus-Cosworth 91	

September 12, ITALIAN GRAND PRIX, Monza
1	René Arnoux	Renault RE30B turbo	(136.39mph)
2	Patrick Tambay	Ferrari 126C2 turbo	
3	Mario Andretti	Ferrari 126C2 turbo	
4	John Watson	McLaren-Cosworth MP4	
5	Michele Alboreto	Tyrrell-Cosworth 011	
6	Eddie Cheever	Ligier-Matra JS19	

September 25, CAESARS PALACE GRAND PRIX, Las Vegas
1	Michele Alboreto	Tyrrell-Cosworth 011	(100.10mph)
2	John Watson	McLaren-Cosworth MP4	
3	Eddie Cheever	Ligier-Matra JS19	
4	Alain Prost	Renault RE30B turbo	
5	Keke Rosberg	Williams-Cosworth FW08	
6	Derek Daly	Williams-Cosworth FW08	

DRIVERS' WORLD CHAMPIONSHIP

Posn	Driver	Points
1	Keke Rosberg	44
2	Didier Pironi	39
	John Watson	
4	Alain Prost	34
5	Niki Lauda	30
6	René Arnoux	28
7	Patrick Tambay	25
	Michele Alboreto	
9	Elio de Angelis	23
10	Riccardo Patrese	21
11	Nelson Piquet	20
12	Eddie Cheever	15
13	Derek Daly	8
14	Nigel Mansell	7
15	Carlos Reutemann	6
	Gilles Villeneuve	
17	Andrea de Cesaris	5
	Jacques Laffite	
19	Mario Andretti	4
20	Marc Surer	3
	Jean-Pierre Jarier	
22	Manfred Winkelhock	2
	Mauro Baldi	
	Bruno Giacomelli	
	Eliseo Salazar	
26	Chico Serra	1

CONSTRUCTORS' CHAMPIONSHIP

Posn	Constructor	Points
1	Ferrari	74
2	McLaren	69
3	Renault	62
4	Williams	58
5	Brabham	41
6	Lotus	30
7	Tyrrell	25
8	Ligier	20
9	Alfa Romeo	7
10	Arrows	5
11	ATS	4
12	Osella	3
13	Fittipaldi	1

1983

The one inevitable lesson learned by the Formula 1 community during 1982 was that cornering speeds were increasing quite dramatically. Nelson Piquet, for example, had qualified on pole position for the Austrian Grand Prix at an average speed of over 151mph. It was mind-boggling stuff which, allied to the worrying collision between Jochen Mass's March and Mauro Baldi's Arrows, a pair of Cosworth-engined also-rans, at Paul Ricard raised the temperature concerning safety.

That collision had seen Mass's March lightly injure a handful of spectators when it came to rest up against a wire mesh fence on the edge of the public enclosure. The horrifying spectre of a third party insurance claim, particularly in the USA, was enough to send a nasty chill down the spine of many race organisers. FISA decided that it had to act and, again tossing aside the notional two-year stability rule, agreed a very fundamental rule change to start from the first race of the 1983 World Championship season.

Ground-effect aerodynamics, as they had come to be known up to that point, were swept away with the implementation of a regulation which demanded that all cars had flat-bottoms from the start of the 1983 season. More welcome was the news that there was to be stability of engine regulations until the end of 1985 – an assurance taken with a large pinch of salt in some quarters – plus a reduction in minimum weight to 540kg and, from the start of the 1984 season, plans to reduce the maximum permissible fuel tankage from 250 to 220 litres.

The banning of shaped underbody profiles was sprung on the Formula 1 fraternity as late as 3 November 1982. Not only did Formula 1 designers see about 60 per cent of the total downforce available to them go out of the window at a stroke, but several of their number almost had seizures as months of intensive ground-effect design and development went the same way.

Ironically, one of those most dramatically affected was Brabham chief designer Gordon Murray. His proximity to FOCA president Ecclestone, the owner of the Brabham *equipe*, did not always work in his favour. Throughout the summer of 1982, Bernie assured Gordon that, yes, ground-effect aerodynamics

BMW's 4 cylinder, production-based M12/13 engine would eventually produce in excess of 1,000bhp in qualifying trim, aided by dense toluene-based fuel and 3.5 bar plus boost pressure. It would power Nelson Piquet to the first turbo Championship in 1983.

would continue to be permitted for 1983. As a consequence, Gordon pursued a very specific route when it came to designing his Brabham-BMW package for the new season.

Throughout the FOCA/FISA wars there had been a gathering feeling from some sections of the Formula 1 Constructors' Association that Murray had perhaps been given access to advanced information as far as changes to the technical regulations were concerned. He has always firmly denied this, saying that, if anything, Bernie was over-scrupulous in this respect and he tended to be one of the last to know which way the prevailing winds were blowing. On this occasion, he got badly caught out by Bernie's confidence that the rules would not be changed.

As a result, for 1983, Murray produced a fixed-skirt ground-effect design, dubbed the BT51. Effectively, it was a neat little 'half tank' pit stop car based round the agile BT49D chassis which had previously used a Cosworth V8. Murray also designed a radical new transmission for the BT51, specifically in line with his ground-effect thinking. On the morning of 3 November 1981, the whole project was scrapped. Murray had to start again with a clean sheet of paper. The new car had to be ready in time for the Brazilian Grand Prix at Rio the following March 13.

Moreover, there was no question of missing this date. The brand new BT52 just had to be finished in time; there was no possibility of running some sort of flat-bottomed, uprated BT50. Murray had specifically asked BMW to alter the routing of the exhaust pipes and turbocharger to fit the new car, and these revised engines, which by the end of the year would be setting the pace with outputs of 640bhp at 11,000rpm, at 2.5 bar boost pressure, would no way fit into the back of the previous year's cars. What followed was one of those remarkable, flat-out displays of burning the candle at both ends which makes Formula 1 such a uniquely stimulating business.

BMW had already got used to thinking in such ambitious terms. The company's competition department had been forced to cast aside traditional motor industry thinking quite early on in its partnership with Brabham. Murray particularly recalls a mid-1982 test session at Paul Ricard where Paul Rosche and his engineers had produced a new experimental camshaft for the M12/13 engine. Piquet was delighted with its performance, so Murray inquired when Rosche anticipated fitting this modified component to all the engines in the team's float. 'For next season,' replied the German engineer confidently. Murray shot back, 'How about the weekend after next . . ?' More than ever as the turbo era gathered pace, the Formula 1 business was about instant response and adaptation.

The BT52 was the most distinctly different new car to appear on the Grand Prix scene in 1983. Murray threw away every vestige of the BT49/50 concept to produce an ultra-slim machine devoid of the now-familiar side pods, its weight bias concentrated very much towards the rear. Yet his continued, underlying conservatism could be judged from the fact that the main outer chassis structure was still manufactured from aluminium alloy honeycomb. Carbon-fibre was employed only for internal panels and bulkheads.

Elsewhere on the Grand Prix scene, the new flat-bottomed chassis regulations met a mixed response. Ferrari were already well down the road to a ground-effect 126 'C3' for the 1983 season when FISA dropped its November bombshell. They intended to run a brand new carbon-fibre development of the previous year's chassis, now fitted with a tailor-made longitudinal gearbox to replace the transverse gearbox which had been a feature of Formula 1 Ferraris for many years up to that point. Now they had to change direction, reverting to the older

The Brabham mechanics leap into action, refuelling and changing tyres on Nelson Piquet's BT52 en route to second place in the British Grand Prix.

transmission. Flat-bottomed versions of the Championship-winning 126 'C2's would serve Rene Arnoux and Patrick Tambay well through the first half of the 1983 season, pending the arrival of the re-worked new car. Ferrari would continue with the Agip water injection system which helped to boost the V6 power output to the 620bhp mark at 11,500rpm.

Water injection was now also employed over at Renault, their system being a less complex fine spray into the inlet manifold, where the chassis design team was working towards the completion of its first carbon-fibre monocoque, the RE40. When news of the rule changes came through the team decided to rely on an interim RE30C, the second update of the alloy chassis which had made its debut two years earlier. Renault assumed, rightly perhaps, that most of the opposition would take a similar route, but when word got out of Gordon Murray's plans for the Brabham BT52, the French team suddenly realised that it might well be wrong-footed. The RE40 programme was accelerated to the best of the team's ability, but there was still insufficient time for the new car to be readied for the first race.

The 1983 season would mark the swansong of the front-line Cosworth-engined car, for Lotus would now be joining the Renault ranks with a French V6 in the back of its new type 93T, a bulky looking challenger, only one of which would be ready in time for the Brazilian Grand Prix. Lotus had been in turmoil throughout the winter following Colin Chapman's sudden death in the early hours of 16 December 1982, but the team's major sponsor, John Player, pledged its continued support. Everybody pulled together as best they could now they faced the first season

In the 1982 German Grand Prix it was Patrick Tambay who won in the ever-improving Ferrari 126C2.

without 'The Old Man' breathing down their necks in his uniquely inspirational manner.

However, those who thought that Cosworth Engineering would now capitulate in the face of the inevitable turbo flood tide, had reckoned without the determination of the Northampton-based specialist engine builders whose naturally-aspirated V8s had been the lynchpin of Formula 1 over the previous fifteen years. For those willing to take one final shot at keeping in play with a non-turbo power unit, Cosworth unveiled its DFY, a short stroke version, higher-revving version of the legendary DFV. Ken Tyrrell put his money where his mouth was, ordering ten. McLaren and Williams, both with turbo engines in the pipeline, ordered a handful each. With an absolute maximum of 515bhp available, the strongest card in the Cosworth deck was clearly going to be reliability. All things being equal, it seemed unlikely they would run from the front.

For these two teams who would go on to carve up the turbo era between them from 1984 onwards, the 1983 season was simply a matter of keeping in play until their new engines from Porsche and Honda became available towards the end of the year. In that respect, McLaren's Ron Dennis had executed a major coup when it came to the financing of his Porsche-built turbo, snatching backing for the project from one of the Williams team's major sponsors.

Amongst the retinue of enthusiastic investors in the Williams team, produced by Frank's assiduous courting of the Saudi Arabians, had been the Paris-based high technology corporation Techniques d'Avante Garde (TAG). Founded by entrepreneur Akram Ojjeh – one of whose more celebrated business deals had been the purchase of the super liner, the *France*, which he subsequently sold on to become a Norwegian cruise ship – TAG dealt in a wide range of hardware from aircraft to missile systems, providing a useful and profitable conduit between the Saudi Arabian and European business communities. Mansour Ojjeh, his eldest son, was heavily involved in the company and was a passionate motor racing enthusiast largely responsible for TAG's backing for the Williams team.

Ron Dennis rightly judged that a Porsche-built, state-of-the-art turbocharged Grand Prix engine might be just the vehicle to project TAG's high technology image to a wider business audience. If there was any tension between him and Frank Williams when he pulled off this commercial coup, none of it was allowed publicly to penetrate the good relationship between the two top team owners.

Dennis had made the McLaren International team's commitment to the Porsche programme long before he attracted TAG as

Prost on Renault's Failure

Alain Prost had experienced a less-than-comfortable 1982 season with Renault, the most disappointing moment of which was his defeat at the hands of René Arnoux under unsatisfactory circumstances in the French Grand Prix. Arnoux had moved to Ferrari for 1983, allowing Prost's position as unchallenged team leader to be consolidated. The French national team seemed set for its most successful ever season.

Sadly, what started on a promising note spiralled downwards to a disappointing result. To start with, Prost found himself wasting too much time in a public relations role rather than concentrating, one hundred per cent, on the business of race driving.

'I seemed gradually to get more involved in the company's public relations campaigns which were incidental to the racing programme,' he explained, 'and, to be honest, I think my relative lack of experience prevented me from understanding all the issues and implications involved. Had I been more seasoned in these matters, I think I would have put my foot down. It certainly detracted slightly from my main purpose of the year.'

Later in the season Alain's equilibrium would be ruffled by the accident at Zandvoort where, desperately attempting to catch Nelson Piquet's Brabham-BMW (which was much quicker on the straight) off-guard, he made a crucial error in colliding with the Brazilian. Then there were death threats at Monza and Renault's failure to grasp the nettle of BMW's late season power surge.

'Not only did Renault fail to heed my warnings on that front,' Alain shrugs, 'they specifically blamed me. By that stage it had got to the point where just about anything I said at Renault was wrong. Everybody was concerned about the corporate image and you had to be careful what was said in public. When I realised that I was to be the fall-guy, I was almost relieved...'

a potential sponsor. It was in the winter of 1981/82, just as Niki Lauda was being lured back into the cockpit of one of the team's MP4Bs, that Dennis opened negotiations with the German company whose experience of turbocharging sports car engines extended back beyond the previous decade.

Knowing the mentality of most Grand Prix team owners, Porsche may have been expecting Dennis's approach to be along the age-old lines they had rejected on many occasions in the past. No, the German company did not wish to build a Grand Prix engine off its own bat and supply it to any specific team. But Dennis was already carving himself a reputation for not conforming to any stereotypes as far as Formula 1 team principals went.

His approaching Porsche as a customer, interested in securing their paid-for professional services, was something they had not altogether expected. Not until December 1982 was the deal finalised with TAG, by which time the first of the Porsche-built turbo engines was ready to be run up on the test bed.

Labelling the price of this project in a world all too accustomed to buying a nice Cosworth DFV off-the-shelf at £25,000 apiece, or whatever, is difficult. But it would be surprising if the cost of developing and building the first such engine were less than £750,000. And that was just the start. The real expenditure came later. The more you think it over, given the volatile nature of Grand Prix racing's rule-makers, the more audacious Dennis's project becomes in retrospect. The consequences of Balestre and his cronies deciding to ban turbocharged engines overnight, for whatever grounds, could not have been something Dennis even dared think about.

As a condition of becoming involved in the project, I understand that Mansour Ojjeh actually laid down that the Williams team could also avail itself of the new engine if it felt so inclined, a course of events which very definitely was not envisaged by Ron Dennis. But Frank and Patrick Head knew as well as Dennis that an exclusive turbo engine deal would become an absolute top priority over the next few years. There was no future in sharing an engine project with another team, so Williams, having rejected the possibility of using a BMW turbo on much the same basis, turned to Honda for their salvation.

The famous Japanese company was no newcomer to the Grand Prix scene, having made an ambitious foray into Formula 1

Nelson Piquet's Brabham-BMW BT50 leads the 1982 German Grand Prix at Hockenheim prior to being eliminated in a collision with Eliseo Salazar's ATS.

between 1964 and 1968. Honda clearly intended to barnstorm a path to the sort of success it had already achieved on the World Championship motorcycle stage.

Honda was at the head of the Oriental invasion of international motorcycle racing, arriving in Europe in 1959 with a fairly orthodox 125cc machine. From such modest beginnings, they set out on the climb to worldwide domination and, throughout their nine years of major international competition, achieved no fewer than sixteen World Championship titles. Yet, ironically, the brightest jewel in motorcycling's crown, the 500c World Championship, continued to elude Honda throughout the 1960s, despite the acknowledged brilliance of the legendary Mike Hailwood, easily their most successful rider. But they won the 350cc title for an amazing six years in succession. Surely, reasoned the pundits, such domination would translate to Formula 1 with ease?

Not one bit of it. Honda's first foray into the world of Formula 1 was low budget and somewhat half-hearted, compromised in no small way by elements of resistance within the company's management hierachy. Initially a tentative deal was done to supply their high-revving, transverse V12 cylinder 1½ litre engine to Team Lotus for 1964. But Colin Chapman slid out of the deal at the last moment, leaving Honda with little alternative but to build its own chassis if it wanted to go Grand Prix racing.

The company did just that and, at the end of 1965, the late Richie Ginther won the Mexican Grand Prix, the final race of the 1½ litre Formula 1. Honda stayed around to contest the new 3 litre Formula 1, but while its new V12 engines were undeniably powerful, the cars were too heavy. John Surtees drove for them in 1967 and 1968, winning the Italian Grand Prix at Monza in the former season. The team pulled out at the end of 1969 and would not be seen in the Formula 1 arena until the early 1980s.

This time, of course, Honda would do it properly, albeit from modest beginnings. In 1980 the company returned to Formula 2 with an 80 degree iron block 2 litre V6 engine to test. It was quickly developed into the engine to beat in this junior category and, at the end of 1982, it was decided to produce a turbocharged 1.5 litre version for a Grand Prix application.

In order to learn the ropes as unobtrusively as possible, without producing an air of over-expectancy, Honda came to an agreement with the tiny Spirit team for which it was already supplying Formula 2 engines. Initially using a modified Formula 2 chassis uprated into an Formula 1 travelling test bed, Swedish driver Stefan Johansson was signed to drive in the 1983 Brands Hatch Race of Champions, later joining the World Championship trail in time for the British Grand Prix.

Knowing Honda's track record and highly competitive approach, it was quite clear from the outset that Spirit represented merely a staging post on a longer journey. Sure enough, at the 1983 Austrian Grand Prix meeting, Frank Williams and Honda's Nobuhiko Kawamoto held a joint press conference to confirm a two-year Anglo-Japanese alliance, initially running to the end of 1985. At that stage nobody was saying when the first Williams-Honda would race, but Frank was clearly keen to be up and running as soon as he possibly could.

Nelson Piquet started as he meant to go on, taking the 'pit stop' Brabham BT52 to a well-judged maiden victory in front of his home crowd at Rio. At one stage it seemed as though it might be a 1-2 for Gordon Murray's sleek new design, but Riccardo Patrese's car succumbed to a cracked exhaust, and consequent loss of turbo boost pressure, whilst holding second place.

However, having expected the turbos to set the pace from the

Flattering to deceive. Prost and Arnoux squirt their Renaults into an immediate lead at the start of the 1982 Las Vegas Grand Prix, but it was Michele Alboreto's Tyrrell (no. 3) that would win the race and Keke Rosberg (Williams no. 6) who would clinch the Drivers' Championship.

Above and opposite: *Derek Warwick tests the new Toleman TG183, designed for the current sliding skirt Formula 1 regulations, at Silversone in late 1982 just before the flat-bottomed 1983 regulations were announced. Based round the team's first carbon-fibre chassis, it featured a much neater Hart engine installation than the superseded TG181B. Of course, it had to be completely revamped for 1983 to conform with the new rules.*

outset, it was quite a surprise to find the dynamic Keke Rosberg popping up on pole position at the wheel of his Cosworth-engined Williams FW08C, a flat-bottomed re-work of the car that had taken him to the 1982 Championship title. Williams had concluded that fuel stops were worthwhile not only for turbos and, starting with a reduced fuel load, Keke confounded many of the pundits by leading for six glorious laps.

Piquet then took over at the front, never relinquishing his advantage even through a routine refuelling stop at two-thirds distance. Williams strategy, meanwhile, called for the flying Finn to make his fuel stop on Lap 28. Everything seemed to be going smoothly until a slight seepage of fuel from around the neck of the filler caused a momentary flash fire.

Keke popped his belts and shot from the cockpit like a jack rabbit, by which time the fire was already out and Williams designer Patrick Head almost hurled him back into the car once again. Strapped up once again, Rosberg hurtled back into the fray and stormed home to second place behind Piquet, only to be subsequently disqualified for receiving a push-start from his mechanics. That promoted Lauda to second place ahead of Williams's new recruit, Jacques Laffite, in the second Williams FW08C.

Gradually, throughout the season, most of the opposition decided they could not afford to ignore the performance advantage offered by the fuel stop strategy, even though many people were concerned about its very real potential hazards even before the Rosberg episode at Rio. Supporters of the cause pointed to the Indianapolis-type cars in the USA, pointing out that refuelling stops had formed an integral part of this category's attraction since time immemorial.

In fairness, this was no valid comparison. At Indianapolis the pit lane is kept scrupulously clear of extraneous personnel, unlike Formula 1 where the same area is more like a boulevard for hangers-on out for a stroll. Since neither Balestre, nor Ecclestone, ever did, or have, managed to clear the Grand Prix pit lanes of all those people not wanted on voyage, so to speak, the biggest hazard implicit in Formula 1 fuel stops was always destined to be the prospect of an arriving car mowing down a couple of dozen poseurs. The question of the procedure immolating the pits seemed to be of secondary concern.

Either way, an enormous amount of effort and intricate engineering went into manufacturing the necessary machinery in order to practise the fuel stop routine throughout 1983. Each team had its own ideas about the technique, so although Brabham had been the trendsetters in this respect, they were soon caught up by the likes of Renault and Ferrari when it came to slick performances in the pit lane.

The competitive pitch of the Formula 1 game meant there was no time for a gravity refuelling system, the relatively leisurely method employed in sports car racing. In Formula 1, the fuel was being pumped in at anything between 15 to 60psi, so it was necessary to vent the tank on the opposite side of the car, allowing the displaced air an escape route without which the tanks — and monocoque — would have almost certainly blown apart. In fact, at the McLaren factory, one chassis actually suffered that fate during an experiment in the workshop, news of which was prudently kept from John Barnard's ears for some time.

Even though the turbos were obviously getting the upper hand in a big way now, still the Cosworth-engined runners raised a few eyebrows by performing quickly enough to keep them on the turbos. Number one in the 3 litre brigade was undoubtedly Rosberg, the Williams team leader by his own admission going through a potentialy rather precarious spell with the flat-bottomed FW08C.

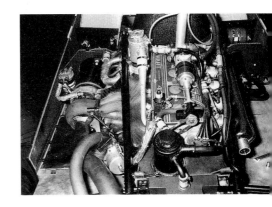

Typical of Keke's over-exuberance was his performance at Long Beach, the second race of the season. Patrick Tambay and René Arnoux buttoned up the front row of the grid in their Ferrari 126C2 turbos, but Keke and Jacques Laffite were third and fourth. As the starting light blinked to green, Rosberg made a superb getaway, his left rear wheel side-swiping Arnoux's right front as he fishtailed through the gap between the two Ferraris, aching to take the lead.

Down into the first right-hander, Tambay just scrambled into the braking area ahead, the Ferrari leading by a length as they juggled their way round that opening lap. Coming into the hairpin at the end of the long back straight, Rosberg dived for the inside of the Ferrari, the Williams went light as it crested a particularly notorious bump and, in a split-second, locked its rear brakes.

Keke spun like a top right in front of a massed field of twenty-four closely packed cars! Amazingly, though, he gathered it all up again and managed to complete the opening lap in third place, overtaken only by Laffite. Second time round, he was back into second place again, harrying Tambay mercilessly. But Patrick was doing his best to conserve rubber, aiming for a non-stop run in this gruelling race. This cat and mouse act continued until Lap 26 when Keke's impetuosity got the better of him. He lunged inside Tambay going into one of the hairpins and the Ferrari rode over the Williams's left front wheel.

The disappointed Patrick was out on the spot, while Keke lasted only until the next corner where his action-packed race finally came to an end as Jean-Pierre Jarer's Ligier ran into the back of the Williams, eliminating it for good. In the end, it was the McLaren MP4/1Cs of John Watson and Niki Lauda who came pounding through to finish first and second, having qualified only twenty-second and twenty-third.

At the time this enormous performance disparity between their qualifying and race performance was shrugged aside as one of dear old 'Wattie's' peculiar weekends. That, of course, ignored the fact that Lauda had been hamstrung by the same performance constraints. The truth was that, after struggling to work their tyres up to suitable operating temperature during qualifying, the higher ambient temperature prevailing on race day allowed the McLaren's Michelin radials to work a treat. This, in itself, highlighted a major problem which would surface repeatedly to compromise the McLaren's performance in those last few pre-TAG turbo months.

Michelin's front-line team was obviously Renault, so the French firm's radial tyres were primarily pitched at suiting the high power, high downforce demands of the yellow turbocars. The McLaren's DFV power and low drag profile could not make the tyres work hard enough, but John Barnard persuaded Michelin to come up with a construction more suitable for his lightly laden cars. The tyre makers agreed, but they were not ready to prevent Watson and Lauda both failing to qualify through the streets of Monaco.

By mid-summer, McLaren had asserted itself as the fastest of the Cosworth runners, but Watson's Long Beach success would stand as the team's lone Grand Prix victory of the season. In

John Watson leads Niki Lauda en route to a McLaren 1-2 in the 1983 Long Beach race, the two MP4/1Cs having qualified out of the top 20 after their Michelin rubber failed to warm up to optimum temperature in the cool conditions of qualifying. The temperature went up on race day – and the two Cosworth-engined cars simply flew through the field.

some ways it was a rather tense period, a question of marking time with outdated machinery, waiting for the TAG turbo – and hoping it would be good enough to get the job done.

The partnership between Lauda and Watson renewed their 1978 association when they had driven together at Brabham. They both knew each other pretty well, got on extremely well and each spent plenty of time rubbishing the other behind his back. At Monaco the previous year, both cars had been beset by terminal understeer at one stage during practice. 'Yes, we've both got understeer,' sad Niki acidly, 'the only difference between John and me is that I know why.' This was typical Lauda gamesmanship.

Niki had a fairly well-developed sense of his own value to the

McLaren team, particularly after his 1982 return season. He started that year on an arrangement whereby McLaren could drop him after four races if he had not proved to be fast enough. That hurdle successfully cleared, he then negotiated a very high price contract for 1983 and 1984. Insiders say they were surprised that its terms did not turn what was left of Ron Dennis's hair grey overnight. Moreover, just to keep things bubbling along nicely, Lauda wasn't averse to revving up the McLaren boss by reminding him he'd only got such massive Marlboro sponsorship because of his presence.

This wasn't quite the case, of course, but such fine detail never stood in Niki's way. As John Watson recalls: 'If Niki made his mind up to take a particular stance, then he would take it and nothing or nobody could change his mind. I mean, once he assumed he was number one driver, that was it. It was fixed in his mind. In that respect, I think he was a more determined individual than myself when we were out of the cockpit. I always felt I was every bit as agressive and committed when I was driving, but perhaps not so much outside the car.'

The first few races of the 1983 season amounted to preliminary limbering up, no firm contender for Championship honours really emerging until the second half of the season. After an inconclusive, troubled debut at Long Beach, the carbon-fibre Renault RE40s, whose V6s engines were now built round

Third at Long Beach, 1983, was René Arnoux's Ferrari 126C2/B, its 120 degree twin turbo V6 now developing a reliable 750bhp with the aid of Agip water injection.

aluminium alloy rather than cast-iron cylinder blocks, stormed to first and third places in the third round of the title chase, the French Grand Prix at Paul Ricard. Prost sailed to his second home win in three years while his new American team-mate Eddie Cheever, who had replaced Arnoux, came home a fine third behind Piquet's Brabham.

In fairy-tale style, Patrick Tambay carried the late Gilles Villeneuve's race number 27 to a splendid, emotional victory in the San Marino Grand Prix at Imola. A late challenge from Riccardo Patrese's Brabham-BMW evaporated when the Italian crashed heavily a few laps from the finish, seconds after surging through into the lead.

As an aside, the romance surrounding number 27, and its associations with the charismatic Villeneuve was, in fact, often misrepresented. Gilles only used this number through 1981 and up to his death in 1982, carrying it to a mere two race victories. Long before that, it had been the property of Alan Jones at Williams, the rugged Australian winning nine races before he was awarded the number one as a World Champion's due. In the years that followed, number 27 would also be carried by Michele Alboreto, Nigel Mansell and Ayrton Senna, fine drivers to a man.

Monaco saw Keke Rosberg and Williams take a real gamble, starting his FW08C on dry weather slicks even though the track was still damp at the start. Fortunately, the rain did not return,

Elio de Angelis gives the first of the ungainly Lotus 93T-Renaults its first test run along the drive in front of the Group Lotus road car factory at Hethel, early in 1983. Gérard Ducarouge would later examine it in detail – and conclude that a new chassis was required.

Fuel stop action. Nigel Mansell's debutant Lotus 94T replenishes its tank during the Englishman's fine run to fourth place in the 1983 British Grand Prix. Pit stop pioneers Brabham do the same for Piquet's Brabham BT52 during his run to second place in the same event.

and those of his rivals who started on wet weather tyres lost much crucial time coming in for a change of rubber. Rosberg had that little Williams-Cosworth dancing from lock to lock through the streets of the principality on his way to the team's only win of the year.

Before the World Championship circus embarked on its two-race North American tour, Formula 1 returned to Spa-Francorchamps for the first Belgian Grand Prix to be held at this traditional venue for thirteen years. Shortened imaginatively from 8.7 to 4.3 miles per lap, the revised circuit through the pine forests of the Haute Fagnes region in the south of the country still threw out a tremendous challenge. Most of the grid had been in short trousers when Pedro Rodriguez stormed to victory at the wheel of his Yardley BRM in 1970, but, to a man, they relished its unique challenge.

Prost qualified on pole position but, amazingly, it was Andrea de Cesaris whose Alfa Romeo 183T burst into an immediate lead and ran away from the opposition for the first eighteen laps. Ever since Brabham abandoned its Alfa Romeo engines at the end of 1979, the Italian marque had been pursuing its own rather erratic Formula 1 programme with the same V12 engine. Now, for 1983, Alfa Romeo entered the turbo era with a compact 74 x 43.5mm V8, claimed to develop 640bhp at 11,500rpm. It certainly looked that way as de Cesaris, driving with a discipline he seemed only able to muster on tracks where the hazards were obvious, left Prost floundering in his wake.

Only two laps after his routine fuel stop, de Cesaris retired out on the circuit with engine trouble, almost certainly the legacy of running more boost pressure than the engine could cope with. Prost, ever easy on the machinery, drove smoothly home to his second victory of the season with Tambay's Ferrari, Cheever's Renault and Piquet's Brabham-BMW in line astern behind him. It was a success which moved him into the World Championship points lead for the first time that season.

Prost would retain his Championship lead through the Detroit and Canadian Grands Prix, although these two events would yield him only a troubled fifth place at Montreal. Michele Alboreto ducked through to score a lucky win in the naturally-aspirated Tyrrell-Cosworth through the streets of MoTown, while René Arnoux's Ferrari blitzed the opposition from start to finish in Canada. Now came the make-or-break stuff.

Elsewhere on the Formula 1 scene, some major changes were in hand. Over at Lotus, the type 93T had been less than totally successful, although it was only regarded as a pilot effort to bring the British team into the turbo era. Moreover, before his death, Chapman had gone after a big budget deal with Pirelli, such was his conviction that radial rubber was essential to get the best out of a turbo car. In the immediate aftermath of Chapman's death, Peter Warr completed that deal. It turned out to be the wrong way to go.

Standing by a 'naked' Ferrari 126C2, Patrick Tambay makes a point to chief engineer Mauro Forghieri at Paul Ricard during the 1983 French Grand Prix meeting. Forghieri regarded Patrick as one of the best test and development drivers he had ever worked with.

Brabham's Recipe for Success

Nelson Piquet's World Championship success with the BMW turbo was spawned by the congenial environment provided for him within the Brabham enclave, conditions diametrically opposite to those endured by his Championship rival Prost in the Renault camp. Nelson had always been the pampered baby of Ecclestone's team, his genuinely close personal friendship with the mechanics being repaid by unswerving loyalty and commitment to his cause.

The Brabham team embodied all the qualities which had made the British FOCA-aligned teams such formidable contenders in the pre-turbo era. With Gordon Murray at the design helm, supported by an enthusiastic and professional workforce, it combined engineering ingenuity with youthful panache. Piquet blended into this happy environment as one of the boys.

While Prost was out, being formally wined and dined by the Renault corporate big guns, Piquet would, like as not, be whooping it up with the Brabham lads, throwing cakes around and acting like an uninhibited child. Yet it was an approach which allowed him to conserve all his professionalism and driving guile for the serious business of a Grand Prix weekend.

Away from the intense activity in the cockpit of his Brabham-BMW, Nelson shrugged aside the promotional obligations which hamstrung the efforts of so many of his colleagues.

'If I have to get out of bed early to make ten thousand dollars,' he once remarked, 'then I'd rather not do it. I like all the sleep I can get. Some days I'll sleep until noon – and after that I'll be quite happy to sleep again.'

Small wonder that, after taking the 1983 title, Piquet remarked: 'I'd like to go on racing for another ten years.' Or that, when he took his third Championship in a Williams-Honda four years later, he reserved his real celebration for when he met up with his old pals from the Brabham team.

Two 93Ts were built and such were the limitations on Renault engine supply in the first part of the year that only Elio de Angelis raced the machine. Mansell would be left to struggle through the first half of the 1983 season with a Cosworth-engined type 92, running at Rio and Long Beach with the early prototype of the computer controlled 'active' suspension about which Chapman had been so enthusiastic. We will return to this topic in some detail in the chapter dealing with the 1987 season, throughout which Ayrton Senna's Lotus-Honda 99T ran equipped with a much-refined version of this system and actually won two Grands Prix.

After only a handful of races, it had become clear that de Angelis was never going to get much out of the Lotus 93T and, as spring turned to summer, Peter Warr detected a certain amount of understandable impatience from John Player. What, the sponsor demanded to know, was Warr going to do about it? The meeting to consider whether or not to renew the team's sponsorship was scheduled to take place prior to the German Grand Prix at Hockenheim. It was crunch time. Team Lotus had to deliver.

Coincidentally, respected French engineer, Gérard Ducarouge

had recently come on to the Formula 1 market. Having contributed an enormous amount of effort by massaging the Alfa Romeo Formula 1 programme into shape, 'Duca' became the sacrificial lamb when de Cesaris had his first day's practice time disallowed at Paul Ricard. His car's on-board fire extinguisher bottle was empty. The Frenchman was fired, but quickly joined Team Lotus the week after the Belgian Grand Prix.

Warr outlined the challenge. Ducarouge looked over the old 93T and told the Lotus manager that, in truth, he would like to produce a new chassis... 'That's fine,' replied Warr. 'Just make certain that two of them are ready in time for the British Grand Prix.' Ducarouge and the team had six weeks...

The development of the sleek Lotus 94T taught many members of the media a lesson they should have known already; that is, treat PR bumf with the greatest scepticism... When two Lotus 94Ts were duly rolled out at Silverstone, the John Player PR machine trumpeted about what an unparalleled achievement it was to have built two brand new cars in six weeks. Brand new cars, my foot...

A glance at the old-style rocker front suspension was the first give-away. How come, since the 93T 'truck' had featured a more elegant, up-to-date pull-rod system? The truth of the matter was that, with remarkable initiative and speed, Ducarouge had raided the Team Lotus stores and built up these 'new' cars from discarded type 91-Cosworth chassis.

Of course, this was far from the work of a moment. New suspension geometry was incorporated and a hundred-and-one detail changes needed to be made. The fuel tank bay was cut down – as it could be in the current climate of fuel stops – and the whole package was clad in totally new, sleek bodywork. But the cars were ready in time, allowing Mansell to storm home a splendid fourth in his home race. John Player were delighted. The new contract was in the bag.

Prost scored a canny victory at Silverstone after Ferrari rather shot themselves in the foot on their final outing with the 126C2s. Tambay and Arnoux qualified 1-2, but Mauro Forghieri opted to race the cars with low downforce rear wings, and both men ran too hard, too soon. Their Goodyear rubber did not stand the pace as well as the Michelins on Prost's Renault and Piquet's Brabham which finished the afternoon first and second ahead of a disappointed Tambay. Make no mistake, Silverstone was one of Prost's best wins of the season. But Piquet was emerging – consistently – as the man he would have to beat.

Immediately after the British Grand Prix, Ken Tyrrell popped up like an unwelcome jack-in-the-box and lodged a protest about the water injection systems used on the Ferrari and Renault V6s

Tyre change in the Paul Ricard pit lane just before Elio de Angelis takes the unloved Lotus 93T-Renault out to practice for its last race. This last of the Chapman-inspired Lotus Formula 1 designs would give way to the Ducarouge-engineered 94T in time for the next race on the calendar, the British Grand Prix at Silverstone.

Alan Jones practises his backhand, while Keke Rosberg (in sunglasses), scans the financial pages. Although very different personalities, these two men were the quintessential Williams drivers of the early 1980s.

turbo engines. His objection was grounded on the suggestion that such systems broke the rules on four counts: one, that it enabled the fuel to exceed the permitted octane rating; two, that the fuel's oxygen content exceeded the permitted 2 per cent allowance; three, the fuel was no longer composed of hydro-carbons, 2 per cent oxygen and 1 per cent nitrogen, by weight, as laid down in the regulations; four, the fuel contained illegal power-boosting additives. The protest was rejected, although its outcome was monitored closely by BMW who had also harboured doubts about the legality of such systems. Shortly afterwards, the German 4 cylinder engines would appear in qualifying races with water spraying into the turbo intercooler in order to reduce the charge air temperature.

Tyrrell's actions so incensed Elf, who supplied Renault with its fuel, that Ken's relationship with the French fuel company, extending back sixteen years to the fledgeling days of Jackie Stewart and the Tyrrell Matra-Cosworth, was cancelled on the spot. Sometimes it is better to keep quiet. The establishment would pay back Tyrrell, brutally and with interest, little more than twelve months hence . . .

Although Ferrari raced the 'C2' in the British Grand Prix, the new carbon-fibre chassis 126 'C3' had been brought to the pre-race Silverstone tyre test and made its race debut in the German

The crucial moment at which Alain Prost could be said to have lost the 1983 World Championship. Under braking for the Tarzan right-hander at Zandvoort during the 1983 Dutch Grand Prix, the Frenchman lost control of his Renault RE40 and speared into Nelson Piquet's Brabham-BMW BT52.

Grand Prix at Hockenheim. Maranello's competitions department was now equipped with the necessary ovens required to 'cure' a carbon-fibre composite monocoque and the significantly lighter C3 used much of its immediate predecessor's running gear. Arnoux won, first time out, at Hockenheim, moving Ferrari back into the lead of the Constructors' Championship.

By now, beneath the surface, all was not well in the Renault camp. Prost could detect the first signs of a tremendous push from the BMW camp and his worst fears were realised at the Austrian Grand Prix. On the super-fast Osterreichring, Piquet's Brabham BT52 displayed such a turn of speed that Alain went straight back to his employers with a worrying message. If you do not step up the pace of our engine development, Prost warned Renault Sport, BMW are going to snatch away our World Championship in the last few races of the season. It was an accurate and prophetic assessment.

In his biography, *Life in the Fast Lane* (Stanley Paul, 1989), Prost recounts the way events unfolded. 'There was no point in getting my hopes up – that would have been a futile exercise in self-deception ... I had been sounding the alarm chez Renault ever since my fourth and last win of the season in the Austrian Grand Prix. No-one was better placed than myself to vouch for the remarkable progress made by Brabham and, above all, its BMW turbo engine. I wasn't at all convinced that the Renault people had a grasp on the situation, but it was real and there for all to see.'

What BMW had done was to concentrate on the development of its fuel technology rather than on water injection. Wintershall, a subsidiary of the giant BASF Chemicals concern, settled down to produce a tailor-made fuel, the chemical make-up of which included constituents such as toluene. Used in conjunction with bigger turbochargers, it unlocked considerably more performance from the BMW M12/13 engine and at last allowed Piquet to contest pole position with the Renaults, qualifying fastest for the first time that season at Monza.

By then, Prost had made what turned out to be a vital stumble. Challenging Nelson's Brabham for the lead at Zandvoort, he produced a rare driving error under hard braking for the tight Tarzan right-hander just beyond the pits. Piquet was shunted into retirement on the spot. Fleetingly, it seemed as though Prost had got away with it. But the Renault had sustained damage to its nose wings; further round the lap, Alain understeered into the barrier as one of the wings broke off, upsetting the RE40's handling.

The Dutch Grand Prix was also a turbo landmark for two other reasons. It marked the debut of the keenly awaited TAG-Porsche turbo engine and the first time that Brian Hart's neat little 415T 4 cylinder turbo propelled Derek Warwick's Toleman to a finish in the Championship points.

The Porsche-built TAG turbo was almost unique in terms of contemporary Formula 1 power units in that it owed nothing to any predecessors and everything to John Barnard's absolute insistence on what he regarded as an idealised technical specification. It was built with an 80 degree vee angle because Barnard specified that configuration. It had all its pumps at the front because Barnard said so, just as it had to be installed in the chassis as a stressed member. It was originally designed with tightly upswept exhausts to maximise the possibilities for ground effect, the necessity for which was eliminated with that FISA decision in November 1982, a matter of weeks before the prototype was due to run on the test bed.

Barnard wanted to defer its race debut until the start of the 1984 season, by which time he would have designed a tailor-made chassis for the new V6. However, pressure from sponsors demanded that an uprated MP4/1E development car be pressed into service as quickly as possible. Barnard was agin it, but commercial pressures ruled. On a day which saw Watson storm to a superb third in the Cosworth car, Lauda duly gave the turbo its debut at Zandvoort, qualifying nineteenth and climbing to twelfth before its inadequate 'Cosworth brakes' boiled their fluid trying to deal with all this extra power. Renault and Ferrari looked, aghast, at the tailor-made KKK turbochargers on the new engines. They had to 'make do' with off-the-shelf components. Ominously for the opposition, the new TAG turbo did not miss a beat. McLaren had raised the Formula 1 stakes with the shape of things to come...

Warwick's sliver of success with the Toleman had been a long time coming, throwing a shaft of light on what was a dogged private effort at competing in the turbo era. As long ago as 1980, Formula 2 engine specialist Brian Hart had toyed with a turbocharged 4 cylinder engine, drawing on his extensive knowledge accumulated over more than a decade of developing 4 cylinder engines for this second division category, from the Cosworth FVA through to his own Hart 420R which powered Brian Henton to victory in the 1980 European Formula 2 Championship.

Toleman was keen to go Grand Prix racing and took the ambitious step of financing the Hart turbo rather than taking the soft, short-term option of a Cosworth DFV. Ahead lay more than two years of frustration, improvisation, heartache and adaptation as this tiny firm attempted to take on the kings of the turbo playground. Now they seemed to have cracked it with the rugged

Prost got away with it in the short term, but damage to the left front aerofoil caused him to lose control and crash further round the next lap.

Warwick storming home fourth at the Dutch seaside circuit. The Toleman TG183B he was driving was itself an uprated version of a fully skirted ground-effect design produced at the end of 1982. Like many of its rivals, its design had to be totally reworked before the start of 1983.

Warwick was described to me by Williams designer Patrick Head as 'the one driver out there today who most reminds me of Alan Jones.' Williams team compliments do not come any better than that. However, at the risk of being cynical, I am bound to wonder why this view never led to Warwick being recruited to drive for the British team. However, I diverge . . .

By this stage, Warwick had been head-hunted by Renault, ostensibly to partner Prost in 1984. He turned down an offer to drive for Lotus on the basis that the works team would make better use of the V6 than one of its customers. Had he gone to Lotus, Mansell would have been dropped. As it was, Warwick went to Renault, a path which led virtually to oblivion. Mansell stayed with Lotus, on Warr's sufferance but John Player's insistence, and then picked up a Williams-Honda drive for 1985. It was the passport to more than a dozen Grand Prix wins and hero status. Had the cards fallen differently at the end of 1983, it could have all been dramatically different. Such is the unpredictable nature of the Formula 1 driver's merry-go-round.

There were three races left on the calendar and Piquet had 14 points to make up. It seemed like a long shot, but the momentum was with Brabham and BMW. Like a rabbit frozen in terror by the headlights of an oncoming car, Renault just did not seem capable of responding. This was one of those occasions where the unwieldy management structure of a major international car maker was not capable of the quick response necessary to take corrective action in time. Perhaps they simply did not believe what Prost was saying.

Derek Warwick scored the first Championship points for the Toleman-Hart partnership with this TG183B, a flat-bottomed version of the original TG183 shown testing at Silverstone on page 144. Warwick finished fifth at Zandvoort, but by that time had already agreed to drive for Renault in 1984.

Monza came and went. Nelson won, but Prost retired with a recurrence of the Renault V6's increasing vulnerability to turbo problems. Piquet was now 5 points behind with two races to go, the penultimate round of the title chase being the Grand Prix of Europe at Brands Hatch.

Pirelli qualifying rubber helped Elio de Angelis to give Lotus a morale-boosting pole position on home ground with the 94T, but he tangled with Patrese early on. Piquet whistled home to another commanding victory with a now definitely outclassed Prost trailing in second place. The RE40 no longer looked in the same class as the Brabham BT52. Nigel Mansell was a storming third, saving his bacon for 1984 in the face of a precarious personal relationship with Peter Warr.

Renault's total failure to grasp the seriousness of the situation could be judged by the fact that they romanced a plane load of French journalists to Kyalami for the final race of the season. Come and see our boy win the Championship! Acres of advertising space was reserved in French newspapers, waiting to proclaim the World Championship success of Alain Prost and Renault. An understandable strategy, perhaps; it is just a shame for them that everybody else got to know about it.

In qualifying at Kyalami, Patrick Tambay's Ferrari took pole position from Piquet by 0.2sec, but this was an irrelevance. The Brabham team had a plan up its sleeve that would destroy the opposition almost before the game had started. Suggested by Bernie Ecclestone, no less, it proved a brilliant variation on their pit stop chassis. Why not start Nelson's BT52 with a small amount of fuel and schedule his fuel stop early?

They did just that. Nelson was two seconds ahead at the end of the opening lap, the demoralised opposition left trailing in his wake as the advantage extended at an unbelievable rate. He made his refuelling stop on Lap 28 of the seventy-seven lap event, emerging with his lead intact. Prost's Renault, running breathlessly in fourth place, succumbed to turbo failure. Only Piquet's retirement could save Alain's title now.

Now such eleventh hour reprieve would be granted. Easing back in the closing stages, Nelson allowed Riccardo Patrese's sister Brabham and de Cesaris's Alfa to overtake. Third place was good enough for him to become the first turbo World Champion. Prost was one of the first at his side, offering congratulations. Renault was stunned. It was nothing less than they deserved, under the circumstances. Almost unnoticed, Niki Lauda's McLaren-TAG climbed through to second place before retiring. Keke Rosberg's Williams-Honda was fifth, first time out. It was an indication from which direction the prevailing turbo wind was blowing, although most could be forgiven for failing to understand it as such.

'Alain didn't lose the Championship – Renault did,' said Piquet, pouring fuel on to flaming waters. But even Nelson didn't realise at the time how finely balanced was the outcome of that first turbo title battle. It was Nelson's second drivers' Championship in three seasons.

When his Brabham BMW engine was stripped down after the race, it was found to have stretched its con-rod bolts to the point where the pistons were almost rattling up and down in the bores. It could have fallen to bits at any moment.

By any standards, it had been a damn close run thing...

THE TURBO YEARS' RESULTS 1983

Winner's average speed

March 13, BRAZILIAN GRAND PRIX, Rio
1   Nelson Piquet   Brabham-BMW BT52 turbo   (108.926mph)
2   Niki Lauda   McLaren-Cosworth MP4
3   Jacques Laffite   Williams-Cosworth FW08C
4   Patrick Tambay   Ferrari 126C2B turbo
5   Marc Surer   Arrows-Cosworth A6
6   Alain Prost   Renault RE30B turbo

March 27, UNITED STATES GRAND PRIX WEST, Long Beach
1   John Watson   McLaren-Cosworth MP4   (80.06mph)
2   Niki Lauda   McLaren-Cosworth MP4
3   René Arnoux   Ferrari 126C2B turbo
4   Jacques Laffite   Williams-Cosworth FW08C
5   Marc Surer   Arrows-Cosworth A6
6   Johnny Cecotto   Theodore-Cosworth N183

April 17, FRENCH GRAND PRIX, Paul Ricard
1   Alain Prost   Renault RE40 turbo   (124.191mph)
2   Nelson Piquet   Brabham-BMW BT52 turbo
3   Eddie Cheever   Renault RE40 turbo
4   Patrick Tambay   Ferrari 126C2B turbo
5   Keke Rosberg   Williams-Cosworth FW08C
6   Jacques Laffite   Williams-Cosworth FW08C

May 1, SAN MARINO GRAND PRIX, Imola
1   Patrick Tambay   Ferrari 126CB turbo   (115.151mph)
2   Alain Prost   Renault RE40 turbo
3   René Arnoux   Ferrari 126C2B turbo
4   Keke Rosberg   Williams-Cosworth FW08C
5   John Watson   McLaren-Cosworth MP4
6   Marc Surer   Arrows-Cosworth A6

May 15, MONACO GRAND PRIX, Monte Carlo
1   Keke Rosberg   Williams-Cosworth FW08C   (80.521mph)
2   Nelson Piquet   Brabham-BMW BT50 turbo
3   Alain Prost   Renault RE40 turbo
4   Patrick Tambay   Ferrari 126C2B turbo
5   Danny Sullivan   Tyrrell-Cosworth 011
6   Mauro Baldi   Arrows-Cosworth A6

May 22, BELGIAN GRAND PRIX, Spa-Francochamps
1   Alain Prost   Renault RE40 turbo   (119.135mph)
2   Patrick Tambay   Ferrari 126C2B turbo
3   Eddie Cheever   Renault RE40 turbo
4   Nelson Piquet   Brabham-BMW BT52 turbo
5   Keke Rosberg   Williams-Cosworth FW08C
6   Jacques Laffite   Williams-Cosworth FW08C

June 5, DETROIT GRAND PRIX, Michigan
1	Michele Alboreto	Tyrrell-Cosworth 011	(81.158mph)
2	Keke Rosberg	Williams-Cosworth FW08C	
3	John Watson	McLaren-Cosworth MP4	
4	Nelson Piquet	Brabham-BMW BT52 turbo	
5	Jacques Laffite	Williams-Cosworth FW08C	
6	Nigel Mansell	Lotus-Cosworth 92	

June 12, CANADIAN GRAND PRIX, Montreal
1	René Arnoux	Ferrari 126C2B turbo	(106.044mph)
2	Eddie Cheever	Renault RE40 turbo	
3	Patrick Tambay	Ferrari 126C2B turbo	
4	Keke Rosberg	Williams-Cosworth FW08C	
5	Alain Prost	Renault RE40	
6	John Watson	McLaren-Cosworth MP4	

July 16, BRITISH GRAND PRIX, Silverstone
1	Alain Prost	Renault RE40 turbo	(139.218mph)
2	Nelson Piquet	Brabham-BMW BT52 turbo	
3	Patrick Tambay	Ferrari 126C2B turbo	
4	Nigel Mansell	Lotus-Renault 94T turbo	
5	René Arnoux	Ferrari 126C2B turbo	
6	Niki Lauda	McLaren-Cosworth MP4	

August 7, GERMAN GRAND PRIX, Hockenheim
1	René Arnoux	Ferrari 126C3 turbo	(130.813mph)
2	Andrea de Cesaris	Alfa Romeo 183T turbo	
3	Riccardo Patrese	Brabham-BMW BT52B turbo	
4	Alain Prost	Renault RE40 turbo	
5	John Watson	McLaren-Cosworth MP4	
6	Jacques Laffite	Williams-Cosworth FW08C	

August 14, AUSTRIAN GRAND PRIX, Osterreichring
1	Alain Prost	Renault RE40 turbo	(138.872mph)
2	René Arnoux	Ferrari 126C3 turbo	
3	Nelson Piquet	Brabham-BMW BT52B turbo	
4	Eddie Cheever	Renault RE40 turbo	
5	Nigel Mansell	Lotus-Renault 94T turbo	
6	Niki Lauda	McLaren-Cosworth MP4	

August 28, DUTCH GRAND PRIX, Zandvoort
1	René Arnoux	Ferrari 126C3 turbo	(115.64mph)
2	Patrick Tambay	Ferrari 126C3 turbo	
3	John Watson	McLaren-Cosworth MP4	
4	Derek Warwick	Toleman-Hart TG183B turbo	
5	Mauro Baldi	Alfa Romeo 183T turbo	
6	Michele Alboreto	Tyrrell-Cosworth 011	

September 11, ITALIAN GRAND PRIX, Monza
1	Nelson Piquet	Brabham-BMW BT52B turbo	(135.178mph)
2	René Arnoux	Ferrari 126C3 turbo	
3	Eddie Cheever	Renault RE40 turbo	
4	Patrick Tambay	Ferrari 126C3 turbo	
5	Elio de Angelis	Lotus-Renault 94T turbo	
6	Derek Warwick	Toleman-Hart TG183B turbo	

September 25, EUROPEAN GRAND PRIX, Brands Hatch

1	Nelson Piquet	Brabham-BMW BT52B turbo	(123.165mph)
2	Alain Prost	Renault RE40 turbo	
3	Nigel Mansell	Lotus-Renault 94T turbo	
4	Andrea de Cesaris	Alfa Romeo 183T turbo	
5	Derek Warwick	Toleman-Hart TG183B turbo	
6	Bruno Giacomelli	Toleman-Hart TG183B turbo	

October 15, SOUTH AFRICAN GRAND PRIX, Kyalami

1	Riccardo Patrese	Brabham-BMW BT52B turbo	(126.1mph)
2	Andrea de Cesaris	Alfa Romeo 183T turbo	
3	Nelson Piquet	Brabham-BMW BT52B turbo	
4	Derek Warwick	Toleman-Hart TG183B turbo	
5	Keke Rosberg	Williams-Honda FW09 turbo	
6	Eddie Cheever	Renault RE40 turbo	

DRIVERS' WORLD CHAMPIONSHIP

Posn	Driver	Points
1	Nelson Piquet	59
2	Alain Prost	57
3	René Arnoux	49
4	Patrick Tambay	40
5	Keke Rosberg	27
6	John Watson	22
	Eddie Cheever	
8	Andrea de Cesaris	15
9	Riccardo Patrese	13
10	Niki Lauda	12
11	Jacques Laffite	11
12	Michele Alboreto	10
	Nigel Mansell	
14	Derek Warwick	9
15	Marc Surer	4
16	Mauro Baldi	3
17	Elio de Angelis	2
	Danny Sullivan	
19	Johnny Cecotto	1
	Bruno Giacomelli	

CONSTRUCTORS' CHAMPIONSHIP

Posn	Constructor	Points
1	Ferrari	89
2	Renault	79
3	Brabham	72
4	Williams	38
5	McLaren	34
6	Alfa Romeo	18
7	Tyrrell	12
	Lotus	
9	Toleman	10
10	Arrows	4
11	Theodore	1

1984

Renault had unquestionably dropped the ball at the end of 1983, but although the French team seemed in some disarray following the South African Grand Prix, most observers believed it would pick itself up, dust itself down and try again. That it did, of course, but if anybody had predicted the Renault works team had won its last Grand Prix and that it would withdraw from the Grand Prix stage, tired, bruised and utterly defeated, less than two years hence, they would have been branded as unduly pessimistic.

However, the Regie took its first step towards the precipice a few days after the South African Grand Prix. Somebody would have to pay for this very public fiasco, made all the more uncomfortable by BMW's offer to take over some of the success-advertising space lying fallow in the French national newspapers.

Gerard Larrousse had some very personal and private reasons for wanting Prost's head on a plate and, under the circumstances, his wish was granted. Alain's place in the executioner's tumbril was reserved almost before he had undone his harness in the Kyalami pit lane. He found himself unceremoniously booted out of the French corporate door only a few days after Kyalami, his place eventually to be taken by Patrick Tambay. Renault's loss would turn out to be McLaren's, and Prost's, gain.

Marlboro's John Hogan had been monitoring the Prost situation for a few weeks prior to Kyalami, for Alain benefited from a Marlboro personal sponsorship contract. Meanwhile, over at McLaren, there was an increasing body of feeling which suggested that perhaps John Watson had come to the end of the competitive road. Only a hint, perhaps, but the team's management recalled the start of the season and how John had led them a merry old dance when it came to finalising the details of his contract. After Kyalami 1983, they did not rush to embrace a continuation of his deal.

Then Prost exploded on to the driver market. A couple of days after being turned out on to the street by Renault, Prost was signing a McLaren contract at Philip Morris's Lausanne headquarters. He was in no position to haggle too much, so Ron Dennis got himself a bargain, serving to remind him just what an expensive proposition Niki Lauda really was. Watson, of course, was out of a job.

Lauda, meanwhile, was obliged to take stock of what, for many other drivers, would be seen as a tricky situation. But he had been comfortable with Watson alongside him. OK, so John was occasionally quicker, and would now and then prove capable of giving Niki a nasty surprise. But Lauda was shrewd enough to know that Prost was a completely different proposition. He was quick.

There is a large body of suitably informed Formula 1 opinion tending towards the view that Lauda was never really quick in the Rosberg/Villeneuve/Senna sense of the word. He was not a slouch, by any means, but his overwhelming advantage as a Grand Prix driver was an ability to detach himself from the immediacy of the scene, retaining a broad overview of what was going on around him, even during the frantic hubbub of a Grand Prix weekend. He knew what was needed to win Grand Prix races, World Championships even – and that quality was not simply speed.

During the winter, John Barnard honed his definitive McLaren MP4/2 design in preparation for the forthcoming season. But off-season testing had to be carried out with the MP4/1E interim cars because there was no hurrying this design genius. Barnard's philosophy was to experiment, investigate and accumulate data for as long as possible. To him, Grand Prix car design was a complex, continuing process, evolving almost by the day. He was reluctant to 'rule off' and say, right, OK, this is the definitive design. He would frequently remark that, even as new cars were being built, he could see further ways of improving them which he had not been able to incorporate in the concept.

Such an approach obviously placed considerable pressure on the McLaren factory workforce to build three definitive MP4/2 cars at the last possible moment. But it also served to unsettle the opposition which started the season not really knowing what to expect from the McLaren-TAG alliance. The engines were equipped with a highly sophisticated Bosch electronic engine management system which took time to develop, as did the relationship itself between the German electronics company and McLaren.

Bosch had been dealing with Porsche for many years, but the relationship with McLaren was a little tricky. It took some time for Bosch to appreciate that, whilst it was supplying its services to Porsche, John Barnard was calling the technical shots because McLaren paid the bills.

At this point it is worth a slight detour to consider the implications for engine performance of the 220 litre fuel

Below: *Niki Lauda stands in the Zandvoort pit lane while McLaren mechanics work on the first 80 degree TAG turbo V6 installed in the interim McLaren MP4/1E test car. To his immediate right is engineer Steve Nichols who would later design the MP4/4-Honda driven to the 1988 World Championship by Ayrton Senna. Overleaf: the new car in action during the race.*

regulations. With no refuelling stops permitted as from the start of the 1984 season, the business of operating a turbocharged Grand Prix engine to its maximum potential assumed another very complex dimension, pressing the very outer limits of the manufacturers' technology. It was now a matter of running as lean a mixture as possible to eke out the fuel load as efficiently as possible. But there was still the task of producing maximum possible power. Fuel could no longer be forced through the engine and turbos, fulfilling the role of a coolant and reducing the considerable thermodynamic loadings, as it could when stops to replenish the tank offered the luxury of fuel to squander.

Renault had been amongst the pioneers of such a system with their Kugelfischer mechanical injection back in 1982, working in conjunction with a cam that would allow response to throttle setting and boost pressure. But this had its limitations in the sense that it was only sensitive to engine load, not speed, so the same amount of fuel would be injected into the combustion chambers for a given load, whatever the revs. What Bosch was developing was a far more sophisticated, all-embracing engine management system, using microprocessors, which would provide instant changes to the engine settings, depending on boost pressure, ambient and charge air-temperature, air flow, fuel pressure and water temperature.

Such systems produced a host of incidental challenges, such as programming the system in the first place — 'mapping' — which was done by a painstaking process of dynomometer testing, taking readings progressively all the way up the rev and turbo boost scale to determine ignition and injection settings for a wide range of engine speed and loading. Seemingly endless problems with the Bosch system on the early TAG turbos caused a great deal of frustration during those 1983/84 winter tests, perhaps throwing the opposition off the McLaren scent.

Not that McLaren seemed likely to have things its own way. Over at Brabham, Gordon Murray had produced a 220 litre tank version of the BT52, featuring longer side pods for enhanced aerodynamic performance. BMW's 4 cylinder development was proceeding apace while Renault held out high hopes for its new RE50 chassis design. Supply of its latest specification V6 turbo engines was now available to Ligier as well as to Lotus. Meanwhile, Gerard Ducarouge's Lotus type 95 concept was a further logical refinement of the 'bitza' 94T, now sporting more up-to-date pull-rod suspension all round.

Ferrari now had Michele Alboreto aboard alongside René Arnoux, poor Patrick Tambay having been jettisoned on the three-into-two won't go basis. And, of course, there was the unknown quantity of the Williams-Honda.

Having got the green light from Honda in the middle of 1983, Williams found itself flung in at the deep end when the first RA163-E V6 arrived at the team's new Didcot factory in a box, with a couple of turbochargers thrown in. This was real 'teach yourself technology' with the Williams team having to work out for itself the best exhaust and intercooler system to go with its new engine. Precious little had been learned from the Spirit programme on that particular score.

Back at Kyalami at the tail end of 1983, the Williams-Honda had been operating with insufficient intercooling capacity which restricted its power output. But Keke Rosberg was optimistic about the future. His deal with Williams for 1984 had been tied up early on and here they were, race testing the prototype of their new machine in the last race of the 1983 season. 'I'm feeling really relaxed and confident about the future,' he told me. A few months later, the outspoken Keke would have some less charitable remarks to make about the Williams-Honda FW09!

Finally, the shadow-boxing stopped and the 1984 Brazilian Grand Prix started the new season. Elio de Angelis, now revelling in Goodyear grip, planted his Lotus 95T on pole position ahead of Alboreto's new Ferrari 126C4, Derek Warwick's Renault RE50 and Alain Prost's McLaren MP4/2. Everywhere on the starting grid, aluminium foil sheeting could be seen covering fuel tanks brimming with 220 litres of pre-cooled fuel. This was truly the start of a new and exciting period in the turbo era.

Alboreto eased into the lead from the start, but a brake caliper malfunction spun him out of contention as early as Lap 8. That allowed Niki Lauda to surge through in the new McLaren, only relinquishing the lead when a minor electrical problem sluiced away his chances. With two-thirds of the race completed, Warwick now went ahead, seemingly set for a maiden victory in the Renault. But an earlier wheel-banging moment with Lauda had weakened the RE50's front suspension, causing it to collapse with only ten laps to go, mercifully at the slowest point on the circuit.

From behind the curtain of Renault's understandable chagrin, Alain Prost came through to win, a remarkable fairy-tale success for the McLaren-TAG. Metaphorically it also enabled him to raise two fingers aloft to the French team which had discarded him so ruthlessly only four months earlier. The account had been settled, a psychological battle won. Moreover, Lauda now fully appreciated the magnitude of the challenge he faced from within his own team.

The irony of Prost's personal standing in his native land was not lost on the intelligent young driver. Throughout his time at Renault he had increasingly become something of an anti-hero in France. When his cherished Mercedes 500SEC was vandalised in the streets of his home town, St Chamond, it provided just one more reason to leave the country, to escape from this peculiar situation where public opinion seemed to be against him. With his wife Anne-Marie and young son Nicolas, he moved to Switzerland. Paradoxically, once he became an expatriate, driving for a foreign team, his personal popularity amongst his fickle countrymen went up again!

Further down the grid at Rio, a handful of bright new lads had burst on to the Formula 1 scene. German rising star Stefan Bellof joined the still-Cosworth-propelled Tyrrell line-up alongside Martin Brundle. Meanwhile Ayrton Senna, Brundle's arch-rival in their battle for British Formula 3 Championship honours, replaced Warwick as Toleman team leader.

Senna had already forged a reputation as a pretty single-minded operator, as Brundle recounted: 'I remember at Snetterton on one occasion, when we were racing in Formula 3, he came over

Jean-Pierre Jabouille trails round at the back of the field with the first Renault RS01 in the 1977 British Grand Prix. Some laughed, but others, far-sightedly, didn't . . .

Winning ways. This was the view the opposition got of Rene Arnoux's Renault RE20B on its way to a commanding victory in the 1980 Brazilian Grand Prix at Interlagos.

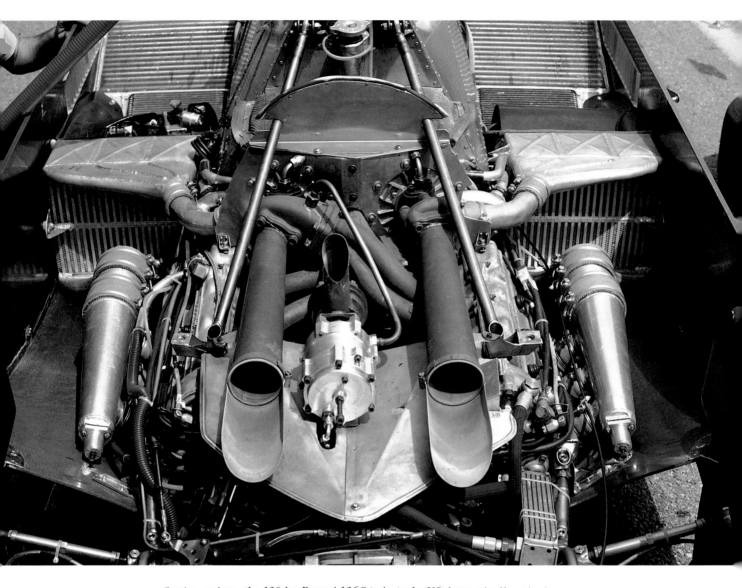

Getting serious: the 120deg Ferrari 126C twin turbo V6 dramatically raised the turbo stakes on its introduction in 1981.

John Watson in the John Barnard-designed McLaren MP4. The Ulsterman's Cosworth V8-powered victory in the 1981 British Grand Prix was the first for the newly formed McLaren International team, paving the way for an avalanche of success during the turbo era.

Helmet and gloves waiting for Didier Pironi on the side pod of his Ferrari
126C2 turbo. He should have become the first turbo World Champion, as well
as the first French title holder, but tragedy would intervene at Hockenheim.

Buried beneath this mass of ducts and plumbing is the four-cylinder Brian
Hart 415T engine which Toleman brought into F1 during the 1981 season.

Keke Rosberg in the ground-effect Williams-Cosworth FW07C during the 1982 Brazilian Grand Prix at Rio. Keke finished a storming second, only to join winner Nelson Piquet's being disqualified in the 'water tank' controversy.

Nigel Mansell's Lotus 91-Cosworth was the final 'skirted' F1 design to emerge from the famous British team under the auspices of Colin Chapman at the start of the 1982 season. Later that year, the dynamic Lotus founder would die suddenly.

Cool Keke. The bouncy Finn, seen here on the eve of his Championship at Las Vegas in 1982, would be the last man to win the title in a naturally aspirated car before F1 was engulfed in the turbo era.

The four-cylinder BMW M12/13 single turbo, production-based engine, seen here installed in a Brabham BT50, would become one of the most powerful forced induction engines of all during the turbo era.

Niki Lauda – seen here lapping Derek Warwick's Toleman during the 1982
South African Grand Prix – would become one of the most accomplished
performers of the turbo era. His cool, controlled and disciplined style earned
him a third World Championship in 1984 with the McLaren-TAG.

As the Cosworth naturally aspirated era came to an end, the long-lived V8
still occasionally outlasted the turbos to win the odd Grand Prix. Here
Michele Alboreto's Tyrrell 011 heads to victory at Las Vegas in 1982, the race
in which Rosberg clinched his Championship.

New dawn from the Far East. Stefan Johansson's Spirit 101 in the 1983 British Grand Prix at Silverstone – powered by Honda. It marked the Japanese firm's return to F1 for the first time since 1968.

The first Honda V6 turbo, packed rather untidily into the engine bay of the Spirit 101. It was horrifyingly unreliable to begin with, but Honda soon rectified that state of affairs.

Keke Rosberg battling the unloved Williams-Honda FW09, a machine he affected to dislike intensely, but which helped him to win the 1984 Dallas Grand Prix. Even designer Patrick Head concedes it probably wasn't the best car Williams have produced . . . but he insists it was nowhere near as deficient as Rosberg always grumbled!

Nigel Mansell battling with Alain Prost in the rain at Monaco in 1984. The sight of these two at – or near – the head of the field was common-place in the latter years of the turbo era.

State of the art. The superb Porsche-built, TAG turbo V6 was tailor-made for the McLaren team between 1984 and 1987. It raced for four seasons and won World Championships in three of them.

Renault-powered pair. Derek Warwick's works Renault RE50 rounds Druids hairpin at Brands Hatch, heading for second place in the 1984 British Grand Prix, a few feet ahead of the 'customer' Lotus 95T of Elio de Angelis. Generally speaking, Lotus made far better use of the French V6 turbos than the home team which withdrew from F1, battered and dejected, at the end of 1985.

Birth of a great new talent. Ayrton Senna's undisputed talent shone brightly during 1984, his first F1 season, and the fine-handling Toleman-Hart TG184 allowed him to put his ability on very public display.

Ayrton Senna was an outstanding contender with the Lotus-Renaults in 1985 and 1986. Here he leads through a rain-slicked La Source hairpin on the opening lap of the 1985 Belgian Grand Prix. Immediately behind, Nelson Piquet starts to spin his Brabham-BMW in front of Alain Prost's McLaren-TAG MP4/2B and Michele Alboreto in the Ferrari 156/85.

Niki Lauda won the 1984 season's World Championship by an infinitesimal half-point margin from McLaren-TAG team-mate Alain Prost.

Nelson Piquet at the wheel of the Brabham-BMW BT54 turbo during 1985. Although it was a highly competitive tool, its Pirelli race rubber was no match for Goodyear's and Piquet only managed a single Grand Prix win.

Honda introduced a new dimension to F1 engine technology during the turbo
era. Here, three of its technicians monitor the huge computers in the pit
garage which receive radio signals from the cars' engine management
computers, giving the engineers even more information about the performance
of the machinery than is available to the drivers.

Keke Rosberg's last F1 season before retirement was spent partnering Alain
Prost in the McLaren-TAG line-up. The Finn hated 'fuel consumption racing'
but now concedes that he probably retired too early.

Honda's turbo V6, equipped with the mandatory FISA-provided boost control valve at the leading edge of its plenum chamber atop the engine intakes. Set at 4-bar for 1987 and 2.5-bar the following year, they were introduced by FISA to put a ceiling on F1 turbo power outputs. With considerable technical ingenuity, some manufacturers found a way to run beyond 4-bar, even with the valves fitted...

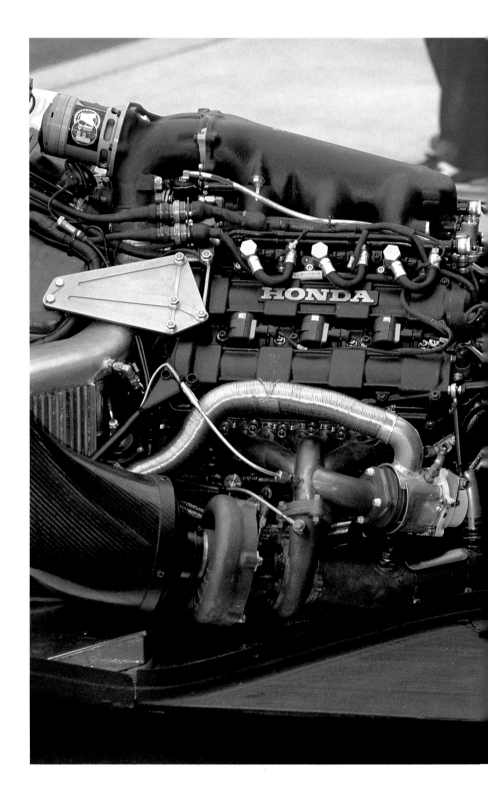

The turbos ran through 1988 with their performance constrained by a 150-litre fuel limit and 2.5-bar boost, so the margin between success and failure was minimal. While Alain Prost's McLaren-Honda won the Portuguese Grand Prix at Estoril, Ayrton Senna had a more difficult time. Here he is seen unsuccessfully trying to fend off Ivan Capelli's naturally aspirated March-Judd 881 which eventually stormed past to finish second.

Ayrton Senna's McLaren-Honda MP4/4 in amongst slower traffic on its way to a momentous 1988 Japanese Grand Prix victory which secured the Brazilian his first World Championship. He has just lapped the Ferrari turbo of Michele Alboreto and the naturally aspirated 3.5-litre Benetton-Ford B188s of Thierry Boutsen and Alessandro Nannini.

Alfa Romeo designed this four-cylinder 1.5-litre turbo for the 1987 season, but found an excuse for withdrawing from its deal with Ligier after Rene Arnoux had complained to the Italian press that it was a lousy engine. Almost certainly, he was right...

Where we came in. Dawn of the new, naturally aspirated era, with Riccardo Patrese's 3.5-litre Judd-engined Williams FW12 leading the Cosworth-powered Benetton B188s of Alessandro Nannini and Thierry Boutsen in the early stages of the 1988 San Marino Grand Prix at Imola.

the top of me to the point where I could count the rivets on the underside of his car's monocoque. Even when he came crashing down on the track, with all his wheels pointing in different directions, he still tried to drive into me before spearing off down an escape road and colliding with an ambulance!'

An episode at their first Formula 1 race together sheds an interesting light on some of Senna's subsequent behaviour. 'He came to me just before the start and suggested, "Look, let's take things easy between us in our first Grand Prix,"' Brundle remembers, '"So whoever gets off the grid first, the other one won't pass." As it happened, I qualified behind him and got the better start. Ayrton soon forgot our deal. On the second corner, he came tearing past me, all four wheels on the grass . . .'

Niki Lauda won the South African Grand Prix at Kyalami after Nelson Piquet's pace-setting Brabham-BMW faded and Prost's challenge was defused when he had to switch to the spare car shortly before the start. But despite starting from the pit lane, Prost drove majestically through to finish second behind his team-mate.

The third round of the Championship was totally a Ferrari affair. Michele Alboreto's Goodyear-shod, Lucas mechanically fuel-injected 126C4 proved the class of the field in the Belgian Grand Prix at Zolder, starting from pole position and leading throughout to beat Derek Warwick's Renault by a comfortable margin. Both McLaren-TAGs retired with fuel-related engine failures. The opposition breathed again; so the super team was vulnerable. But not for long.

Prost won at San Marino, surviving a spectacular spin caused by a faulty brake master-cylinder. Lauda retired with engine failure after racing with an extrovert zest that surprised everybody. Then Niki took the French Grand Prix at Dijon-Prenois after a great battle with Tambay's pole position Renault. Prost, delayed after a lurid moment when front-wheel securing bolts worked loose, was out of the points in seventh place. Niki spun off at Monaco, where monsoon conditions prevailed and half points were awarded when the race was stopped at half distance. Prost was just ahead, but about to be gobbled up by the dynamic Senna's new Toleman TG184.

You might be forgiven for wondering what had happened to FISA and Jean-Marie Balestre at this point in the narrative. He was still right there in the forefront of attention. The sport's governing body was embroiled in a complex battle with the Monaco organisers over the question of lucrative television-coverage rights, so Balestre eagerly sprang to the attack when it became clear that administrative irregularities had surfaced after the event had been flagged to a halt.

Peter Warr, Nigel Mansell and Gérard Ducarouge deep in thought during Silverstone testing. The Lotus 95T twice led races in Mansell's hands, but failed to score a single victory.

Nigel Mansell in the Renault-engined Lotus 94T pulls every trick in the book to fend off Keke Rosberg's Williams-Honda FW09 in the 1984 Dallas Grand Prix. The Finn (opposite) would later make some scathing comments about Mansell's driving tactics, only later to learn that the English driver would be joining him in the Williams squad for 1985.

Clerk of the course Jacky Ickx, a respected former Grand Prix driver who had come second at Monaco for Ferrari in similarly appalling conditions twelve years earlier, had correctly used a red flag to stop the race. But, implicit in the use of a red flag, was the possibility of a restart over the balance of the race distance. However, the president of the Automobile Club de Monaco, Michel Boeri, also took it upon himself to show a chequered flag, even though he had no right to be out on the circuit giving signals.

FISA homed in on that irregularity and the race finished in a mood of bad feeling and tension with Jacky Ickx subsequently admonished for his apparent transgression in stopping the race when it did not need to be terminated. From some quarters there was also the disgraceful, albeit veiled, slur that Ickx, as a Porsche works sports car driver, had some sort of vested interest in letting the TAG/Porsche-engined McLaren win the race. Ickx later had his clerk of the course licence suspended and was fined $6,000, a manifestly stupid action by FISA. In a sport administered by so many blue-blazered theorists, officials like Ickx, who really know their stuff and understand the business, are at a premium.

Reigning World Champion Nelson Piquet had not been able to do much about defending his title for the first half of the 1984 season. The undeniably quick BT53 succumbed to a worrying series of largely unrelated mechanical problems as Paul Rosche and his team of BMW Motorsports engineers concentrated on developing more power and enhanced economy from its production-based 4 cylinder engine. Time and again, Piquet would be on pole position, only to see an initial advantage squandered with turbo failures, piston breakages, timing problems, fuel difficulties and gearbox malfunctions. Yet the mid-season North American tour provided Piquet with a respite from this sequence of disappointing performances.

At Montreal, Nelson won commandingly, beating Lauda and Prost into second and third places. The following weekend at Detroit saw him savaged at the start when Nigel Mansell, starting fast from the second row in his Lotus 95T, attemped to squeeze between Prost's McLaren and the pole position Brabham. There was not quite enough room to pull it off, Mansell triggering a multiple pile-up for which he was later fined $6,000.

Piquet's race car was wrecked in the impact, but despite feeling bruised and battered, he took over the spare car to win the race, scraping home a few lengths ahead of Martin Brundle's naturally-aspirated Tyrrell 012. Lauda retired with serious electronic trouble while Prost, whose hatred of Detroit was possibly due to the McLaren team's consistent failure ever to make the Barnard-designed cars really perform well through its twists and turns, wound up a lack-lustre fifth.

Meanwhile, what of the Williams-Hondas? Over the winter, the aluminium honeycomb chassis FW09 was fitted with significantly better intercooling thanks to a typically intensive programme of wind tunnel development carried out by the team's own aerodynamicist Frank Dernie. The FW09 had also made its debut fitted with FW08-style rocker arm rear suspension, but the incorporation of a definitive pull-rod rear end had now endowed it with more grip. The improved intercooling had proved the key to unlocking the Honda engine's fierce power delivery and Rosberg, never one to mince his words, quickly reported that the car's abiding characteristic was understeer. Then the engine would explode into sudden life as it entered its narrow power band, pitching the FW09 into violent oversteer. As a result, it was tiring to drive and displayed a voracious appetite for its Goodyear rubber.

It certainly irritated Patrick Head as well. The Williams designer was convinced that the fundamental cause of Rosberg's complaint was the abrupt power delivery rather than his number one driver's much-trumpted assertion that the chassis was flexing. In fact, the 1984 engine was still basically built round the old Formula 2 block, so it was perhaps no surprise that the block was flexing under load, contributing to bearing failures, the engine mounts were also distorting and a problem with restricted water flow to one bank of cylinders alone also proved a constraint on maximising the engine's potential.

Rosberg converses with Williams chief designer Patrick Head. There was some tension between the two men over precisely why the FW09 handled so precariously, Head attributing much of the blame to the Honda engine's abrupt power delivery while Rosberg initially believed the chassis flexed excessively.

Just prior to the Montreal and Detroit races, Patrick Head introduced a McLaren-style, waisted rear-end, complete with aerodynamic 'ramps' à la John Barnard, and the FW09 had to revert to its older rocker arm rear suspension set-up in order to accommodate this. Then the team went to Dallas for the inaugural, controversial and sole Formula 1 race to be held on the challenging Fair Park circuit in the Texas city.

Most of the controversy throughout the weekend centred round whether the track surface would survive the rigours of practice, let alone the race itself. Crumbling like a meringue in the sweltering 100°F plus temperatures, the race itself was in doubt right through to race morning. Even when the cars lined up on the starting grid, behind Nigel Mansell's pole position Lotus 95T, there were many who believed it would be flagged to a halt after only a handful of laps. Rosberg, who had invested $2,500 in a water-cooled skullcap to wear beneath his helmet, knew otherwise. By the end of the day, that skullcap was to look like the bargain of the age.

Mansell led from the start, but Warwick soon moved through to challenge, determined to get on with the business as he feared the race would be stopped. He challenged Mansell with an excess of brio, spinning broadside into a tyre barrier as he attempted to draw level with the Lotus as early as Lap 11. He walked back to the pits, furious with himself, and rightly more worried about what his wife Rhonda would say rather than any ticking off he might expect from the team. Derek always had his priorities in the right order!

As the race wore on, Rosberg gradually picked up the pace. Formula 1's great improvisor, Keke was always at his best when the variables were unpredictable and this was one of those days. All the balls were up in the air like never before in recent memory. Eventually, Rosberg came up behind Mansell and had a great deal of trouble dislodging the Lotus driver from the lead. Eventually, aided by a touch of shameless 'brake-testing', he shook himself free of the Englishman and went on to win, dodging every hazard on a day when both McLaren drivers, red-faced with embarrassment, hit the wall.

You might have expected most drivers to forget the frustrations of the race in their moment of glory, but that was not Keke's style. His capacity to call a spade a shovel was all but unmatched during my time in the Grand Prix business. No sooner had he mounted the winner's rostrum than he began giving television viewers all over the world a piece of his mind on the subject of Nigel Mansell's driving tactics. None of it was complimentary, no punches were pulled.

Mansell, in the meantime, was busy collapsing on the track

The essence of 1984 as Alain Prost's McLaren-TAG MP4/2 surges away from the pack during the early stages of the Dutch Grand Prix at Zandvoort. Further back, Niki Lauda's sister car is battling through traffic from its starting position further back on the grid.

after an over-dramatic attempt to push his out-of-fuel Lotus home into sixth place. It was just the sort of theatrical performance which made many of us wince. But we were wrong. In truth, it was an index of his monumental determination which would finally flower, ironically, at the wheel of a Williams-Honda, in years to come.

Sadly, after his splendid showing in Detroit, Martin Brundle crashed during practice at Dallas, sustaining ankle injuries which were to keep him away from the cockpit for the balance of the season. His spell of enforced absence would coincide with another Formula 1 witch hunt, this time centred round the Tyrrell team, following routine samples taken from the contents of the 'water injection reservoir' and fuel tank on Brundle's car after his second place in the first of the preceding US street races.

A quantity of lead balls was found in the Tyrrell's water tank, Ken explaining this away as ballast. However, when he found himself called in front of a FISA Executive Committe meeting in July, he was informed that the water sample contained 27.5 per cent aromatics. He now found himself facing charges of breaching the fuel regulations on four counts: taking on fuel during the race; using fuel which did not comply with the regulations; equipping the car with fuel lines which did not conform to the correct specification; using lead ballast not fixed to the car in the properly prescribed manner.

Subsequent inquiries by Tyrrell revealed that there was, in fact, less than 1 per cent hydrocarbon content in the water. His evidence suggested that FISA had wrongly interpreted their own evidence. However, on appeal, the FISA Court of Appeal switched the charges, a technique which was to become unpleasantly familiar in ensuing years. Now he was accused of having holes in the supposedly flat undertray of the Tyrrell, unsecured mobile ballast and the presence of hydrocarbons in the water.

The FISA Court of Appeal was now poised, in the view of most observers, to blunder into another ill-judged decision. Tyrrell was found guilty on three counts: illegal hydrocarbons in the water, unsecured ballast and holes in the flat bottom of the car. The sentence was that his team should take no further part in the 1984 World Championship and be retrospectively excluded from the races run so far. It was a stunning decision, far more worthy

Ayrton Senna's place at the wheel of the Toleman TG184-Hart marked him out as a star of the future during 1984. Here he is heading for third place in the British Grand Prix at Brands Hatch behind Niki Lauda's McLaren-TAG and Derek Warwick's Renault RE50.

of collective indignation and concerted action on the part of other team owners than, say, the disqualification of Senna's McLaren from the Japanese Grand Prix five years later, an event which provoked an enormous furore.

Nobody rushed to Tyrrell's aid. Some felt, uncharitably, that he was paying the price for rocking the turbo boat once too often. But inter-team solidarity goes to pieces on occasions like this. Tyrrell was like the poor schoolboy who, forced to stand in the corner of the class wearing the dunce's hat, finds his discomfiture heighted when he is subjected to a hail of chalk from his supposed pals. But there was more to it than that. Tyrrell had been the only objector in the move to retain the 220 litre fuel limit rather than reducing the capacity, as planned, to 195 litres in 1985.

In order to achieve this rule change, unanimity amongst team owners had to exist. With Tyrrell neatly out of the picture, there was. Nothing was ever proved, but it seemed a shameful affair. The RACMSA claimed there were wider issues at stake and, marshalling all the inertia at its disposal, failed to come to Tyrrell's assistance. Since the RACMSA never made public the nature of those 'wider issues' they also stood condemned in this matter.

Tyrrell was not finally sentenced until the Dutch Grand Prix weekend, a High Court injunction allowing him to compete in the British Grand Prix at Brands Hatch where he got at least some of his own back by earning plenty of television coverage for his new sponsors, Systime Computers, who seemed rather bemused by the whole episode.

The Brands Hatch race itself turned into a three-way affair between the two McLarens and Piquet's Brabham, only Lauda surviving intact to lead past the chequered flag and score an immensely popular win in front of a British crowd, which had always taken him to its collective heart as one of their own. Warwick was second, with Senna, running superbly again in the Toleman TG184, third. In an afternoon, Niki had reduced his points deficit to Prost from 10½ to 1½. All bets were now off.

All things being equal, Prost looked likely to emerge with the title. Over the season as a whole, the Frenchman was faster, particularly when it came to qualifying. Niki confessed that, at his time of life, he was finding it increasingly difficult to screw himself up for an all or nothing lap in order to secure a prime position on the grid. When it came to the race, there was a lot less to choose between the two of them. The strongest firepower in Lauda's armoury was the fact that he had won the World Championship before and displayed none of the pent-up tension so often radiated by a driver aiming at the title for the first time.

Lauda and Prost: Doing it Ron's way

Some people thought it was absolutely inevitable that Ron Dennis would eventually put together the most formidable driver pairing of the early 1980s. Consequently, when circumstances and a shrewd reading of the prevailing political wind presented the possibility of partnering Niki Lauda with Alain Prost. It was no surprise that he jumped at the chance.

Dennis's preoccupation with technical and operational excellence may have marked him out as slightly eccentric amongst certain of Formula 1's old traditionalists, but the 1984 season would set the tone of McLaren International's *modus operandi* for the remainder of the decade. It was an absolutely fundamental tenet of Ron's philosophy that his team should project a first-rate image, a sheen of excellence. Sponsors, or 'investors' as McLaren prefers to call them, would pay handsomely for the privilege of being associated with a classy operation. Moreover, they would come back for more, renewing their associations time and again.

Although Lauda was receptive to the idea of a return to the cockpit at the start of the 1982 season, that he actually took the firm decision to climb back behind the wheel was down to Ron tempting and cajoling him over a long period. Midway through 1982, Dennis commented: 'Niki's the best driver in the car and the best driver out of it. That doesn't mean he's got to be winning races all the time. But he has a total commitment to that end.'

Likewise, when Prost unexpectedly came on to the market at the end of 1982, there was no sentiment over dropping John Watson. Dennis and his colleagues had known, as long ago as 1980, that Prost was the better long-term bet. He won his first Grand Prix on returning to the team. A further twenty-nine victories and two World Championships would fall to the Frenchman's McLaren before he quit the team at the end of 1989.

If Lauda was not going to beat Prost on speed, he would have to do it on strategy. In fact, the record book shows that he really did it on luck. Granted, Prost made a few mistakes, but generally the prevailing wind was with the Austrian. More crucially, the misfortunes of non-McLaren drivers tended to favour Lauda rather than his colleague.

On a personal level, the two men got on extremely well once Lauda allowed his initial barrier of caution and scepticism to fall away. During the winter he had asserted his authority by claiming his contractually-assured priority when it came to testing, a state of affairs which frequently left Prost kicking his heels in the pit lane. But Alain genuinely admired Niki, claiming that he had tried to model himself on the Austrian driver from his early days in Formula 1.

'Alain is extremely quick,' Lauda confirmed. 'Having him as a team-mate has both stimulated me and haunted me. There is no break in the pressure. In qualifying, particularly, he is unbelievable. I have had to drive faster, and try harder, than ever before in my career . . .' All this from a man who, when offered the prospect of joining James Hunt in a Marlboro McLaren 'super team', declined on the grounds that Hunt was too quick. He wanted to stay at Ferrari, protected by its power advantage. Most drivers would

Nelson Piquet, now in the spare Brabham BT53-BMW, gets away cleanly at the restart of the 1984 Detroit Grand Prix ahead of Prost and Mansell. Earlier, his race car had been badly damaged when Mansell triggered off a multi-car pile up at the first start.

cut off their right hand before conceding that a rival was quicker. Lauda was always on more than nodding terms with reality.

In terms of their sparing use of the machinery, McLaren were spoiled like few other teams in recent Grand Prix history. Team director Creighton Brown told me recently that, after a few races, they became so confident in Alain and Niki that they stopped bothering to insure the chassis. The team did not wreck a single car throughout the year; indeed, only three MP4/2s were fielded during the year; two race cars and a spare. That lack of damage was, in itself, remarkable. The mechanics would reflect with sentimental longing on 1984 when Keke Rosberg, Stefan Johansson and Ayrton Senna later went through the McLaren mill. They were different again.

McLaren made a lot of progress during the course of the season, running carbon-fibre brakes – a feature offering prodigious retardation and a worthwhile weight saving – but the Cosworth-based transmission was always marginal. Prost lost possible victory in Austria when he spun in oil dropped by de Angelis's Lotus while holding his McLaren in gear, yet ironically, Lauda won the same race with his transmission virtually destroyed.

Leading his home race after Prost's demise, Niki suddenly heard an enormous bang, followed by an ominous metallic jangling, from the rear of the car. Stirring the gear lever around amongst the broken bits, he was hoping to find enough drive just to get him back to the pits. Then he suddenly realised that he still had third ... and fifth. Encouraged, he limped on.

Nelson Piquet, running second in his Brabham-BMW, concluded that Niki had eased off strategically. Nelson did the same, cruising home for a secure 6 World Championship points. Only as they walked to the winner's rostrum did Niki tell him, almost casually, of his plight. An ashen faced Piquet realised the McLaren had been a sitting duck, and he had been duped into settling for second.

Prost had the upper hand at Zandvoort, thanks to a shrewd tyre choice, but luck intervened at Monza. During the race morning warm-up, both the McLaren race cars suffered loss of power, fluctuating turbo boost pressure and water leaks. Niki insisted on an engine change, wanting to run his race car. Prost was happy to take the spare, mindful that he had won with it in the past. Early in the race Alain suffered an engine failure. Niki, running a softly-softly race, emerged the winner.

At about this time Lauda almost shot himself through both feet thanks to some off-track wheeler dealing. Approached by Renault to lead the French team in 1985, he attempted to keep the negotiations under wraps. To his horror, soon after visiting their Paris headquarters, Ron Dennis phoned him to ask why he had been seen there. Niki was almost speechless, now boxed into a corner on terms for his 1985 contract.

It was a delicate moment. Dennis made it clear that he was not prepared to pay more than half the current rate for Niki's services in 1985, whether or not he was World Champion. Moreover, thanks to some inept bumbling on the part of Renault's senior management, the offer of a drive was withdrawn. Niki seemed isolated, but he was damned if he was going to drive for half-pay. He went behind Dennis's back direct to John Hogan and Marlboro agreed to make up part of the difference.

Inside McLaren itself, there was a preference for Prost to emerge World Champion. It was not a specific anti-Lauda lobby, merely the feeling that another title for Niki would be a case of, 'Oh yes, Lauda can win in anything...' Prost was the new boy, representing the team's future. Despite this, both drivers continued to receive the customary even-handed treatment when it came to machinery.

Prost bounced back to win the Grand Prix of Europe, held at the antiseptic, revamped Nurburgring, while Niki spun, lapping Mauro Baldi's Spirit and could do no better than fourth. After the race, Lauda sought out Baldi to administer a stiff rebuke, only to have the wind taken out of his sails when the Italian tail-ender told him, in no uncertain terms, that the incident was his fault and he could get stuffed. It was one of the few occasions on which Niki was seen publicly lost for words.

Niki now had 66 points, Prost 62½ points, and there was one race to go, the inaugural Portuguese Grand Prix at Estoril. To take the title, Prost would have to win (9 points) with Lauda no higher than third (4 points). If he was second (6 points), Niki would have to be fifth (2 points) or lower. The odds were fairly evenly stacked.

Yet the tension was getting to Prost. He qualified second to Piquet in Portugal with Niki a distant, troubled eleventh; but Alain was the nervous one. Piquet threw away his chances with a first lap spin, and while Keke Rosberg barrelled his bucking bronco of a Williams-Honda into an initial lead, Prost was ahead from Lap 9, driving away to a commanding seventh win of the season.

Lauda, suffering from lack of response when he tried to increase the turbo boost pressure, seemed bogged down in the middle of the pack. But gradually the opposition fell away and, on Lap 33, he moved into third place with only Mansell's Lotus separating him from his third World Championship. On Lap 52 Mansell's gallant run came to an end and he crawled into the pits to retire. One of the pistons had popped out of a front brake caliper, allowing the fluid to leak away, and his final drive for Team Lotus had ended in disappointment.

There was nothing more that Prost could do. Lauda followed him steadily home to take second place, taking the title by the wafer-thin margin of half a point. McLaren had won twelve of the season's sixteen races, Brabham two, Ferrari and Williams one apiece.

Ironically, the most consistent McLaren challenger, the Lotus 95T-Renault, never won a single race. The team enjoyed absolutely first-rate service from Renault and increasingly made better use of the French V6 engines than the factory cars. Yet they were never quite up to the McLaren-TAG mark. Grand Prix racing was more and more about harnessing several crucial variables to best effect – engine, tyres, chassis, fuel consumption, drivers – and in that respect, McLaren was head and shoulders above all the opposition.

In terms of temperament, Mansell and de Angelis were as different as chalk and cheese. The Englishman had yet to refine his over-ambitious driving style, so although he was on the front row at Monaco and Dallas, when it came to the races, often-as-not he fumbled the vital opportunity. In the Texas heat he over-

Keke Rosberg at Hockenheim during the 1984 German Grand Prix where his Williams FW09B retired when its Honda V6 turbo engine suffered one of many piston-related failures.

TAG/Porsche: Taking Technology up a Gear

John Barnard's no-compromise approach to Formula 1 engineering led him to stamp his distinctive identity on the newly formed McLaren International team from the middle of 1980. Just as he discarded all the design concepts of the superseded regime, so he refused to accept second-best when it came to a state-of-the-art turbocharged engine to propel his new generation of McLaren chassis into Formula 1's exciting new era.

Engine manufacturers, in Barnard's opinion, often thought no further than testing their products on a dynomometer. 'Sometimes they tend to forget the fact that a designer has to install it in a chassis,' he observed. When McLaren stood poised on the edge of the turbo era, it would have been all too easy for them to conclude a deal with an existing manufacturer. That was the course of action preferred by established McLaren directors Teddy Mayer and Tyler Alexander, but Barnard had well-reasoned arguments against either option. What he wanted was a brand new engine, and Dennis shared his enthusiasm wholeheartedly.

When Dennis and Barnard sat down for their first meeting with Hans Mezger, chief of Porsche's engine design unit, McLaren's new chief designer had a sheaf of notes detailing the basic requirements for his ideal, bespoke Grand Prix engine. He provided the German company with maximum dimensions, maximum cylinder vee angle (90 degrees) and crankshaft height. He canvassed Porsche's opinion on the number of cylinders which might be best, pondering a V8, but both parties concluded that the V6 option was the way to go.

Barnard vetted every detail of Porsche's workmanship, thumping the table if they attempted to deviate in any way from his specific requirements. It was an unusual experience for the German car maker whose standards were extremely high, but rewarding to find itself working with a like-minded Formula 1 team.

taxed his tyres trying to stay ahead, at Monaco he surged past Prost in the teeming rain, running much faster than was really necessary, almost inevitably skidding into a barrier whilst well ahead.

De Angelis, meanwhile, produced less spectacular, more consistent results. A consistent points gatherer, at Hockenheim he even seemed to have the measure of the McLarens during the early stages of the German Grand Prix only for his engine to break. But it was a tribute to his approach that he retained an outside mathematical chance of winning the Championship as late as the Austrian Grand Prix. By contrast to Renault's carbon-Kevlar RE50 monocoque, which proved alarmingly vulnerable to serious impacts, the carbon-composite tubs of the Lotus 95Ts – built in basically the same fashion as that pioneered on the type 88 three years earlier – proved extremely durable.

Rosberg's Dallas win aside, Williams and Honda spend the season each getting to know how the other worked, juggling chassis and tyre performance to try to match the violent power delivery of the Japanese V6 engine.

'It had been incredibly quick on the straight when I first drove it at Kyalami in 1983,' Rosberg recalls with relish, 'but the following year, once the intercooler problems had been sorted out, its throttle response was quite frightening. It had absolutely no response low down the rev range. In 1984, we started to make progress, but don't forget that our chassis was not stiff enough and we had problems with engine blocks flexing and bearings failing as a result.

'But I think everybody forgets the crucial role played by Patrick Head in educating Honda to the fundamental philosophy of contemporary Formula 1 design. He was the one who showed them that a powerful engine alone was not enough, that it needed to be integrated into an overall package. It was something that I felt wasn't easy for the Japanese to understand, working as they were in a totally new, strange environment.'

Williams, of course, was to be the last of the front-line teams to climb aboard the carbon-fibre composite bandwagon, practical and down-to-earth Patrick Head not willing to make the transition until he had all the specialist manufacturing facilities under his own factory roof. Besides, he knew full well that a good aluminium/honeycomb monocoque could still have qualities of impact resistance and torsional strength every bit the equal of carbon-fibre.

Ever since Alan Jones's FW06 broke a hub shaft at Watkins Glen in 1978, Head always held constructional integrity to be an equal priority in his own personal philosophy alongside competitive performance. This viewpoint had been strengthened after Reutemann slammed an FW07 almost head-on into one of the vertical sleeper retaining walls at Silverstone during a test session in 1980, the Argentine driver walking away almost unhurt from a very high-speed impact.

'Alright, I'll admit we were a bit slow off the mark developing our own composites side at Williams,' he conceded, 'but I've always tried to adopt a practical approach to building our racing cars. I wouldn't take the view that this method may be a little bit nicer, so we'll do it even though it costs ten times as much.' Some 'telephone number' quotes from outside sub-contractors had made Head even more wary of carbon fibre, although he admitted that the biggest limitation involved in building an aluminium structure was the extra weight and greater complexity involved in the manufacturing progress.

For 1985, however, things would be different at Williams Grand Prix Engineering once Honda successfully surmounted the spate of major engine problems, usually involving piston failure, which ruined the second half of the 1984 season.

Ferrari, of course, ended the year as possibly the most disappointed team of all. That early season Zolder triumph must have seemed like a trick of the light in retrospect, but the fact was that their Goodyear tyres were inferior to Michelin's radials

Brabham designer Gordon Murray at his drawing board on the team's Chessington factory during the summer of 1984. Having pencilled the Championship winning Brabham BT52 the previous season, Murray now found its successor, the BT54, let down by a series of unrelated engine and transmission problems.

and competing with an unreliable 680bhp was just insufficient to deal with the consistent 780bhp allegedly produced by the TAG/Porsche turbo on race boost.

Yet, for all McLaren's domination, there were some surprises. If one had to quantify success in terms of brake horsepower-per-pound sterling, then the remarkable achievements of Ayrton Senna in the Toleman-Hart TG184 would unquestionably stand at the top of the pile.

Brian Hart's little Harlow factory did a superb job with its 4 cylinder single turbo 415T, which, having switched from Garrett to turbochargers supplied by the small English Holset company, was capable of developing 600bhp at 10,750rpm using 2.1 bar boost pressure. With the dynamic Senna at the wheel, the engine which oh-so-nearly won at Monaco, was keeping the McLarens in sight before a rear wing breakage at Hockenheim triggered a major accident, and finished a stupendous third at Estoril behind Prost and Lauda. This result was to represent the absolute pinnacle of achievement for the Toleman-Hart alliance.

Even after a single season, the young Brazilian had already outgrown the fledgeling's nest provided for him by Toleman. Yet the manner in which he accepted an offer from Team Lotus for 1985, failing to secure a release from Toleman before he did so, caused all manner of tension. Toleman brought him down to earth with a jolt by suspending him from the Italian Grand Prix, but it was only a minor hiccup in the rise to stardom of this startling talent. Senna was on the way to the World Championship, even at this early stage in his career.

Two beacons of hope for the future survived to shine in the darkness amongst the debris of the opposition's efforts to get on terms with the mighty McLarens. One was Senna's glittering flair, another the potential of the Williams-Hondas.

Nigel Mansell's long-term possibilities remained largely concealed. But no less real for that.

THE TURBO YEARS' RESULTS 1984

Winner's average speed

March 25, BRAZILIAN GRAND PRIX, Rio
1   Alain Prost   McLaren-TAG MP4/2 turbo   (115.43mph)
2   Keke Rosberg   Williams-Honda FW09 turbo
3   Elio de Angelis   Lotus-Renault 95T turbo
4   Eddie Cheever   Alfa Romeo 184T turbo
5   Martin Brundle   Tyrrell-Cosworth 012
6   Patrick Tambay   Renault RE50 turbo

April 7, SOUTH AFRICAN GRAND PRIX, Kyalami
1   Niki Lauda   McLaren-TAG MP4/2 turbo   (126.367mph)
2   Alain Prost   McLaren-TAG MP4/2 turbo
3   Derek Warwick   Renault RE50 turbo
4   Riccardo Patrese   Alfa Romeo 184T turbo
5   Andrea de Cesaris   Ligier-Renault JS23 turbo
6   Ayrton Senna   Toleman-Hart TG183B turbo

April 29, BELGIAN GRAND PRIX, Zolder
1   Michele Alboreto   Ferrari 126C4 turbo   (115.221mph)
2   Derek Warwick   Renault RE50 turbo
3   René Arnoux   Ferrari 126C4 turbo
4   Keke Rosberg   Williams-Honda FW09 turbo
5   Elio de Angelis   Lotus-Renault 95T turbo
6   Stefan Bellof   Tyrrell-Cosworth 012

May 6, SAN MARINO GRAND PRIX, Imola
1   Alain Prost   McLaren-TAG MP4/2 turbo   (116.354mph)
2   René Arnoux   Ferrari 126C4 turbo
3   Elio de Angelis   Lotus-Renault 95T turbo
4   Derek Warwick   Renault RE50 turbo
5   Stefan Bellof   Tyrrell-Cosworth 012
6   Thierry Boutsen   Arrows-Cosworth A6

May 20, FRENCH GRAND PRIX, Dijon-Prenois
1   Niki Lauda   McLaren-TAG MP4/2 turbo   (125.531mph)
2   Patrick Tambay   Renault RE50 turbo
3   Nigel Mansell   Lotus-Renault 95T turbo
4   René Arnoux   Ferrari 126C4 turbo
5   Elio de Angelis   Lotus-Renault 95T turbo
6   Keke Rosberg   Williams-Honda FW09 turbo

June 3, MONACO GRAND PRIX, Monte Carlo
1   Alain Prost   McLaren-TAG MP4/2 turbo   (62.619mph)
2   Ayrton Senna   Toleman-Hart TG184 turbo
3   Stefan Bellof   Tyrrell-Cosworth 012
4   René Arnoux   Ferrari 126C4
5   Keke Rosberg   Williams-Honda FW09 turbo
6   Elio de Angelis   Lotus-Renault 95T

June 17, CANADIAN GRAND PRIX, Montreal
1	Nelson Piquet	Brabham-BMW BT53 turbo	(108.171mph)
2	Niki Lauda	McLaren-TAG MP4/2 turbo	
3	Alain Prost	McLaren-TAG MP4/2 turbo	
4	Elio de Angelis	Lotus-Renault 95T turbo	
5	René Arnoux	Ferrari 126C4 turbo	
6	Nigel Mansell	Lotus-Renault 95T turbo	

June 24, DETROIT GRAND PRIX, Michigan
1	Nelson Piquet	Brabham-BMW BT53 turbo	(81.679mph)
2	Martin Brundle	Tyrrell-Cosworth 012	
3	Elio de Angelis	Lotus-Renault 95T turbo	
4	Teo Fabi	Brabham-BMW BT53 turbo	
5	Alain Prost	McLaren-TAG MP4/2 turbo	
6	Jacques Laffite	Williams-Honda FW09 turbo	

July 8, DALLAS GRAND PRIX, Fair Park
1	Keke Rosberg	Williams-Honda FW09 turbo	(80.28mph)
2	René Arnoux	Ferrari 126C4 turbo	
3	Elio de Angelis	Lotus-Renault 95T turbo	
4	Jacques Laffite	Williams-Honda FW09 turbo	
5	Piercarlo Ghinzani	Osella-Alfa Romeo FA1F turbo	
6	Nigel Mansell	Lotus-Renault 95T turbo	

July 22, BRITISH GRAND PRIX, Brands Hatch
1	Niki Lauda	McLaren-TAG MP4/2 turbo	(124.40mph)
2	Derek Warwick	Renault RE50 turbo	
3	Ayrton Senna	Toleman-Hart TG184 turbo	
4	Elio de Angelis	Lotus-Renault 95T turbo	
5	Michele Alboreto	Ferrari 126C4 turbo	
6	René Arnoux	Ferrari 126C4 turbo	

August 5, GERMAN GRAND PRIX, Hockenheim
1	Alain Prost	McLaren-TAG MP4/2 turbo	(131.60mph)
2	Niki Lauda	McLaren-TAG MP4/2 turbo	
3	Derek Warwick	Renault RE50 turbo	
4	Nigel Mansell	Lotus-Renault 95T turbo	
5	Patrick Tambay	Renault RE50 turbo	
6	René Arnoux	Ferrari 126C4 turbo	

August 19, AUSTRIAN GRAND PRIX, Osterreichring
1	Niki Lauda	McLaren-TAG MP4/2 turbo	(139.11mph)
2	Nelson Piquet	Brabham-BMW BT53 turbo	
3	Michele Alboreto	Ferrari 126C4 turbo	
4	Teo Fabi	Brabham-BMW BT53	
5	Thierry Boutsen	Arrows-BMW A7 turbo	
6	Marc Surer	Arrows-BMW A7 turbo	

August 26, DUTCH GRAND PRIX, Zandvoort
1	Alain Prost	McLaren-TAG MP4/2 turbo	(115.60mph)
2	Niki Lauda	McLaren-TAG MP4/2 turbo	
3	Nigel Mansell	Lotus-Renault 95T turbo	
4	Elio de Angelis	Lotus-Renault 95T turbo	
5	Teo Fabi	Brabham-BMW BT53 turbo	
6	Patrick Tambay	Renault RE50 turbo	

September 9, ITALIAN GRAND PRIX, Monza

1	Niki Lauda	McLaren-TAG MP4/2 turbo	(137.02mph)
2	Michele Alboreto	Ferrari 126C4 turbo	
3	Riccardo Patrese	Alfa Romeo 184T turbo	
4	Stefan Johansson	Toleman-Hart TG184 turbo	
5	Jo Gartner	Osella-Alfa Romeo FA1F	
6	Gerhard Berger	ATS-BMW D7 turbo	

October 7, EUROPEAN GRAND PRIX, New Nurburgring

1	Alain Prost	McLaren-TAG MP4/2 turbo	(119.148mph)
2	Michele Alboreto	Ferrari 126C4 turbo	
3	Nelson Piquet	Brabham-BMW BT53 turbo	
4	Niki Lauda	McLaren-TAG MP4/2 turbo	
5	René Arnoux	Ferrari 126C4 turbo	
6	Riccardo Patrese	Alfa Romeo 184T turbo	

October 21, PORTUGUESE GRAND PRIX, Estoril

1	Alain Prost	McLaren-TAG MP4/2 turbo	(112.18mph)
2	Niki Lauda	McLaren-TAG MP4/2 turbo	
3	Ayrton Senna	Toleman-Hart TG184 turbo	
4	Michele Alboreto	Ferrari 126C4 turbo	
5	Elio de Angelis	Lotus-Renalt 95T turbo	
6	Nelson Piquet	Brabham-BMW BT53 turbo	

DRIVERS' WORLD CHAMPIONSHIP

Posn	Driver	Points
1	Niki Lauda	72
2	Alain Prost	71½
3	Elio de Angelis	34
4	Michele Alboreto	30½
5	Nelson Piquet	29
6	René Arnoux	27
7	Derek Warwick	23
8	Keke Rosberg	20½
9	Nigel Mansell	13
	Ayrton Senna	
11	Patrick Tambay	11
12	Teo Fabi	9
13	Riccardo Patrese	8
14	Thierry Boutsen	5
	Jacques Laffite	
16	Andrea de Cesaris	3
	Eddie Cheever	
	Stefan Johansson	
19	Piercarlo Ghinzani	2
20	Marc Surer	1

CONSTRUCTORS' CHAMPIONSHIP

Posn	Constructor	Points
1	McLaren	143½
2	Ferrari	57½
3	Lotus	47
4	Brabham	38
5	Renault	35
6	Williams	25½
7	Toleman	16
8	Alfa Romeo	11
9	Arrows	6
10	Osella	4
11	Ligier	3
12	ATS	1

1985

The pace of the second generation turbo battle intensified dramatically in 1985. The ideal qualities required from a car in qualifying and race trim continued to diverge to the point where the whole fabric of Formula 1 turbo technology began to come under the microscope. On the one hand, the lure of the turbo age had been responsible for attracting a whole new generation of engine manufacturers into the Grand Prix game. Yet their very presence had been responsible for spawning the costly, high-boost qualifying engines which had no relevance at all to the race specification engines which were still required to run a Grand Prix distance on 220 litres of fuel.

In truth, the very fact that these factors were now being kicked about in public was a portent for the future. Even though the last naturally-aspirated Cosworth DFY did not bow off the Grand Prix stage for the last time until the 1985 German Grand Prix, nagging doubts about the long-term validity of the turbos were now being expressed.

Admittedly, there was a long way to go, and a great deal of technology to be developed, before the turbos would be restricted. But FISA, FOCA and the motor manufacturers between them now found they had created a monster, albeit a magnificent one in the eyes of those who loved motor racing. The cars were becoming faster and more spectacular by the month, demanding a blend of commitment and intelligence from the drivers, which certainly had not been the case in the heyday of the Cosworth V8.

The turbos certainly provided plenty of varied, close and unpredictable racing, yet forces within the sport were already plotting their downfall. Ideas for the future included a 1200cc turbo limit, a revival of the fuel-flow formula which was one of Keith Duckworth's pet subjects, and the spectre of some limit on turbo boost control. Within a year, the last-mentioned option would be settled upon for introduction at the start of the 1987 season.

Ironically, turbo engine development was rushing forward at a pace which produced an increase in lap speeds far more dramatic than that of skirted ground-effect cars. The particular concern over the hazards of qualifying, where drivers were consistently taking mammoth risks lest they should waste their precious two marked sets of qualifying tyres, was such that a host of alternative methods of sorting out the grid order popped up in discussion during the year. They ranged from lining the grid up on the basis of the previous race's results, holding a qualifying race for at least part of the field, or even one-at-a-time Indy-style qualifying runs.

A legacy of some clever negotiating the previous summer had seen Ron Dennis conclude a contract to switch the pace-making McLarens to Goodyear rubber for 1985. Over at Brabham, Bernie Ecclestone pulled off a similarly shrewd deal with Pirelli, touted at the time as being worth $4 million to the BMW-powered team. Only when the signature was dry on those two contracts did the news break that Michelin was withdrawing from the Formula 1 fray.

Dennis had not been formally advised that this news was in the pipeline, but he harboured his suspicions. Had word of Michelin's retirement leaked out ahead of McLaren's deal with Goodyear, the negotiating initiative would have passed to the US company. But Ron could put his hand on his heart and say he did not know . . .

As far as technical regulations were concerned, FISA now outlawed aerodynamic winglets which had sprouted to the maximum width of most cars, aft of the rear axle line, over the

This overhead shot of Nigel Mansell's Lotus 94T-Renault drawing level with Keke Rosberg's Williams FW09B-Honda during the 1984 Portuguese Grand Prix shows clearly the additional aerodynamic 'ears' on either side of the main wing, ahead of the rear axle line. These were prohibited in 1985, forcing chassis designers to devise alternative methods of clawing back the lost downforce.

previous eighteen months. This development had enabled designers to claw back some of the downforce on their flat-bottomed cars, but FISA had now taken it away, throwing the onus back on to the efficiency of conventional aerofoils and, crucially, the upswept aerodynamic diffuser panels beneath the gearbox which were now in almost universal use.

By accelerating the air under the flat bottom and ducting it out from beneath the car via these panels, a worthwhile degree of additional downforce was achieved. Moreover, ducting exhaust outlets through these diffusers, as pioneered on the Renault as early as 1983, further enhanced the effect, although this could only be done with efficiency on vee-configuration engines with two separate exhaust systems. The BMW and Hart 'fours', with their single turbo and exhaust, were ill-equipped to make the most of this advantage.

While McLaren and Ferrari retained their driver pairings in 1985, Lotus and Williams made changes. Mansell's tenure with the team that had given him his Formula 1 break was at an end, but he picked up a plum seat alongside Keke Rosberg at Williams now that Jacques Laffite was pensioned off. In fact, Jacques returned to his old stamping-ground at Ligier which, equipped with Renault turbos since the start of the 1984 season, enabled him to give Frank's lads a gratifying run for their money on a couple of occasions. Senna joined de Angelis at Team Lotus.

Rosberg was quite close to de Angelis and worked himself into a real panic when he heard that Frank Williams was signing

Ambitious small-timer. German Ford turbo specialist Eric Zakowski's tiny Zakspeed team produced its own chassis fitted with a single turbo 4 cylinder engine which campaigned from the start of 1985. It was claimed to develop 820bhp at 10,500rpm from the outset, using 3.5 bar boost pressure.

Mansell. At the time Keke lived in a suitably grand mansion at Cookham Dean, in Berkshire and the moment he heard of Frank's decision he leaped into his car and tore down to the Williams factory at Didcot for a major showdown. He told Frank that he wanted to be released from his contract to accept a Renault offer, upset that Mansell was joining the team. His information, from an admittedly biased de Angelis, was that Mansell meant trouble.

Williams told Keke that releasing him at this late stage in the 1984 season was out of the question because there was no prospect of recruiting a replacement driver of his calibre. So the Finn just had to grin and bear it, although inwardly he was fuming and vowed to leave Williams at the end of 1985 come what may. In retrospect, this looked like a somewhat precipitate decision for the man approaching recognition as the fastest Grand Prix driver in the business.

At Lotus, Peter Warr had been so keen to get Senna that he offered Ayrton a two-year contract as number one driver. Shrewdly, Senna realised he still had plenty to learn and asked to be joint number one with Elio for 1985, but on the understanding that he would be unchallenged number one for 1986. Warr was impressed, but the second element in that agreement would cause aggravation towards the end of the season.

Michelin's withdrawl, meanwhile, had left the Toleman team boxed into an unpleasant political corner. At the 1984 San Marino Grand Prix, Toleman managing director Alex Hawkridge had fallen out with Pirelli in quite a big way with the result that the team switched to Michelin in time for the debut of the new TG184 design. Suddenly, they had no Senna, no tyres and not much in the way of sponsorship.

The promising new Rory Byrne-designed Toleman TG185 struggled through the pre-season Rio test on a couple of rag-end sets of Pirelli tyres discarded by Brabham, but the Italian tyre company showed an understandable lack of interest in welcoming Hawkridge back into the fold. Overtures to Goodyear also proved useless, so contracted team leader Stefan Johansson found himself every bit as isolated as the team.

The excellence of the McLaren-TAG concept was emphasised when Barnard simply uprated the MP4/2 to 'B' specification for the start of the season. This involved revisions to conform with new chassis footbox regulations, slightly revised bodywork and push-rod activation of the rear spring/dampers, to replace the heavy, outmoded rocker-arm system which had survived through 1984. The switch to Goodyear rubber caused the drivers to report the emergence of a slight handling imbalance, rooted in uneven balance between front and rear grip, but otherwise the MP4/2B was a winner straight out of the box.

Gérard Ducarouge in his office at Team Lotus's headquarters. The former Matra/Ligier/Alfa Romeo engineer's role as the English team's technical director involved more conceptual work than hands-on designing.

However, the car which everybody was watching with most interest was the moulded carbon-fibre Williams FW10, whose design had been finalised late the previous autumn. Unlike the McLaren MP4s and the Lotus 97T, third in the line of Ducarouge-inspired Lotus-Renaults, the new Williams did not have separate removable bodywork. In the style of the latest genre of carbon-fibre chassis cars, the monocoque surface was licked by the air stream in the style pioneered by the ATS D6, and continued by Ferrari and Renault. This was more of a serious, no-compromise racing car to replace the 'experimental' and unloved FW09.

Things were looking brighter at Ferrari; the new car carried the out-of-sequence designation 156/85 — as if, by such symbolism, the Scuderia's intense disappointment at the outcome of 1984 might somehow be removed. It certainly looked promising from the start, Alboreto bagged pole from Rosberg's new Williams at Rio, de Angelis and Senna making it an all-Lotus second row with Mansell alongside Prost on row three.

Fifteen seconds into the first race of the season, Nigel Mansell had already blotted his copybook with a manoeuvre which made you wonder if he would ever learn to harness his impetuosity. As Rosberg streaked for the first corner just ahead of the Ferrari, Nigel came charging down the outside in an attempt to follow Keke through the first right hander. As he turned in, he clipped Alboreto's left front wheel and immediately spun off the circuit. Resuming at the tail of the field, he eventually retired with a broken exhaust caused by the damage that earlier episode had wrought on his car's diffuser panel.

Keke led dramatically for nine laps, sliding the new Williams from lock to lock in a dramatic style which was as much a reflection of the Honda engine's continuing abrupt power delivery as his own personal driving style. Then a turbo gave out, leaving Alboreto, his steering slightly awry after swiping Mansell, at the mercies of the remarkable Mr Prost. With Lauda retiring due to a malfunction of the fuel metering system, Prost ran out an unchallenged winner from Alboreto, de Angelis and Arnoux.

René's performance had been quite outstanding. After tangling with Andrea de Cesaris in the Ligier, he had to limp slowly round almost an entire lap before coming into the pit lane to replace a punctured tyre. He then hurtled back from near the tail of the pack, admittedly aided by the retirement of others, to grab three Championship points. Yet it would turn out to be René's last outing at the wheel of a Ferrari.

Enzo Ferrari and the team's management had become increasingly concerned with his erratic race form through much of 1984, problems which they felt mirrored a host of personal problems weighing on the French driver's mind. After Rio,

Arnoux was called for a serious meeting at Maranello, the upshot of which was his departure from the team after only a single race of the 1985 season.

On the basis that one person's disaster can be another's salvation, Arnoux's trauma played right into the hands of the popular Stefan Johansson. Approached by Ferrari, he was generously released by Alex Hawkridge who, seeing no immediate end to the Toleman team's problems, felt he could not stand between Stefan and such a golden opportunity. The Swede joined up in time for the second round of the Championship, the Portuguese Grand Prix at Estoril.

Less than six months after finishing a splendid third in the last race of 1984 at that same circuit, Ayrton Senna finally came of age with a flawless victory in absolutely appalling conditions of torrential rain. Outqualifying Prost for pole position, the Brazilian's Lotus 97T eased into the lead at the start and never looked like being challenged. Elio de Angelis's frustration was almost tangible as he chased Senna as hard as he could in the other 97T, but there was simply no way he could compete. The

Champion car. Alain Prost at the wheel of the McLaren-TAG MP4/2B which carried him to his first World Championship title in 1985.

Lauda on his Formula I Career

Niki Lauda's Formula I career stretched from 1972 to 1979 and from 1982 to 1985. He drove for five teams during that period: March (1972), BRM (1973), Ferrari (1975-77), Brabham (1978-79) and McLaren (1982-85). He won a total of twenty-four Grands Prix and three World Championships (1975, 1977 and 1984).

'When March turned me out on the street after an awful year in 1972, I had absolutely no prospects', he recalls. 'I still had to pay back the money that I'd borrowed to get into Formula I in the first place. Then I managed to do a deal to drive for BRM, but only by digging myself ever deeper in debt by persuading them to accept a complicated arrangement whereby I effectively paid for my drive from the start money I earned.'

These imaginative financial arrangements ended with his signing a contract with the fading English team for 1974 and 1975, but when a Ferrari contract beckoned he signed it and sorted out the legal problems later. On joining Ferrari, he remarked, 'When you see all their facilities at Maranello, you can't help wondering why they don't win all the races.' Three years later, he admitted to 'falling out of love with the team. Suddenly I no longer had the motivation to give the 110 per cent effort needed to be really successful . . .'

Seeking rejuvenation, he switched to Brabham, buoyant with optimism for the prospects offered by Gordon Murray's new car. But consistent mechanical problems again sapped his morale. Rather than trailing round with less than total commitment, he abruptly retired just before the end of 1979.

For two years he hardly took any notice of motor racing. 'I could watch a Grand Prix without feeling a tremble of excitement, but gradually I found myself thinking "I wonder . . ."' At the start of 1982, he was back in the cockpit, en route for his third Championship two years hence.

As Lauda often observed, 'If you're going to make any sense out of this life, you've always got to be looking ahead.' And this pragmatic Austrian driver certainly practised what he preached.

penny must have dropped in Elio's mind that, his status usurped by this newcomer, he no longer had a future with the team that had been his home since the start of 1980.

In conditions which saw Prost spin into retirement when he hit a puddle on the main straight, Alboreto splashed home second from Tambay's Renault RE60, the disappointed de Angelis, a mildly encouraged Mansell and Bellof on the naturally-aspirated Tyrrell. If anybody had harboured any doubts, it was now clear beyond question that Senna's was a quite special talent. Lotus team manager Peter Warr likened his genius to that of the late Jim Clark . . .

Interestingly, Renault engineer Bernard Dudot used the Lotus, not the works cars, as the yardstick by which to judge the performance of his V6 engines, and the British team was afforded ever-increasing access to the French company's research and development department. The different demands of qualifying and racing, touched on earlier, were reflected by the fact that Renault produced two versions of its engine. Lotus availed itself of both the EF4, which would accept prodigious quantities of boost pressure, and the EF15, which was a more fuel-efficient, lower-boost unit intended specifically for racing. Renault also switched from KKK to Garrett turbochargers in 1985 with a perceptible improvement in that component's reliability.

Throughout 1985, Grand Prix racing was more akin to a technical juggling act than ever before, not only as far as fuel consumption was concerned, but also the weight at which the car finished the race. This was dramatically underlined in the third round of the Championship, the San Marino Grand Prix, where the two pace-setters both fell by the wayside for totally different reasons.

Senna proved that Estoril had been no flash in the pan when he planted his Renault EF4-engined Lotus 97T on pole for the Imola race ahead of Rosberg, de Angelis and Alboreto. Just as in Portugal, de Angelis kicked off with as strong a challenge as he could muster, chasing Senna hard for the first ten laps until first Alboreto, then Prost squeezed past him. By Lap 24 Prost had a clear road to Senna's leading Lotus and the fireworks got underway.

Alain duly hauled himself up on to Ayrton's tail and set about attempting to dodge through into the lead. But there was no way the Lotus driver was leaving any doors open, although Prost later stated quite firmly that Senna's Formula 3 tactics should have been left behind once he graduated into Formula 1. Interestingly, in the light of events four years later, Prost had taken a dislike to the Brazilian ever since an apparently innocuous episode at a Marlboro press conference just prior to the Brazilian Grand Prix that same year.

Prost and Lauda's place names were together in the centre of the table with Senna, a John Player driver, provisionally seated on the outer edge of the circle. Before the other drivers arrived, Senna juggled the labels in order to end up sitting next to Lauda, the reigning World Champion. Prost made a mental note that 'Senna is an *arriviste*.'

However, the outcome of the Imola battle was ruled by fuel economy considerations. Prost knew that to continue pursuing the Lotus would be suicide. His tanks would run dry long before the finish. Senna, running without the assistance of a cockpit computer read-out, also cut his revs when it seemed as though the race was in the bag. But with the team's available Renault EF15 engine allocated to de Angelis, Senna had been obliged to race one of the thirstier EF4 units. Both developed around 770bhp in race trim, but Senna's ran out of fuel with three laps to go.

Prost just tiptoed his way home to victory, but his afternoon's work was rendered worthless when the McLaren failed the post-race weight check, weighing in a kilogramme or so beneath the prescribed 540kg limit. Prior to the race, the team had been obliged to guess how much ballast would be needed on Alain's car, taking into account the fuel load, wear on brake pads and tyres, but they had come out frustratingly on the wrong side of the divide. Prost was out and a delighted Elio de Angelis was elevated to a fortunate victory.

Senna was at the centre of a controversy again during practice at Monaco. Having qualified successfully on pole position, his team sent him out again to get in the way of other potential quick runners. His behaviour prompted the one occasion in twelve years of Formula 1 racing that Niki Lauda really lost his temper. Senna had forced him to hit the brakes coming out of a corner when the McLaren was abreast his Lotus. Clearly, he and Lauda were never destined to be bosom buddies...

Prost won again at Monaco, but Senna again set the pace in the early stages before his Renault engine – which had previously jumped out of gear during the race morning warm-up – predictably expired. But then Alain found that Michele Alboreto was going to be a tough nut to crack in the new Ferrari. The Italian driver was on brilliant form and, once through into the lead, had an almost certain victory snatched away by a punctured tyre. He finished second, but he had done well enough to win...

Ferrari had expended a lot of effort developing an in-line 4 cylinder engine, feeling that perhaps BMW's lessons were worth learning, in addition to the feeling that this might be the best technical solution for the 1.2 litre turbo regulations which were still being tossed around as a possible alternative means of reducing power outputs. As it was, the 4 cylinder suffered more

Ayrton Senna splashing to Team Lotus's first victory in three years at Estoril, 1985. He proved that the Lotus 97T-Renault was almost good enough to challenge for the World Championship.

than its fair share of problems on the test bed and the team invested all its effort in the V6-propelled 156/85.

Johansson's arrival on the scene had inspired the team with even more confidence after Arnoux's somewhat confused approach, but it was Michele who really began to show signs of maturing into a really first-rate contender. In the early part of the season his confidence was running at a really high level, particularly after getting to grips with Prost at Monaco. That was a crucially important performance for both him and the team, proving that the Ferrari V6 matched fuel efficiency and race power output of such an order as to match the TAG V6, the benchmark by which all others judged their efforts.

You only had to look at the first six cars on the starting grid for the French Grand Prix at Paul Ricard to appreciate just how wide open the turbo battle had become by mid-1985. The order ran Williams-Honda (Rosberg), Lotus-Renault (Senna), Ferrari (Alboreto), McLaren-TAG (Prost), Brabham-BMW (Piquet) and McLaren-TAG (Lauda). The forced-induction juggling act was at its height; each driver/car combination offered subtly different qualities, one's weak area being the other's strong point. The Formula 1 technical conundrum was thrown into sharp relief and, at that stage in the year, it was conceivable that any one of four drivers might elbow his way through to the World Championship.

Brabham had been having a miserable time up to the French race, but Piquet's Pirelli rubber proved peculiarly suited to the high track temperatures which prevailed on race day. The way in which the performance of the Italian tyres swung dramatically from one extreme to another was extremely unsettling for the Brazilian. Having been reduced to a virtual walking pace at Estoril on rain tyres that absolutely refused to generate any sort of operating temperature, at Ricard, Nelson suddenly found himself endowed with a tremendous performance advantage. He used it to shake free from the pack and disappeared into the distance, scoring the sole Brabham-BMW victory of the season.

A solitary victory was a lot more than Renault could hope for and, with Derek Warwick heading for his home Grand Prix, the Englishman's maiden victory looked as far away as ever it had done. Since the fiasco surrounding his abortive attempt to recruit Lauda in 1984, Gerard Larrousse had found life increasingly difficult within the Renault Sport corridors of power, so he joined Ligier at the end of the season, taking chassis engineer Michel Tetu with him.

Team manager Jean Sage now found himself having to work under the direction of Gerard Toth, the brother-in-law of Renault president Bernard Hanon. Toth had a high opinion of himself which was certainly not shared by many of his colleagues – least of all Warwick and Tambay who struggled through a soul-destroying programme with the new, unwieldy Renault RE60. I was always tempted to wonder what might have happened if Lauda had been forced to deal with Toth. Truth be told, I do not suppose Niki would have given him the time of day. The Renault man would have been booted out of the front door in about three seconds flat . . .

Toth's apparent altruism in expanding Renault's supply of turbo engines to encompass the Tyrrell team during 1985 was also not what it appeared. After the Renault works team withdrew from Formula 1 at the end of the season, he would come a cropper, charged with diverting monies for the Tyrrell engines into his own personal account. From the moment he took over, Renault's Formula 1 team was a lost cause.

The RE60s were further handicapped by the fact that they had been built specifically for the EF15 version engine; unlike the Lotus 97T, there was no question of their using the high-boost EF4s for qualifying. This further compromised their performance and they never managed to struggle clear of the midfield bunch at the very best.

Come the British Grand Prix at Silverstone, Senna and Prost became embroiled in another two-horse race. It was too easy to dismiss Ayrton's pace-setting efforts as wasteful over-boosting with disastrous consequences for the fuel consumption. Lotus's pre-race calculations for his Renault EF15 engine were thrown

Toyota beat Honda!

As Honda's turbo V6 began to establish itself as a consistently competitive force throughout 1985, few people realised that this Japanese company was not the first to build a turbo Formula 1 engine. Back in 1981, Toyota, then minority shareholders in Group Lotus, commissioned the Lotus Engineering subsidiary initially to design a concept for a road car engine from which sprang a project designated 'L9' – an advanced turbocharged V6 cylinder Grand Prix engine!

This not only had twin turbochargers, but also incorporated an ancillary axial supercharger mounted, the purpose of this two-stage forced induction being to use massive air pressure to carry out all the requisite cooling within the combustion chamber. Moreover, it was a compound engine, with fuel/air vapour being ignited within the turbos themselves as well as within the conventional combustion chamber. The engine incorporated a number of novel features, including the injection nozzles being positioned in the side wall of the cylinders, to be uncovered as the piston retreated down the bore.

The brief was for the engine to develop 750bhp at a massively high 5 bar boost pressure, this during a period when most existing turbo engines were producing 2.5 bar. Six were made and duly delivered to Japan, since when they were never seen again. During the course of the development period, Lotus talked informally with Toyota about the possibility of the Formula 1 team using these engines, but by the time the project was signed off at the start of 1984, the Renault V6 was already developing a reliable 780bhp.

The moment for Toyota's Formula 1 onslaught had clearly passed.

into disarray when one sensor went haywire, adjusting the fuel/air mixture on one bank of cylinders to full-rich. His tanks ran dry and Prost, whose McLaren had profited from a minor front suspension modification immediately prior to the meeting, drove commandingly away to another victory.

While Prost continued to run consistently near the front of the field, reigning World Champion Niki Lauda was having a disappointing time. A succession of unrelated, irritating failures were keeping him out of contention. By mid-season he had privately made the decision to retire, this time for good. On his home ground at Osterreichring, he convened a press conference to make the official announcement.

It was typical Niki. 'Thanks everybody, I'm off-goodbye-now' sort of stuff. It was also an occasion which returned to haunt Ron Dennis over the years. The McLaren boss, by his own admission pretty ambivalent about motor racing's press corps, proceeded to enhance his reputation for never being able to pass a mouth without sticking his foot into it.

He had already put Lauda on edge by effectively gate-crashing what Niki thought was Niki's press conference, but what Ron believed should be a McLaren affair. After Niki had finished his say, the McLaren boss suddenly stepped forward and launched into an embarrassing tirade, pointing out that Lauda ought to be thanking John Barnard for all his success because he was the man who really deserved it. Niki stoically stared into the middle distance while the audience tried to look elsewhere.

The moment Dennis walked from this gathering, he knew full-well he had dropped a major clanger. Lauda sought him out and gave him a well-rehearsed piece of his mind. Insiders privately envied Dennis little; they knew just what a juggling act he was involved in, trying to keep relations between the volatile Barnard and his two superstar drivers on an even keel. Still, there was a time and a place . . .

Rosberg's blinding 160mph pole-winning lap at Silverstone, using every ounce of the 1,070bhp unleashed by his Honda in qualifying trim, served as another reminder that the Williams-Honda challenge was gaining momentum, although neither Keke nor Nigel Mansell was in at the finish. Nigel, in fact, was fortunate to be racing in front of his home crowd at all. During pratice at Paul Ricard, his Williams had suffered a tyre failure approaching 200mph on the Mistral straight, cannoning off the circuit and into the catch fencing. Mansell sustained a severe blow on the side of the head and, although a brain scan revealed no damage, he was forced to miss the race and only his legendary determination saw him back for Silverstone.

Honda had taken a fundamental forward stride in time for the

Glum for good reason. Patrick Tambay listens dolefully while 1985 Renault team director Gerard Toth lectures him about the Formula 1 future, of which there was previous little left for Renault.

Preparing for a great day. Nigel Mansell sits strapped in his Williams FW10-Honda during practice for the 1985 Grand Prix of Europe, his first Formula 1 success. In the background, Patrick Head tunes in his radio link with the driver.

Canadian Grand Prix at Montreal where a new 'E' specification engine offered improved structural rigidity and reliability combined with a more usable power curve. In a race where Alboreto and Johansson strengthened Ferrari's advantage at the head of the Constructors' Championship table with a 1-2 finish, Keke finished fourth behind Prost despite having to make two pit stops. Mansell was sixth, but the following week Keke scored the first of the Williams team's four 1985 wins at Detroit, a typical Rosberg balls-in-the-air performance . . .

Mansell crashed at relatively slow speed, jarring his thumb agonisingly. This, added to his Ricard shunt, would cause him a great deal of discomfort over the weeks ahead. But when he went to be checked over by neuro-surgeon, Professor Syd Watkins, FISA's chief medical officer, prior to the British Grand Prix, he was absolutely resolute that he would not as much as wince.

'I went in to see Syd, grabbed his hand and shook it as firmly as I could, ' Mansell recalls. 'My thumb was in absolute agony and the pain was unspeakable, but I'd had so much bad luck in my home race over the years, I was damned if I was going to miss racing at Silverstone!'

Behind the scenes, Patrick Head was still educating the Honda engineers in the art of producing the best possible package. This collaboration was enhanced when the Japanese company opened their engine shop adjacent to the new Williams factory at Didcot. In time for the Grand Prix of Europe at Brands Hatch, Honda came up with revised inlet tracts for the 'E' version of its current V6 which enabled Head to reduce dramatically the height of the engine cover, improving airflow over the rear wing. At the same time, a lighter pull-rod rear suspension was fitted to replace the heavy rocker arms. The Williams-Honda package was now set to fly.

Off-track, Williams had problems, or so Frank thought. Even though Rosberg quickly came to enjoy Mansell as a team-mate, he did not revise his decision to leave at the end of the year. Once Lauda's imminent retirement became more than a rumour, Frank did not need to be clairvoyant to realise that Keke would replace him at McLaren. He needed a front-line driver, and fast. Over at Brabham, Piquet was dissatisfied with Bernie Ecclestone's reluctance to increase his salary to what he regarded as an appropriate level. So, in the car park at Osterreichring, Frank did a deal with Nelson.

The Brazilian came expensive, but Frank reckoned it was a worthwhile investment. Now he could look forward into 1986 with a well-matched team. After all, Mansell was a good number two who might pick up the occasional win after Piquet faltered. Few people were prepared for what happened next.

The Belgian Grand Prix at Spa, originally scheduled for 2 June, had been postponed to mid-September after the recently resurfaced track broke up during practice and the early summer meeting had to be abandoned. It is interesting to speculate on the way the Championship battle might have developed had that race actually taken place, for Alboreto's Ferrari, at the zenith of its competitiveness, was comfortably quickest in qualifying up to the point at which the meeting was abandoned. By the time the September race came along, Ferrari was nowhere. Senna won splendidly in tricky wet/dry conditions with Mansell scoring his best result so far, second ahead of Prost.

It did not remain his best result for long. The Grand Prix of Europe saw Mansell qualify third behind Senna and Piquet, and ahead of Rosberg. Ayrton went into the lead at the start, but the Finn lost time in a tangle which eliminated Piquet and forced the Detroit winner into the pits to replace a punctured tyre. He resumed just ahead of Senna, holding up the Lotus to such good effect that Mansell was able to nip by into the lead. Senna fans deemed this poor sportsmanship, but Mansell supporters simply regarded it as good team-work.

Mansell now had a clear track ahead of him and successfully dodged every hazard to win a memorable first Grand Prix victory in front of his home crowd. Over the last few laps, the Williams pit crew threw away their lap board and chose not to give Nigel any more signals, not wanting to risk flustering him. In any case, the reaction from the grandstands signalled his progress towards the chequered flag better and more dramatically than any signal from a pit board.

In the emotion surrounding Nigel's great day, one could almost have been forgiven for overlooking the fact that Alain Prost, by finishing fourth, had become the first Frenchman to win the World Championship. It would take McLaren through to the end of the season to button up the Constructors' Championship beyond doubt, but that was little more than a formality. Under pressure from opposition on three sides – McLaren, Lotus and Williams – Ferrari's defence of that early points advantage had collapsed amidst the wreckage of broken engines, over-boosted in a vain attempt to keep up during the second half of the year.

Mansell's Brands Hatch success had been well deserved, although some initial grumbling from the Lotus camp to the effect that Nigel had overtaken Senna under a yellow flag briefly raised the worrying spectre of a protest. But it was Hazel Chapman, Colin's widow, who firmly vetoed such a move. 'We're not protesting, Nigel,' she told team manager Peter Warr unequivocally. Three years later she would remark somewhat wistfully, 'I sometimes don't understand this business of choosing drivers . . . I never really understood why we let Nigel go in the first place.'

So often, once a driver finally wins a race, subsequent success flows freely. So it was for Mansell. After years of struggling, he had finally hit on the combination that unlocked the door to success. At Kyalami, he qualified for the South African Grand Prix on pole position and led every lap but one to a second resounding success. He was learning a lot about strategy as well, waving Rosberg through into the lead when it appeared that Keke was using more boost pressure than was good for his fuel consumption prospects.

Unwittingly, by letting Keke through, he did himself a major favour. An oil slick dropped by Ghinzani's expiring Toleman created a skating rink at the tricky Crowthorne right-hander at the end of Kyalami's long start/finish straight. Rosberg, first on to the slick, pirouetted several times, allowing Mansell to duck back into the lead. Thereafter Nigel ran out a comfortable winner, demonstrating great expertise in fending off pressure from Prost's just-not-quick-enough McLaren-TAG which the fast-recovering Rosberg pushed back to second place at the finish.

The weather in this publicity shot of Peter Warr, Johnny Dumfries and the new moulded carbon-fibre Lotus 98T, with lower 195 litre fuel cell, was nowhere near as frosty as the relationship between Derek Warwick and Ayrton Senna at the end of 1985.

Mansell steers his Williams FW10-Honda up through Surtees during his run to victory in the Grand Prix of Europe at Brands Hatch. By now Honda's work on the V6 twin turbo unit had produced a more usable power curve and dramatically improved reliability.

Lauda's relationship with Ron Dennis had now deteriorated to the level of Warwick's disenchantment with Renault. Renault had announced that they would be quitting the Formula 1 stage at the end of the season, but after Lauda injured a wrist in a silly, low speed shunt during practice at Spa, the French team steadfastly refused to loan Derek to McLaren for the Grand Prix of Europe.

Instead, McLaren invited the rusty John Watson down from the shelf. The Ulsterman duly brushed himself down, dug out his old set of McLaren overalls, and turned up to finish a distant seventh. Then Renault found it would have to toe the French government anti-apartheid line, leaving Warwick and Tambay sidelined for Kyalami. With only one more race on the schedule before turning its discarded men on to the streets, it would not have been too much to ask permission for Derek to drive that McLaren at Brands Hatch.

Lauda, meanwhile, returned to the Kyalami pits to find that he had not been allocated the spare McLaren, even though it had been his turn for this privilege. Ron Dennis told him, with sledge-hammer subtlety, that he was not sure whether or not Niki was sufficiently recovered. Lauda warned him to be very careful, unless he wanted to make an enemy for life. In the event, Niki had the spare car. 'Just so that you haven't got any excuses,' said Dennis.

The striking low-line Brabham
BT55, with its angled BMW turbo
engine, should have been
dramatically quick. But as Riccardo
Patrese, seen here on opposite-lock
at Adelaide, came to learn, it was
short on development as well as
straight-line speed.

Knowing Ron, I half wonder whether those remarks were made in jest. But knowing Niki, whose grasp of English was arguably better than his employer's, I have the feeling that the McLaren boss was being unfortunately serious.

With retirement finally beckoning for good, Niki found himself wavering at the last moment as Brabham boss Bernie Ecclestone put a $6 million proposition to him for 1986. Pirelli and Olivetti, having committed a vast investment to the Brabham-BMW programme based round Piquet's proven testing skills, were highly unamused when the Brazilian slipped through Bernie's fingers. The prospect of picking up the ball again with Lauda on board was tantalising. Niki thought it over, but rejected the idea at the end of the day.

There was one glorious moment left for the man who had won three World Championships over ten seasons. In the first Australian Grand Prix to be held through the streets of Adelaide, Niki drove through the pack to take the lead. But there was no fairy-tale ending awaiting him. Caught out by a grabbing brake, he crashed lightly under the uncompromising gaze of the television cameras. No matter, he walked away.

Rosberg rounded off the season with his second win of the year. Any clairvoyant suggesting it would be the last of his career would have been shown the door. But so it proved. Prost, meanwhile, had finally done it after all those years of close shaves.

Patrick Tambay best summed up the outcome of the title battle. 'In my time,' he opined, 'I have seen three drivers with that little bit extra, something which marks them apart from their rivals. Villeneuve, Prost and Senna...'

By the end of the turbo era, few would look back and dispute that conclusion.

THE TURBO YEARS' RESULTS 1985

Winner's average speed

April 7, BRAZILIAN GRAND PRIX, Rio
1	Alain Prost	McLaren-TAG MP4/2B turbo	(112.795mph)
2	Michele Alboreto	Ferrari 156/85 turbo	
3	Elio de Angelis	Lotus-Renault 97T turbo	
4	René Arnoux	Ferrari 156/85 turbo	
5	Patrick Tambay	Renault RE60 turbo	
6	Jacques Laffite	Ligier-Renault JS25 turbo	

April 21, PORTUGUESE GRAND PRIX, Estoril
1	Ayrton Senna	Lotus-Renault 97T turbo	(90.198mph)
2	Michele Alboreto	Ferrari 156/85	
3	Patrick Tambay	Renault RE60 turbo	
4	Elio de Angelis	Lotus-Renault 97T turbo	
5	Nigel Mansell	Williams-Honda FW10 turbo	
6	Stefan Bellof	Tyrrell-Cosworth 012	

May 5, SAN MARINO GRAND PRIX, Imola
1	Elio de Angelis	Lotus-Renault 97T turbo	(109.17mph)
2	Thierry Boutsen	Arrows-BMW A8 turbo	
3	Patrick Tambay	Renault RE60 turbo	
4	Niki Lauda	McLaren-TAG MP4/2B turbo	
5	Nigel Mansell	Williams-Honda FW10 turbo	
6	Stefan Johansson	Ferrari 156/85 turbo	

May 19, MONACO GRAND PRIX, Monte Carlo
1	Alain Prost	McLaren-TAG MP4/2B	(89.65mph)
2	Michele Alboreto	Ferrari 156/85 turbo	
3	Elio de Angelis	Lotus-Renault 97T	
4	Andrea de Cesaris	Ligier-Renault JS25 turbo	
5	Derek Warwick	Renault RE60 turbo	
6	Jacques Laffite	Ligier-Renault JS25 turbo	

June 16, CANADIAN GRAND PRIX, Montreal
1	Michele Alboreto	Ferrari 156/85 turbo	(108.54mph)
2	Stefan Johansson	Ferrari 156/85 turbo	
3	Alain Prost	McLaren-TAG MP4/2B turbo	
4	Keke Rosberg	Williams-Honda FW10 turbo	
5	Elio de Angelis	Lotus-Renault 97T turbo	
6	Nigel Mansell	Williams-Honda FW10 turbo	

June 23, DETROIT GRAND PRIX, Michigan
1	Keke Rosberg	Williams-Honda FW10 turbo	(81.7mph)
2	Stefan Johansson	Ferrari 156/85 turbo	
3	Michele Alboreto	Ferrari 156/85 turbo	
4	Stefan Bellof	Tyrrell-Cosworth 012	
5	Elio de Angelis	Lotus-Renault 97T turbo	
6	Nelson Piquet	Brabham-BMW BT54 turbo	

July 7, FRENCH GRAND PRIX, Paul Ricard
1   Nelson Piquet   Brabham-BMW BT54 turbo   (125.09mph)
2   Keke Rosberg   Williams-Honda FW10 turbo
3   Alain Prost   McLaren-TAG MP4/2B turbo
4   Stefan Johansson   Ferrari 156/85 turbo
5   Elio de Angelis   Lotus-Renault 97T turbo
6   Patrick Tambay   Renault RE50 turbo

July 21, BRITISH GRAND PRIX, Silverstone
1   Alain Prost   McLaren-TAG MP4/2B turbo   (146.27mph)
2   Michele Alboreto   Ferrari 156/85 turbo
3   Jacques Laffite   Ligier-Renault JS25 turbo
4   Nelson Piquet   Brabham-BMW BT54 turbo
5   Derek Warwick   Renault RE60 turbo
6   Marc Surer   Brabham-BMW BT54 turbo

August 4, GERMAN GRAND PRIX, New Nurburgring
1   Michele Alboreto   Ferrari 156/85 turbo   (118.773mph)
2   Alain Prost   McLaren-TAG MP4/2B turbo
3   Jacques Laffite   Ligier-Renault JS25 turbo
4   Thierry Boutsen   Arrows-BMW A8 turbo
5   Niki Lauda   McLaren-TAG MP4/2B turbo
6   Nigel Mansell   Williams-Honda FW10 turbo

August 18, AUSTRIAN GRAND PRIX, Osterreichring
1   Alain Prost   McLaren-TAG MP4/2B turbo   (143.618mph)
2   Ayrton Senna   Lotus-Renault 97T turbo
3   Michele Alboreto   Ferrari 156/85 turbo
4   Stefan Johansson   Ferrari 156/85 turbo
5   Elio de Angelis   Lotus-Renault 97T turbo
6   Marc Surer   Brabham-BMW BT54 turbo

August 25, DUTCH GRAND PRIX, Zandvoort
1   Niki Lauda   McLaren-TAG MP4/2B turbo   (119.97mph)
2   Alain Prost   McLaren-TAG MP4/2B turbo
3   Ayrton Senna   Lotus-Renault 97T turbo
4   Michele Alboreto   Ferrari 156/85 turbo
5   Elio de Angelis   Lotus-Renault 97T turbo
6   Nigel Mansell   Williams-Honda FW10 turbo

September 8, ITALIAN GRAND PRIX, Monza
1   Alain Prost   McLaren-TAG MP4/2B turbo   (141.40mph)
2   Nelson Piquet   Brabham-BMW BT54 turbo
3   Ayrton Senna   Lotus-Renault 97T turbo
4   Marc Surer   Brabham-BMW BT54 turbo
5   Stefan Johansson   Ferrari 156/85 turbo
6   Elio de Angelis   Lotus-Renault 97T turbo

September 15, BELGIAN GRAND PRIX, Spa
1   Ayrton Senna   Lotus-Renault 97T turbo   (117.943mph)
2   Nigel Mansell   Williams-Honda FW10 turbo
3   Alain Prost   McLaren-TAG MP4/2B turbo
4   Keke Rosberg   Williams-Honda FW10 turbo
5   Nelson Piquet   Brabham-BMW BT54 turbo
6   Derek Warwick   Renault RE60B turbo

October 6, EUROPEAN GRAND PRIX, Brands Hatch

1	Nigel Mansell	Williams-Honda FW10 turbo	(126.52mph)
2	Ayrton Senna	Lotus-Renault 97T turbo	
3	Keke Rosberg	Williams-Honda FW10 turbo	
4	Alain Prost	McLaren-TAG MP4/2B turbo	
5	Elio de Angelis	Lotus-Renault 97T turbo	
6	Thierry Boutsen	Arrows-BMW A8 turbo	

October 19, SOUTH AFRICAN GRAND PRIX, Kyalami

1	Nigel Mansell	Williams-Honda FW10 turbo	(124.84mph)
2	Keke Rosberg	Williams-Honda FW10 turbo	
3	Alain Prost	McLaren-TAG MP5/2B turbo	
4	Stefan Johansson	Ferrari 156/85 turbo	
5	Gerhard Berger	Arrows-BMW A8 turbo	
6	Thierry Boutsen	Arrows-BMW A8 turbo	

November 3, AUSTRALIAN GRAND PRIX, Adelaide

1	Keke Rosberg	Williams-Honda FW10 turbo	(95.71mph)
2	Jacques Laffite	Ligier-Renault JS25 turbo	
3	Philippe Streiff	Ligier-Renault JS25 turbo	
4	Ivan Capelli	Tyrrell-Renault 014 turbo	
5	Stefan Johansson	Ferrari 156/85 turbo	
6	Gerhard Berger	Arrows-BMW A8 turbo	

DRIVERS' WORLD CHAMPIONSHIP

Posn	Driver	Points
1	Alain Prost	73
2	Michele Alboreto	53
3	Keke Rosberg	40
4	Ayrton Senna	38
5	Elio de Angelis	33
6	Nigel Mansell	31
7	Stefan Johannson	26
8	Nelson Piquet	21
9	Jacques Laffite	16
10	Niki Lauda	14
11	Patrick Tambay	11
	Thierry Boutsen	
13	Marc Surer	5
	Derek Warwick	
15	Philippe Streiff	4
	Stefan Bellof	
17	René Arnoux	3
	Andrea de Cesaris	
	Ivan Capelli	
	Gerhard Berger	

CONSTRUCTORS' CHAMPIONSHIP

Posn	Constructor	Points
1	McLaren	99
2	Ferrari	82
3	Williams	71
	Lotus	
5	Brabham	26
6	Ligier	23
7	Renault	16
8	Arrows	14
9	Tyrrell	7

1986

Before the wraps came off the new generation of 195 litre turbo challengers, the British Formula 1 scene was rocked by a highly publicised controversy. Ayrton Senna, having driven an exasperated Elio de Angelis from what he now considered his personal domain, laid down to Peter Warr his requirements for a team-mate in 1986.

In a nutshell, Senna rightly believed the Lotus-Renault partnership would be right on the outside edge of its technological capability shaping up to the opposition. He was not so worried about the McLaren-TAGs, more about the enormous amount of obvious investment and technology which Honda was applying to its partnership with Williams. Personally doubting whether Lotus had the ability to field two reliably competitive front-line cars, he vetoed the inclusion of Derek Warwick in the line-up as his number two.

This caused a highly emotional outcry from the British specialist press corps, the author being amongst those near the front of the pack. Warwick had briefly tested a Lotus 97T at Brands Hatch shortly before the end of the season and Gerard Ducarouge expressed satisfaction with the Englishman's technical feed-back. Derek was fighting for survival and Lotus seemed his only option. He agreed to play a subordinate role.

One of Senna's great strengths is his utter and complete candour — even if it sometimes tends to make one wince. Publicly, he aired his reservations about Lotus's ability to prepare two front-running machines. Peter Warr privately huffed and puffed in response, pointing to the fact that both Elio and Ayrton had run at the front during 1985. He was right. But Senna's emphasis was on 'reliably'. The 97T had not been sufficiently reliable to pose a Championship challenge.

These reservations aside, Senna had his doubts that Warwick would abide by the deal. Once he had got his foot in the door, thought the Brazilian, I will be battling with my team-mate. There was nothing personal, as he proved by sending the rather bemused Warwick a Christmas card, but he was not having Derek in the team. Lotus acceded to his requirements and former British Formula 3 Champion Johnny Dumfries got the nod.

Alain Prost was undoubtedly the driver of the decade, winning consecutive Championships in 1985 and 1986 and later adding a third in 1989.

Gérard Ducarouge took the chance to revise Team Lotus's chassis construction techniques for 1986, replacing the concept of panels folded round internal bulkheads with an integral unified moulding, although separate outer bodywork was retained. The small fuel cell enabled the section behind the driver to be lowered slightly and, to guard against the traumas experienced by Senna at Imola and Silverstone the previous year, the new type 98T had a consumption read-out on the cockpit dash.

With Renault Sport's Formula 1 team now history, Team Lotus got what amounted to full factory backing (although Lotus was still paying for the privilege) and their engine supply emanated from the French competitions department at Viry-Chatillon rather than the Bourges-based sub-contractors Mecachrome operating at Bourges. Bernard Dudot and his team produced their latest EF15B version of the Renault V6 in two very different forms; standard or Distribution Pneumatique.

The 'DP' version featured an ambitious and ingenious system of pneumatic valve-closing, replacing the conventional valve spring, and was Renault's answer to the need for more revs. Tested in as much secrecy as Lotus and Renault could muster, installed in a type 97T during the pre-Christmas Rio test at the end of 1985, the 'DP' engine worked a treat. It seems likely that this little secret would have been kept amongst Renault and its customer teams had it not been for the defection of Renault Sport engineer Jean-Jacques His to Ferrari. He had been one of the key personnel who worked on the project and, once away from Renault, was not too worried about spilling the beans...

In place of each valve spring was a flange on the valve stem, itself forming a tiny piston which ran in a nitrogen-filled chamber, each one being part of a larger network. Pressurised to an average of 1.5 bar, when compressed by the flange as the valve lifted, the expansion of the nitrogen snapped the valve closed again cleanly and efficiently. The saving in mass and weight enabled the engine's rev limit to be increased, initially from 11,000 to 12,500rpm, but later to over 13,000rpm which unlocked around 900bhp for the races.

In qualifying, Lotus would use EF15 spec V6s with water injection and their wastegates blanked off, surviving concentrated doses of 5 bar boost pressure to propel Senna to nine pole positions out of the sixteen races. Running amidst a shower of sparks with minimal ground clearance to generate as much downforce as possible, a haze of unburnt hydrocarbons hovering ominously in its wake, the all-black Lotus 98T and its yellow helmeted ace driver created a visually formidable combination, shimmering with suppressed menace and power.

Yet Ayrton would have his World Championship aspirations

sacrificed on the altar of poor fuel efficiency relative to the superb new Williams-Honda FW11s, the first product of the Didcot-based team's considerable financial investment in the latest General Electric 'Calma' computer-aided design/manufacture system. However, in registering that fact, one must remember that fuel consumption in these straitened 195 litre days was not merely the product of a powerful engine matched to a highly efficient electronic management system. Aerodynamic efficiency, or otherwise, played a crucial role and there is persuasive evidence that Lotus's subsequent plans for 1987 were at least partially founded on an incorrect assumption.

The FW11 represented a watershed in terms of Williams design and manufacturing technology, its superbly detailed carbon-fibre composite monocoque and associated bodywork enveloping the car's mechanical components like a skin-tight leather glove. The car was significantly lower than the FW10 thanks to the smaller cell needed to accommodate the 195 litres of toluene-based Mobil fuel, manufactured by the petroleum company whose close collaboration with the team was to prove enormously beneficial for both parties.

Enlisting the assistance of Mobil's chemists, Honda was by now hotly pursuing the same route as that pioneered by Wintershall for BMW a couple of years before, opting for high density aromatic 'hydrocarbon' fuels. Much of Honda's increase in power output, to over 900bhp in race trim, was achieved during 1986 by persuading the injection to atomise its fuel more completely, ensuring that none was wasted within the combustion chamber.

Niki Lauda (right) and Keke Rosberg both partnered Prost at McLaren at different times during the TAG turbo era. Both found him a tough nut to crack, although Niki beat him to the 1984 title by the scant margin of half a point.

The Arrival of Nigel Mansell

If Alain Prost was the outstanding driver of the 1980s, then Nigel Mansell was the one who produced the biggest surprise. His four seasons driving for Team Lotus had seen him establish a reputation as a bullishly determined youngster who frantically over-drove for much of the time and seemed continually prone to fundamental errors of judgement.

Off-track, he earned a reputation as a moaner, a driver who would always offer a complex excuse for what, on the surface, might appear as a straightforward, clottish mistake. Anybody who witnessed his rambling, over-intense explanation to BBC television's Murray Walker as to how he threw away victory in the rain-soaked 1984 Monaco Grand Prix will have cringed with embarrassment.

Yet, like the ugly duckling who turned into the beautiful swan, Mansell's metamorphosis into a winner was as sudden as it was unexpected. Offered more congenial surroundings in the Williams-Honda team for 1985, he put it all steadily together until, in the Grand Prix of Europe at Brands Hatch, he finally cracked the winning combination.

Once into the way of winning, this bluff Birmingham-born driver produced a succession of blistering victories throughout 1986 and 1987, perhaps becoming more famous for not winning the World Championship than if he had in fact managed to grasp that elusive tag. Granted he still made silly errors, but as Ayrton Senna would prove, he was not alone in that distinction. By the end of 1988, when he quit Williams to join Ferrari, he was regarded as one of the best in the world, possibly the fastest of all.

But Mansell never doubted he would make it to the top. As his close friend Peter Windsor, now running Ferrari's Formula 1 satellite in England explained: 'what you must understand about Nigel is that, after his first Formula 1 drive with Lotus in Austria, back in 1980, he came away absolutely knowing in his own mind that he was faster than the team's two regular drivers, Andretti and de Angelis. There was no shred of doubt in his mind.'

It was that sort of determination which carried Nigel Mansell all the way to the top.

As the team's aerodynamicist Frank Dernie explained to *Autosport* magazine at the start of the 1988 Formula 1 season, the CAD/CAM system was a Godsend in that it enabled the chassis designer to come up with the three-dimensional image on the computer screen, allowing experimentation with a whole host of varying concepts before manufacturing a single component.

'The conceptual stuff comes first,' he explained, 'so the first thing to do is to think it all out, check radiator ducts, wing positions or whatever, before you even produce the quarter scale drawings from which the wind tunnel models are produced.

'We also wanted to make the bodywork on FW11 as tight fitting as possible because the Honda V6 was really gargantuan from a dimensional point of view when compared with the Renault or the TAG engines, for example. It was quite a job to fit the whole package in, so it was a real luxury to be able to take the engine management box, for example, in 3-D and then take sections, check clearances and be able even to show that we would have to remove some of the honeycomb from the engine cover in order to make it fit. It can save a tremendous amount of time in the prototype shop.'

In addition to providing the facility to alter or improve the design at quite a late stage, the CAD/CAM system enabled Williams to obtain a detailed structural anlysis of all the complex component parts.

Enhancing the Williams-Honda package, not only did the Honda V6 sport an even more sophisticated engine management system, it also offered car-to-pit telemetry which would allow the engineers to check what the driver was doing almost as he was doing it. A radio link complemented this facility, so more than ever since the days of fuel stops back in 1983, the Formula 1 business became a true team effort even during the races for the Williams-Honda alliance throughout 1986.

Unhappily, Frank Williams would not be at the pit wall during his team's most successful season. A couple of weeks prior to the Brazilian Grand Prix, Frank was driving back to Nice airport from the final pre-season test at Paul Ricard when his Ford Sierra rental car left the road and crashed into a field. The team's public affairs manager, Peter Windsor, was in the car as a passenger and emerged thankfully unhurt, but Frank sustained very serious back injuries.

In the immediate aftermath of the accident it was feared that he might succumb to these injuries, but he fought back with astonishing resolution and single-mindedness. The qualities which enabled him to build up one of the best Grand Prix racing teams in post-war history now helped him to pull through this latest crisis, but he would, henceforward, be confined to a wheelchair with the limited mobility that this inevitably involves.

The team pulled together 'for Frank' and Nelson Piquet rewarded his new employer with a well-judged maiden victory at Rio, soundly beating Senna's Lotus 98T into second place. Mansell, who qualified third behind the two Brazilians, forced his way inside Senna at the end of the long back straight. The two cars touched and Mansell speared off into the barrier, taking off a wheel. It seemed an all-too-familiar story.

Piquet could be forgiven for thinking that his third World Championship success might be little more of a formality to judge by the way in which he outclassed the opposition at Rio. But although the McLaren-TAGs found the Constructors' Championship slipping from their grasp, there was no trace of the post-World Championship blues on the part of Alain Prost. The McLaren team lost the Championship due to a shortfall in the strength which had secured it for the past two years, namely two drivers on the payroll who regularly won races.

If this sounds slightly demeaning for Keke Rosberg, it certainly is not meant to. But the hard facts are that Keke, used to a nervous, over-steery car during his spell at Williams, simply could not adapt his style to accommodate the abiding understeer of the McLaren MP4/2C. Moreover, John Barnard, for reasons that he knew best, steadfastly declined to make alterations to the chassis set-up in order to accommodate Rosberg's requirements.

Mind you, when Keke says he never really developed a close relationship with Barnard we may find a clue to understanding just why, if we consider his first test session with the car at Rio. As Prost reminds us with wry amusement, 'Keke wasn't any old driver arriving at McLaren grateful for the opportunity.' Ignoring Barnard's counsel to do a couple of slow laps, then come into the pits, before really pressing on hard, Keke embarked on what looked like a very fast run without more ado.

Like a schoolboy who knows his friend is about to be put through the wringer by the headmaster, Prost was aghast when he saw the cloud of dust kicked up at the end of the back straight. Rosberg had dropped it, good and proper, scything through a couple of layers of catch fencing before his badly damaged McLaren shuddered to a halt. 'You think very seriously before ignoring Barnard's steely-eyed counsel,' said Alain admiringly.

During his season driving with Prost at McLaren, Keke remarked admiringly, 'You know, I thought I was the fastest driver in the world until I came into the same team as Alain Prost.' Three years later, when I spoke to him during the course of preparing this book, he had changed his tune slightly.

'I still think I was fundamentally the fastest driver out there in

Enzo Ferrari at Maranello, September, 1986, flanked by team director Marco Piccinini (left) and his son, Piero Lardi-Ferrari.

214

McLaren mechanics working on the TAG V6-engined MP4/2Cs during practice for the 1986 British Grand Prix at Brands Hatch. John Barnard, by now on the verge of a terminal rift with Ron Dennis, always insisted that a top priority was serviceability in the field for all his cars.

1986,' he reflected with typical breezy confidence, 'and I'm sure I could have given Alain a good run for his money in a different car. The TAG didn't have the top end power of the Honda, of course, but the real problem was that understeer. I found it so bad that I was only really able to harness about 70 per cent of my potential. On the other hand, it was difficult to come into the pits and say, "Look, this car is undriveable" when Alain was producing the results.

'Quite honestly, it was like having two horses. His had a saddle and mine didn't . . . .' Keke has not got the analogy right, of course. It would have been more accurate to say that Prost was better riding bare-back!

Either way, it seems that the Rosberg/Barnard relationship never quite recovered. 'There was never any real contact between us,' Keke shrugged. 'No rapport ever got going. He just didn't take any notice . . .'

McLaren followed its traditional practice of not preoccupying itself with high boost qualifying engines, preferring to concentrate on race settings and banking on their two drivers being able to compete with around 850bhp from wherever they started on the grid. This had worked superbly in 1984, when their race capability was superior to the opposition, and less so in 1985. But in 1986 the odds were starting to pile up against them because the Williams-Hondas could qualify and race almost as fast as they liked.

Prost and Rosberg were assisted in their endeavours by the

latest in Bosch Motronic engine management softwear, but Keke was temperamentally unsuited to this business of 195 litre fuel consumption racing. There was no problem running as fast as Alain, but he used more fuel to do so. Both men had fuel read-outs in the cockpits, so they knew precisely where they were at any time in the race. Keke's most celebrated failure came at Montreal, where he elbowed his way to the front of the field, but eventually had to drop back to fourth at the finish.

At Hockenheim, where Bosch produced some improvements to the management system, Keke qualified on pole and did a fair share of leading. When he and Alain eventually ran out of fuel on the last lap it was, ironically, down to the fuel computer going on the blink. Nothing to do with them!

The second round of the title chase, the maiden Spanish Grand Prix to be staged at the new Jerez circuit, produced an absolutely electrifying confrontation between Senna and Mansell. This was a race where fuel consumption would not be quite such a stifling constraint, allowing Senna to lead from pole position, but with Piquet's Williams breathing down his neck from the word go. This was to be perhaps the first day that Nelson Piquet got the message that Mansell was not all he might have seemed in years past.

Ayrton Senna's Lotus 98T-Renault takes a last-gasp victory by a couple of feet from Nigel Mansell's Williams FW11-Honda in the 1986 Spanish Grand Prix at Jerez.

Nigel dropped back as low as fifth in the early stages, anxious to conserve fuel, but soon picked up the pace once he had his consumption bang on target. Then he picked off Prost and Piquet before settling down to deal with Senna. He had boxed Ayrton in behind Brundle's Tyrrell-Renault as they came up to lap the slower car and, once through, quickly opened a cushion of three seconds or so.

Just when it seemed as though Nigel had it in the bag, he began to realise his Williams had the first sign of a problem. It started with a hint of instability at the rear. The car was spinning its wheels a little more than he had come to expect, losing grip at the rear. The diffuser panel was becoming detached and, to make matters worse, he had picked up some debris on a rear tyre which had caused a slow puncture. Senna gradually came back at him as the problem worsened.

It was clear he would not make it to the flag with his lead and, midway round Lap 68 – with only four laps to go – the Lotus slipped through again. Mansell now headed straight for the pits where a replacement set of pre-heated Goodyears was waiting.

In less than ten seconds, the Williams crew slammed on the replacement wheels and Nigel erupted back on to the circuit. From a standing start, his next lap was only 1.3sec slower than his fastest all afternoon!

It seemed an impossible task. He slashed away at Ayrton's advantage, the gap coming down 15.3sec, 12.8sec, 8.67sec . . . on successive laps. Briefly baulked by Prost, who later apologised – 'If I'd realised you could have caught him, I'd have let you through quicker' – Mansell was 5.3sec adrift with two laps to go. Senna was paying out the line. On Lap 71 the gap was 1.5sec. Out of the hairpin for the last time and Mansell drew level with the Lotus, surging by almost the instant they passed the chequered flag. It was Senna's race by one-hundredth of a second, the closest winning margin in Grand Prix history and a dramatic testimony to Mansell's fast-rising maturity.

The battle for the Championship was destined to be as much between Mansell and Piquet themselves as between the Williams drivers and the rest of the pack, a reality which aided Prost immeasurably in his quest for a second successive Championship. Alain unquestionably enjoyed some good wins.

At Imola, the efficiency of the Bosch Motronic system was displayed when his McLaren began to stutter, low on fuel, as he accelerated towards the chequered flag on the last lap. This race also marked the debut of the new Cosworth-built Ford TEC 120 degree turbo which had been developed exclusively for the new Haas/Lola team for whom veterans Alan Jones and Patrick Tambay were driving.

At the height of their spellbinding battle for victory, Nelson Piquet leads Nigel Mansell round Druids hairpin at Brands Hatch during the 1986 British Grand Prix. The Williams-Honda FW11s had the race to themselves, balancing power and fuel economy in a manner not matched even by the McLaren-TAGs.

Sponsored by the giant Beatrice Group, an enormous US-based food and consumer products conglomerate, this organisation came into Formula 1 with a massive budget and high hopes. Based round a cast aluminium block and, unusually, with chain drive for its valve gear, the engine gained much publicity through using Ford's own EECIV engine management system, a link which Detroit enjoyed stressing had a direct relationship with its production car technology.

However, the task of sorting out these advanced electronics preoccupied Cosworth until February 1986, obliging the team to use Hart 415T engines from their race debut in mid 1985. Jones used the Ford V6 at Imola, commenting that it felt like a Le Mans engine: 'It gave me the impression that it would just run on and on and on.' That was part of the problem. Cosworth took an essentially conservative route, never willing to build high-boost qualifying engines. The Haas Lolas proved midfield runners at best and, even before sampling the Ford V6, lost their Beatrice backing as the result of a buy-out by a corporate raider. The team evaporated at the end of the season.

At Monaco, Prost was in a class of his own, beating Rosberg

and an extremely disgruntled Senna in a straight fight. But it was Mansell's onslaught against Piquet's number one status at Williams which really captured everybody's imagination in the first part of the year.

At Spa, Nelson looked well in command when the engine failed, allowing Nigel to score his first win of the season. But at Montreal, Mansell took the race by the throat from the start. This was a newly relaxed, assured and confident Mansell, looking neat and tidy without a care in the world. He would have won the following weekend in Detroit but for brake problems which dropped him to fifth. Nelson destroyed his FW11 against one of the circuit's unyielding walls as he attempted to close on Senna, the Brazilian taking his second victory of the season.

It was Mansell again at Paul Ricard, where Patrick Head's strategy of two tyre stops rather than one earned him a memorable victory over Prost's McLaren. Then, at Brands Hatch, Nigel was granted a fortuitous second chance after a driveshaft cage broke just as he was accelerating away from the start, leaving his Williams-Honda slowing suddenly right at the head of the pack.

In his wake, all hell broke loose. Thierry Boutsen's Arrows-BMW snapped wildly out of control going into Paddock Bend, unleashing a multiple collision which caused the race to be red flagged to a halt. Unhappily, amidst this chaos, Jacques Laffite crashed his Ligier very heavily and sustained serious leg injuries which brought to an end a long and distinguished Formula 1 career.

Enzo Ferrari was still in charge of the automobile dynasty which bore his name when these shots were taken in September 1986, but his lack of a Formula 1 wind tunnel facility was costing his Grand Prix team dear.

There was no question of repairing the damaged driveshaft cage on Mansell's car in the time available, so Nigel took over the spare car which had been set up for Piquet. At the restart the Brazilian shot away into the distance, Mansell falling in behind Gerhard Berger's Benetton-BMW for the first couple of laps while he played himself in at the wheel of an unfamiliar machine. Then he overtook the Austrian and went after Piquet with a vengeance. Such was their pace that Berger had dropped to five seconds behind in third place with only six laps completed.

By Lap 20, Nigel was right on his team-mate's tail, and when Nelson missed a gear going on to the straight after Surtees, Nigel surged through into the lead. There were no team orders and, as the two drivers sailed through their routine stops for fresh tyres on Laps 30 (Piquet) and 32 (Mansell), it was clear this would be a fight to the finish.

Mansell just scampered back on to the track again with his lead intact, but had to slam the door firmly in Nelson's face at South Bank to protect his advantage. It was hard stuff, but fair enough. Two laps later, Nelson had a clear run through Paddock Bend, but just as he tried to take the inside line for the climb up to Druids he found Alessandro Nannini's Minardi occupying the section of track he had earmarked for this manoeuvre.

Mansell and Piquet continued to trade lap records for the rest of the race, but there was nothing Piquet could do. He had been beaten fair and square and there could no longer be any doubt in his mind what he was up against with Nigel Mansell. Alain Prost was third, a lap down, keeping private his grief over the death of his brother Daniel a few days before.

With half the season run, three teams and four drivers had monopolised the winner's circle, but with the ratio of Williams victories standing 3:1 in Mansell's favour, Piquet was preparing himself for a counter-attack at Hockenheim. Meanwhile, neither Brabham nor Ferrari had so much as looked remotely like winning anything.

The Brabham team's plight was particularly tragic, for all the disappointment they had experienced with Gordon Murray's new low-line BT55 paled into insignificance alongside the sense of loss felt when Elio de Angelis died as the result of injuries sustained in a testing accident at Paul Ricard immediately after the Monaco Grand Prix.

It was the first time that the Brabham Grand Prix team had lost one of its drivers and the entire workforce felt a profound sense of grief over the disaster. Elio was a new boy with the team, having switched from Lotus at the end of the previous season, sharing Gordon Murray's trials and tribulations as they attempted to come to terms with the complicated new BT55.

Elio de Angelis: Gentleman Player

The death of Elio de Angelis following an accident during testing at Paul Ricard was understandably a shattering blow to the Brabham team in general and designer Gordon Murray in particular, the first time anybody had been killed in one of their cars. The tragedy emphasised the wild and unpredictable nature of the sport, the spectre of disaster always lurking in the shadows no matter how much progress might be made in terms of car technology or circuit security.

It was doubly ironic that such a fate should befall the debonair Italian driver. Most members of the pit lane community agreed that he was the last driver one would have expected to fall victim to such a disaster. Although evidence pointed to loss of control being caused by partial breakage of the rear wing, the failure of the safety services to rescue him from the burning, upturned car was an absolute scandal. Having suffered only superficial injuries in the impact, de Angelis died from lack of oxygen. It was inexcusable.

The son of a wealthy and influential Roman building contractor, the young Elio was powerboat racing in company with his father Giulio in his teens. But his path to motor racing was achieved through karting, the traditional nursery for the single seater star. His initial progress was meteoric. At 19, he won the Monaco Formula 3 supporting race at the wheel of a Chevron; at 20, he finished seventh on his Formula 1 debut driving a Shadow DN9 in the 1980 Argentine Grand Prix.

Cultured and civilised, Elio de Angelis's accomplishments included performing, to classical concert standards, at the piano where he was good enough to consider this as an alternative career. On the track, six years with Lotus, during which he won two Grands Prix, saw his early impetuosity replaced with a driving technique as well-honed and refined as his own personality. The man had a lot of style.

This striking, low-line challenger sounded the Last Post for Gordon as far as his relationship with Bernie Ecclestone was concerned. Most aerodynamic development over the years has centred round picking up the odd fraction here and there and, of course, the size and shape of the engine was always bound to be a constraining factor. Now Murray aimed for a quantum leap forward, taking on monumental technical challenges on several different fronts at the same time.

The tall, upright 4 cylinder BMW engine had always been awkward to package properly, by its very nature defying all Gordon's efforts to achieve a decent airflow over its rear wing. 'It kept nagging at me that we were tending to forget some basic principles of Formula 1 design,' he pondered, 'and we could spend all week in a wind tunnel with the BT54 without picking up so much as half a second. It was really frustrating.'

Piquet had been pressing Murray to do a 'low line' car for some time, remembering the days in his Formula 3 Ralt when he would try to tuck down an inch or so lower in the cockpit than any of his rivals in a quest for a tiny aerodynamic advantage. Murray got the green light from Ecclestone and the complex BT55 went into production.

BMW produced a batch of specially engineered 4 cylinder engines canted over at 72 degrees, built round his first all-carbon-fibre monocoque with a bevel-drive, seven-speed transmission developed by Californian gearbox specialist Pete Weismann who had collaborated with Brabham in the past on several experimental transmission projects. With a projected 30 per cent reduction in frontal area as compared with the old BT54, the concept should have worked. But it was overwhelmed by lack of development time.

It was also projected that the concept would produce 'between 22 and 32 per cent more downforce', but the fact remains that the car was handicapped by crushingly poor engine response out of the corners. The angled BMW engine clearly had oil scavenging problems which were preventing it from releasing its pent-up potential. It was a nightmare problem which the team never looked like overcoming. Derek Warwick was recruited to take the place of de Angelis alongside Riccardo Patrese. Both men gave it their best shot, but it proved an impossible task.

'What I had completely underestimated was the length of time it would take to build a new, all-carbon-fibre car from the ground up, with transverse transmission, canted engine and a brand new monocoque which was no more than 16½in high,' concedes Murray. They needed another six months, but that sort of luxury does not exist in the fast-moving Formula 1 stream.

Early the previous season, the Benetton knitwear company – which already sponsored the chronically unreliable Alfa Romeos – came to the rescue of Toleman in time for the Monaco Grand Prix. Teo Fabi debuted the new TG185 under the 'United Colors of Benetton' promotion. The team got on the road by dint of purchasing a Pirelli tyre contract from the Spirit team which was on the verge of closing its doors, but the Benetton deal only went through on the strict condition that the Italian firm retained an option to purchase Toleman Group Motorsport at the end of the season. They duly exercised that privilege, abandoned Brian Hart's gallant engine programme and switched to 'upright' BMW fours prepared by Heini Mader.

With BMW power and Pirelli rubber, the Benetton squad severely embarrassed the floundering Brabham *equipe*, and while Teo Fabi was never really going to mature into a great talent, his newly recruited team-mate Gerhard Berger was clearly something quite special. Switching to Benetton after a year's 'training' alongside Thierry Boutsen at Arrows, Berger took maximum advantage of Rory Byrne's aerodynamic package which had been developed through exclusive access to the wind tunnel at the Royal Military College at Shrivenham.

It was probably the failure to invest in its own wind tunnel facility which most contributed to the also-ran status of the Ferrari team throughout 1986, such a facility only being completed at Fiorano towards the end of that season. The arrival of Jean-Jacques His from the Renault design team heralded a change from KKK to Garrett turbos, initially only for racing, but also for qualifying from the British Grand Prix onwards.

Despite developing around 830bhp early in the season, leap-frogging up to almost 900bhp towards the end of the season, Alboreto and Johansson never had chassis performance to match and the whole package never looked like a winner throughout the year.

Piquet's counter-attack at Hockenheim produced a fortuitous victory when the McLarens both ran short of fuel, Senna trailing home a fuel-constrained second with Mansell, lacking grip from a partially detached diffuser panel, third. The rivalry between the two Williams drivers was now gaining pace, Piquet feeling that Williams should intervene to advise Nigel that, according to Nelson's understanding of his contract, the English driver should defer to his number one status. But the Williams *équipe* were racers to the core and felt that, having provided absolute top-line equipment for both drivers, the best man should win. Piquet rightly felt that he could not bother Frank himself with this problem, but the matter would surface again in 1987.

Grand Prix racing went behind the Iron Curtain on its first visit to the Eastern Bloc a fortnight after Hockenheim, the superb Hungaroring facility near Budapest offering Senna a better chance with the Lotus-Renault. Ayrton led the opening lap chased by Mansell, but it would be Piquet who eventually stormed through to displace his compatriot from the front of the field. At the end of the chase the order was Piquet, Senna, Mansell, Johansson's Ferrari and Johnny Dumfries, the Scot scoring his first Championship points for Team Lotus.

Mansell near-as-damn-it accused Piquet of a duplicity by running a more effective differential, the benefits of which he had not been acquainted with. But the Williams team denied that there had been any secrecy in this connection, a reassurance which did not completely mollify the English driver.

Nevertheless, Mansell was still leading the Championship with 55 points to Senna's 48. Then both Williams-Hondas failed to survive the distance in the Austrian Grand Prix, allowing Prost through to win by over a lap from the Ferraris after both Benettons had led, then been delayed. Suddenly Alain was only 2 points behind Mansell and 5 points ahead of Senna. It was getting a little too close for Nigel's comfort.

FISA bounced back into the limelight at Monza where Nelson Piquet gambled on a last minute change of wing setting to beat Mansell in a straight fight. Fast circuit stuff was Nelson's forte, heroic victories against the odds, Nigel's. At this race we were

Above and opposite: *Amazing sight at the start of the 1986 Italian Grand Prix as Nigel Mansell's Williams FW11-Honda and Gerhard Berger's Benetton B186-BMW have a clear run from the second row of the grid. Front row qualifiers Teo Fabi and Alain Prost had hit technical snags and neither was able to take up his allotted position.*

treated to the quite extraordinary sight of a starting grid without a front row. Fabi's Benetton-BMW had stalled just before the parade lap and Prost's McLaren suffered an alternator failure and steadfastly refused to fire up. Too late, as events would transpire, Prost switched to the spare car and prepared to start from the pit lane.

While Mansell, Piquet and, briefly, Alboreto's Ferrari battled for the lead, Prost came hurtling through to sixth place by Lap 18. By now, half an hour into the race, the stewards had decided that, by the scant margin of five seconds, Alain had switched cars after the green flag had been shown to signal the cars away on the parade lap. That was a major offence punishable with disqualification. Out came the black flag at the end of Lap 26.

It may seem incredible that Alain had been permitted to risk his neck for nothing for such a long time, even making a quick pit stop to change the McLaren's collapsed nose cone, but Ron Dennis had spent much of that time attempting to prevail upon

the stewards to let him run to the finish and argue about the matter later. It was no consolation that his TAG V6 expired expensively on Lap 28, just as he was about to return to the pits.

Prost sounded off quite vociferously on the subject of FISA's behaviour and was rewarded in time-honoured fashion with a $6000 fine. Unlike the Belgian race, where a stupendous charge through the field with a bent chassis following a first corner collision with Berger yielded a single Championship point, a similar display of Prost's enormous determination came to nought in Italy. Now the Championship table read Mansell (61 points), Piquet (56 points), Prost (53 points) and Senna (48 points).

Ayrton's chances of the title finally died at Estoril during the closing stages of the Portuguese Grand Prix. A pair of experimental Garrett turbos, rushed from testing on Renault Sport's Viry Chatillon dynomoter, earned Senna's Lotus 98T a staggering pole position by the huge margin of eight-tenths of a second over

Mansell. But Nigel took the lead at the start, leading from start to finish in a style befitting a World Champion elect.

Prost finished next to collect six points after Piquet had a late race spin and, more crucially, Senna dropped from second to fourth on the last lap when, after a great race, his Lotus ran out of fuel despite the cockpit instrumentation telling him all was well. Mansell led the Championship by ten points. Williams had long since clinched the Constructors' title and now it seemed as though Nigel was on the verge of becoming the first English World Champion in a decade.

The penultimate round of the title battle proved to be a scrappy, untidy and inconsistent affair in Mexico, that country gaining restoration to the Championship calendar for the first time since 1970. The Autodromo Hermanos Rodriguez – the Brothers' Rodriguez – had an abrasive surface, was bumpy and extremely dusty. It proved absolute anathema for the Goodyear runners, most of whom had to make several stops.

Senna was on pole from Piquet, Mansell, Berger, Patrese and

Elio de Angelis; a tragic victim of technical malfunction.

Prost. Nigel stalled on the grid, losing the initiative to Piquet in his private battle. He was way down near the tail of the field at the end of the opening lap. Both Williams-Hondas made two pits stops for fresh Goodyears. Prost, worried that his TAG turbo had lapsed on to 5 cylinder and, if stalled, might not start again, used all his delicacy to coax his second set through to the finish. That strategy paid off as he finished second, promoted when Senna made a second stop for tyres. Berger, running non-stop on Pirellis which seemed ideally suited for the conditions, emerged a worthy winner in the Benetton-BMW.

The final season of unrestricted boost Grand Prix racing wound up with a memorable finale in Adelaide, where Mansell, Piquet and Prost started the weekend with a shot at the Championship. For the Williams drivers, the story is an agonising one, a tale that has gone down in Formula 1 folklore, Mansell started from pole with Piquet alongside him, so it seemed as if the battle might be exclusively between the two Williams men.

Mansell got the jump at the start, but wisely moved over at the second corner to allow Senna and Piquet to go hurtling by. He was demonstrating all the subtlety and stealth needed in this sort of situation. Piquet led at the end of Lap 1, but it did not take Rosberg long to elbow through to the front of the pack. Running his last race before retirement, Keke found his McLaren was magically devoid of its customary dreaded understeer for only the second time that season. Although he had privately pledged to help Alain, he pulled quickly away from the pack.

Everybody watching thought his boost was off the dial. Keke says no. 'I swear to you, I was using 2.8 bar boost and everything ran perfectly,' he insists. 'I only had to snap my fingers to open out an advantage. I remember wondering to myself, well, if it's this easy, why the hell am I retiring?'

Prost quickly asserted himself as an equally onimous threat. By Lap 12 he was third ahead of Mansell, by Lap 21 second ahead of Piquet. Nelson then had a quick spin, dropping to fourth. On Lap 32 came one of those remarkable incidents by which the outcome of Championships can be resolved. Prost clipped Berger's Benetton whilst lapping the Austrian, the McLaren sustained a punctured front tyre and Alain dropped to fourth after stopping to have it changed.

On Lap 63, with only nineteen to go, Rosberg's swansong went the same way as Lauda's twelve months earlier when he retired whilst leading. After hearing an ominous rumbling from the McLaren, he switched off the engine and coasted to a halt, certain that the bearings were about to fail. In fact, after he had climbed out, he realised a rear tyre had started to fail. What he had heard was wayward chunks of rubber battering against the bodywork.

Mansell and Piquet had a tense relationship in the Williams team, but between them, they squeezed the best out of the Williams-Honda FW11 and FW11Bs. They are seen here on the winner's rostrum at Monza after their 1986 1-2.

Was there a tyre problem? Prost's discarded Goodyears looked fine, but the covers on the Williams FW11s, now running 1-2 in the order Piquet-Mansell, had been looking in bad shape for several laps now. Before anybody made a decisive decision, Nigel's left-rear Goodyear exploded at almost 200mph on the long back straight, the fastest section on the Adelaide circuit.

The Williams-Honda squatted down on its left rear corner in a shower of sparks, its right front wheel lifting off the circuit. Somehow – who knows how? – Mansell steered it away from the unyielding concrete walls and his Championship hopes were virtually snuffed out as he slid up the escape road. Prost and Piquet would have to retire now, if he was to emerge with the crown.

Goodyear counselled bringing in Piquet's leading Williams for fresh rubber. Williams agreed, but there was nothing wrong with his old tyres. Prost was now first, but Piquet began rattling off a whole series of fastest laps, desperate to catch the McLaren.

As for Alain, he inwardly knew he did not have a hope. The fuel computer read-out was flashing him dire warnings; he just knew he would run out of fuel before the end. Piquet would snatch his third World Championship.

But the read-out was wrong. Prost, amazingly, had fuel in hand and cruised home to clinch his second consecutive Championship title, snatching it from the grasp of Williams and Honda at the 59th minute of the 11th hour.

THE TURBO YEARS' RESULTS 1986

Winner's average speed

March 23, BRAZILIAN GRAND PRIX, Rio

1	Nelson Piquet	Williams-Honda FW11 turbo	(114.94mph)
2	Ayrton Senna	Lotus-Renault 98T turbo	
3	Jacques Laffite	Ligier-Renault JS27 turbo	
4	René Arnoux	Ligier-Renault JS27 turbo	
5	Martin Brundle	Tyrrell-Renault 014 turbo	
6	Gerhard Berger	Benetton-BMW B186 turbo	

April 13, SPANISH GRAND PRIX, Jerez

1	Ayrton Senna	Lotus-Renault 97T turbo	(104.07mph)
2	Nigel Mansell	Williams-Renault FW11 turbo	
3	Alain Prost	McLaren-TAG MP4/2C turbo	
4	Keke Rosberg	McLaren-TAG MP4/2C turbo	
5	Teo Fabi	Benetton-BMW B186 turbo	
6	Gerhard Berger	Benetton-BMW B186 turbo	

April 27, SAN MARINO GRAND PRIX, Imola

1	Alain Prost	McLaren-TAG MP4/2C turbo	(121.918mph)
2	Nelson Piquet	Williams-Honda FW11 turbo	
3	Gerhard Berger	Benetton-BMW F186 turbo	
4	Stefan Johansson	Ferrari F186 turbo	
5	Keke Rosberg	McLaren-TAG MP4/2C turbo	
6	Riccardo Patrese	Brabham-BMW BT55 turbo	

May 11, MONACO GRAND PRIX, Monte Carlo

1	Alain Prost	McLaren-TAG MP4/2C turbo	(83.657mph)
2	Keke Rosberg	McLaren-TAG MP4/2C turbo	
3	Ayrton Senna	Lotus-Renault 98T turbo	
4	Nigel Mansell	Williams-Honda FW11 turbo	
5	René Arnoux	Ligier-Renault JS27 turbo	
6	Jacques Laffite	Ligier-Renault JS27 turbo	

May 25, BELGIAN GRAND PRIX, Spa

1	Nigel Mansell	Williams-Honda FW11 turbo	(126.47mph)
2	Ayrton Senna	Lotus-Renault 98T turbo	
3	Stefan Johansson	Ferrari F186 turbo	
4	Michele Alboreto	Ferrari F186 turbo	
5	Jacques Laffite	Ligier-Renault JS27 turbo	
6	Alain Prost	McLaren-TAG MP4/2C turbo	

June 15, CANADIAN GRAND PRIX, Montreal

1	Nigel Mansell	Williams-Honda FW11 turbo	(110.74mph)
2	Alain Prost	McLaren-TAG MP4/2C turbo	
3	Nelson Piquet	Williams-Honda FW11 turbo	
4	Keke Rosberg	McLaren-TAG MP4/2C turbo	
5	Ayrton Senna	Lotus-Renault 98T turbo	
6	René Arnoux	Ligier-Renault JS27 turbo	

June 22, DETROIT GRAND PRIX, Michigan
1   Ayrton Senna   Lotus-Renault 98T turbo   (84.97mph)
2   Jacques Laffite   Ligier-Renault JS27 turbo
3   Alain Prost   McLaren-TAG MP4/2C turbo
4   Michele Alboreto   Ferrari 156/85 turbo
5   Nigel Mansell   Williams-Honda FW11 turbo
6   Riccardo Patrese   Brabham-BMW BT55 turbo

July 6, FRENCH GRAND PRIX, Paul Ricard
1   Nigel Mansell   Williams-Honda FW11 turbo   (116.85mph)
2   Alain Prost   McLaren-TAG MP4/2C turbo
3   Nelson Piquet   Williams-Honda FW11 turbo
4   Keke Rosberg   McLaren-TAG MP4/2C turbo
5   René Arnoux   Ligier-Renault JS27 turbo
6   Jacques Laffite   Ligier-Renault JS27 turbo

July 13, BRITISH GRAND PRIX, Brands Hatch
1   Nigel Mansell   Williams-Honda FW11 turbo   (129.77mph)
2   Nelson Piquet   Williams-Honda FW11 turbo
3   Alain Prost   McLaren-TAG MP4/2C turbo
4   René Arnoux   Ligier-Renault JS27 turbo
5   Martin Brundle   Tyrrell-Renault 015 turbo
6   Philippe Streiff   Tyrrell-Renault 015 turbo

July 27, GERMAN GRAND PRIX, Hockenheim
1   Nelson Piquet   Williams-Honda FW11 turbo   (135.74mph)
2   Ayrton Senna   Lotus-Renault 98T turbo
3   Nigel Mansell   Williams-Honda FW11 turbo
4   René Arnoux   Ligier-Renault JS27 turbo
5   Keke Rosberg   McLaren-TAG MP4/2C turbo
6   Alain Prost   McLaren-TAG MP4/2C turbo

August 10, HUNGARIAN GRAND PRIX, Budapest
1   Nelson Piquet   Williams-Honda FW11 turbo   (94.32mph)
2   Ayrton Senna   Lotus-Renault 98T turbo
3   Nigel Mansell   Williams-Honda FW11 turbo
4   Stefan Johansson   Ferrari F186 turbo
5   Johnny Dumfries   Lotus-Renault 98T turbo
6   Martin Brundle   Tyrrell-Renault 015 turbo

August 17, AUSTRIAN GRAND PRIX, Osterreichring
1   Alain Prost   McLaren-TAG MP4/2C turbo   (141.56mph)
2   Michele Alboreto   Ferrari F186 turbo
3   Stefan Johansson   Ferrari F186 turbo
4   Alan Jones   Lola-Ford THL-2 turbo
5   Patrick Tambay   Lola-Ford THL-2 turbo
6   Christian Danner   Arrows-BMW A8 turbo

September 7, ITALIAN GRAND PRIX, Monza
1   Nelson Piquet   Williams-Honda FW11 turbo   (141.9mph)
2   Nigel Mansell   Williams-Honda FW11 turbo
3   Stefan Johansson   Ferrari F186 turbo
4   Keke Rosberg   McLaren-TAG MP4/2 turbo
5   Gerhard Berger   Benetton-BMW B186 turbo
6   Alan Jones   Lola-Ford THL-2 turbo

September 21, PORTUGUESE GRAND PRIX, Estoril

1	Nigel Mansell	Williams-Honda FW11 turbo	(116.59mph)
2	Alain Prost	McLaren-TAG MP4/2C turbo	
3	Nelson Piquet	Williams-Honda FW11 turbo	
4	Ayrton Senna	Lotus-Renault 98T turbo	
5	Michele Alboreto	Ferrari F186 turbo	
6	Stefan Johansson	Ferrari F186 turbo	

October 12, MEXICAN GRAND PRIX, Mexico City

1	Gerhard Berger	Benetton-BMW B186 turbo	(120.11mph)
2	Alain Prost	McLaren-TAG MP4/2C turbo	
3	Ayrton Senna	Lotus-Renault 98T turbo	
4	Nelson Piquet	Williams Honda FW11 turbo	
5	Nigel Mansell	Williams-Honda FW11 turbo	
6	Philippe Alliot	Ligier-Renault JS27 turbo	

October 26, AUSTRALIAN GRAND PRIX, Adelaide

			(101.04mph)
1	Alain Prost	McLaren-TAG MP4/2C turbo	
2	Nelson Piquet	Williams-Honda FW11 turbo	
3	Stefan Johansson	Ferrari F186 turbo	
4	Martin Brundle	Tyrrell-Renault 015 turbo	
5	Philippe Steiff	Tyrr' -Renault 015 turbo	
6	Johnny Dumfries	Lotus-Renault 98T turbo	

DRIVERS' WORLD CHAMPIONSHIP

Posn	Driver	Points
1	Alain Prost	72
2	Nigel Mansell	70
3	Nelson Piquet	69
4	Ayrton Senna	55
5	Stefan Johansson	23
6	Keke Rosberg	22
7	Gerhard Berger	17
8	Jacques Laffite	14
	Rene Arnoux	
	Michele Alboreto	
11	Martin Brundle	8
12	Alan Jones	4
13	Philippe Streiff	3
	Johnny Dumfries	
15	Teo Fabi	2
	Riccardo Patrese	
	Patrick Tambay	
18	Christian Danner	1
	Philippe Alliot	

CONSTRUCTORS' CHAMPIONSHIP

Posn	Constructor	Points
1	Williams	141
2	McLaren	96
3	Lotus	58
4	Ferrari	37
5	Ligier	29
6	Benetton	19
7	Tyrrell	11
8	Lola	6
9	Brabham	2
10	Arrows	1

1987

Irrespective of what Honda might inwardly have felt about the failure of either Piquet or Mansell to clinch the 1986 Drivers' World Championship, the Japanese continued to put maximum effort behind the Williams team's effort throughout 1987, a season which has come to be regarded as the turbo's last hurrah. Granted, there was now a thinly supported naturally-aspirated secondary league, but this would not develop into anything of consequence until 1988, by which time the turbo brigade would definitely be in the minority.

The technical regulations retained the 195 litre fuel maximum for the new Championship programme, but this was now coupled with a 4 bar boost restriction which was enforceable both during qualifying and the race. This was achieved by the provision of a pop-off valve by FISA which was designed to vent the system when the prescribed level of four times ambient barometric pressure was achieved. The valves, manufactured in the USA specially for this purpose, were retained by FISA between races and distributed on a 'pot luck' basis prior to the first qualifying session at each Grand Prix. Wise to the enterprising approach adopted by most Formula 1 teams, there was no way in which the sport's governing body was going to risk handing out valves for the entire year, just in case a little 'custom tuning' to circumvent their intended purpose should be applied.

In truth, one of the biggest sources of gossip throughout the season would centre round which teams had found a means of running in excess of 4 bar boost pressure. There was the danger that consistent over-boosting would weaken the springs to the point where they began operating at around 3.7 or 3.8 bar, a problem which was definitely to be avoided. In qualifying, however, the chase for front row grid positions saw some teams using big turbos with massive doses of boost being forced through the engines, the key factor being how the engine responded to this back-pressure under such circumstances.

Ferrari, Honda and BMW fitted single pop-off valves, but the TAG and Cosworth turbos had two, reflecting the fact that their engines effectively worked as two 3 cylinder engines joined only

Philippe Streiff at the wheel of the Tyrrell DG/016 with which he and team-mate Jonathan Palmer contested the 1987 Jim Clark and Colin Chapman Cups for naturally-aspirated competitors.

by the crankshaft. Each bank had its own separate induction tract, oil and water systems, so there was a strongly persuasive body of technical thought which regarded two separate pop-off valves as preferable, bearing in mind the slight variations in boost pressure which could occur between both sides of the engine.

Whilst Porsche's Rolf Hahn and Udo Zucker of Bosch – the two companies' engineers who were most closely involved – propounded this argument successfully in the case of the TAG turbo, the McLaren design staff frequently asked whether it would be possible to run a single valve. 'Those valves were rather agricultural affairs, big and bulky,' explained Steve Nichols. 'On the MP4/3 they interfered with the oil tank attachment and made the car a little complicated to package round the rear end.'

As far as Williams was concerned, Frank, his disabilities

notwithstanding, was becoming involved once more in the running of his company by the start of the year. Patrick Head and aerodynamicist Frank Dernie came up with a significantly revised 'B' version of the Constructors' Championship-winning FW11, a major re-design of the internal bulkheads enabling the driving position to be further reclined, benefiting the airflow over the rear wing. Dernie revealed with understandable pride that the FW11B generated significantly improved downforce as compared with its immediate predecessor, but with no penalty in terms of added drag.

Honda, of course, had been storming away on engine development, the latest RA168G version of the V6 now capable of working up to 13,000rpm. Later during the season there would be a revised version of the Japanese engine, offering enhanced economy, which reverted to the 12,000rpm rev maximum used the previous season. Honda Formula 1 project leader, Osamu Goto, admitted to four specifically different specification engines being used during the course of the year, the maximum output being at least 950bhp in race specification.

These potent units would also be available to Team Lotus for the first time. This not only allowed the gifted Ayrton Senna into the Honda enclave at long last, but enabled Satoru Nakajima to be placed in the Team Lotus line-up as his number two, part of the quid-pro-quo involved in making the engines available in the first place.

There had been a major shake-up on the design side at McLaren International during the second half of 1986, following a somewhat unsettling period. John Barnard, increasingly at odds with Ron Dennis since the end of 1985 over various aspects of McLaren corporate structure and policy, began negotiations with a view to joining another company. This came to a head in August 1986 when Dennis felt these unsubtle negotiations, notably with BMW Motorsport over the possible design of its own chassis, had gone too far, and he was asked to leave. In the event, BMW did not proceed with the project, but by that point Barnard had carefully laid the groundwork for his other new challenge, walking straight into the role of Ferrari's technical director.

From the outset, John had shown no interest in negotiating with the Italian team if a condition of employment involved relocating to Italy. Some saw this as a rather insular attitude, but, be that as it may, Barnard never made any bones about it and Maranello took him on with that strict understanding very firmly in mind. He quickly established a design office at Shalford, near Guildford, operating under the title of Guildford Technical Office, thus producing the incredibly corny acronym GTO...

Although Barnard's top priority was the development of a brand new, state-of-the-art, naturally-aspirated car for 1988 or 1989, he inevitably became embroiled in the development of the team's brand new turbocar for the 1987 Championship campaign. The design of this machine had been initiated by Austrian designer Gustav Brunner, who would be amongst the early critics of Barnard's intensely autocratic technical regime at Maranello.

Almost from the outset, Barnard's authoritarian approach would put people's backs up, but John never made any apology for this strategy. 'If I'm the one who's going to be blamed if things go wrong, then if I don't instigate a system where things are done my way, I'm being a fool to myself,' he concluded firmly.

Although one of Barnard's requirements had been a longitudinal gearbox, he had little input to the 90 degree V6 engine development programme, apart from carrying out some torsion testing of the block which resulted in the whole structure being stiffened up slightly. The development of this 81 x 48.4mm unit was largely directed by Fiat engineer Ildo Renzetti. The use of a linerless cast-iron block was intended to sustain the thermodynamic loads more effectively than the previous aluminium alloy block used on the 120 degree V6.

Prior to his arrival in the Ferrari fold, Barnard had given the team what he felt to be some fundamental chassis specification

Ayrton Senna's active suspension Lotus-Honda 99T, seen here winning the 1987 Monaco Grand Prix, was a formidable tool, but even the gifted Brazilian could not get on terms with the similarly powered, but more fuel efficient Williams FW11Bs.

The Cosworth-built 120 degree Ford TEC V6 was originally employed in the Team Haas Lolas, but not until it was installed in the Benetton B187 at the start of the 1987 season were its aerodynamic assets capitalised on by a chassis manufacturer.

parameters: pull-rod suspension geometry and upright design. He had even arranged the manufacture of the wishbones by BS Fabrications, the Luton-based specialist racing sub-contractors with whom he had worked on the development of the Chaparral 2K seven years earlier.

When Barnard took up his post at GTO, he would produce further cosmetic changes, such as slight modifications to the top of the fuel cell and the addition of his own distinctive trademark, the sharply waisted rear bodywork complete with aerodynamic ramps. Ferrari's drivers for 1987 would be Gerhard Berger, transferring from Benetton, and resident incumbent Michele Alboreto. The Italian driver would soon develop into a staunch critic of Barnard's methods; he likened John operating from GTO to 'A surgeon trying to carry out a complex operation down a telephone.'

Back at McLaren International, Barnard's protégé Steve Nichols was charged with picking up the design gauntlet as Formula 1 project leader, the balance of the 1986 season spent sustaining the Championship challenge while at the same time endeavouring to work out the most suitable route by which to tackle 1987. The resultant MP4/3 represented yet another logical development of what had gone before, although this time the monocoque was revised to incorporate a reduced fuel cell tailor-made for only 195 litres, replacing the MP4/2C's original 220 litre outer moulding, the initial 1986 reduction to 195 litres having been achieved by internal changes alone. This, allied to other minor bodywork alterations, produced a worthwhile aerodynamic benefit.

Suspension configuration remained substantially unchanged, as did the transmission, but Porsche made considerable strides matching the TAG turbo's engine development programme to the requirements of the 4 bar, 195 litre regulations. Prospects for the season seemed excellent, particularly when Alain opened the year with another shrewd, winning performance in the Brazilian Grand Prix at Rio.

John Barnard recalled: 'When I strolled down the pit lane and glanced over Alain's detailed race set-up, I remember thinking, "Yes, that's the way to go..." I just wish we'd had more time to work out a similar approach at that race for the Ferraris...' As usual, Alain's qualifying performance was nothing spectacular. But the fact that he lined up 'only' fifth was merely a reflection of the team's continuing policy of eschewing high boost qualifying engines.

In race trim, the TAG turbo proved ever competitive, Prost coaxing his McLaren home with only two tyre stops rather than the three required by his rivals. Shades of Mexico, 1986...

The TAG turbo engine's two separate cylinder banks, which were not interlinked, required a FISA pop-off valve apiece. While this meant that there were two potential leaks in the system rather than one, in practice the German-built V6 thrived at around 3.7 bar, at which point it developed around 900bhp at 13,000rpm. Any over-boosting showed a tendency to scramble the latest induction sensing equipment in the Bosch engine management system and, in any case, throttle response became significantly poorer beyond this point.

On the human front, Keke Rosberg's departure from the scene meant that McLaren had to recruit a new partner for the Frenchman. The man chosen for the job was ex-Ferrari driver Stefan Johansson, the genial Swede proving his worth with a steady run to third place behind Prost and Piquet's Williams FW11B in the first race of the season.

However, Johansson was an unusual choice by McLaren's established standards, even though he had previously driven for Ron's Project Four team to win the 1980 British Formula 3 championship. He was certainly no slouch, but did not stand comparison with either Lauda or Rosberg in terms of proven status. His inclusion in the team raised certain questions which were answered, in part, only at the end of the year.

Ron Dennis would later confess that he had been keeping an eye on Ayrton Senna ever since the start of 1983. In fact, Dennis had been so impressed by the Brazilian's form in Formula Ford 2000 that he volunteered to finance Senna's 1983 British Formula 3 programme in return for an option on his services the following year. In that respect, Ayrton's performances in Formula Ford 2000 supporting races at a handful of 1982 Grands Prix, had really paid off. But, as Ron acknowledged, he rather misjudged the state of the game.

'I wanted a situation where I simply had the option on whether or not to use his services,' he remembers. 'I didn't want to get into a situation where I was obliged to give him a Formula 1 drive in 1984. What I underestimated was how strong a position he was actually in to come up with his own Formula 3 budget.'

Senna's subsequent Formula 1 form, driving for Toleman and Lotus, convinced Dennis that his original assessment had been correct. Thus, when Lotus became involved with Honda – an occurrence which took place after Dennis's first contact with the Japanese manufacturer – the likelihood of Senna driving for McLaren at sometime in the future strengthened with each race. Whether or not McLaren had come to a provisional agreement with Senna for the 1988 season even before the start of 1987 remains unclear; either way, signing Johansson for a single season makes it look, in retrospect, as though Ron was either keeping his options open or deliberately clearing the decks for Ayrton's arrival.

In retrospect, although Prost was the only McLaren runner capable of mounting a winning challenge, had the outcome of two crucial races been different he would have contested the Championship battle all the way down to the wire. At Imola, he was breezing along in second place, confident that he could deal with Mansell's then-leading Williams-Honda, when an alternator belt snapped. Then, less than four laps from the finish of the German Grand Prix at Hockenheim, Alain lost a certain victory for the same reason.

Detailed examation of the engine after the first such failure made it clear that this was a random breakage. But it was not until new 'double vee' belts were supplied from a US manufacturer in time for the Hungarian Grand Prix in August that the problem was finally licked. Prost by then had also won in Belgium and would go on to score a record twenty-eighth career victory at Estoril, hounding Gerhard Berger's Ferrari into a late-race spin before moving triumphantly ahead to eclipse at last Jackie Stewart's record of twenty-seven wins which had lasted for thirteen years.

Stewart has always been a great Prost fan and was typically effusive in his praise: 'He produced a faultless performance to win that race. I think Alain is absolutely in a class of his own

The Cosworth-built Ford V6 turbo was abandoned at the end of 1987 – most now agree that it would have been a formidable tool through to the end of the following year.

The Future for the Small Teams

With FISA now firmly fixed on the long-term aim of ridding Formula 1 of what was now regarded in some quarters again as the turbo scourge, the smaller teams were granted some relief with the introduction of a category for 3.5 litre naturally-aspirated cars. Whilst this would form the basis of the universally applied engine regulations when turbos were outlawed two years later, in the short-term it provided a refuge for teams that were out of their depth in the world of forced induction. It also provided a lowered 'bottom rung' to the ladder for incoming aspirants.

It came as no surprise that Ken Tyrrell opted for the naturally-aspirated division. With Renault withdrawing from the Formula 1 stage, albeit temporarily, and when Lotus opted for Honda power, his source of turbocharged engines suddenly dried up. Instead, he chose to contest Formula 1's newly instigated second division which had been endowed with a whiff of respectability with its own private contest for the Jim Clark (drivers) and Colin Chapman (constructors) trophies.

With all due respect to Jonathan Palmer and the Tyrrell team recipients of these who were meaningless accolades, tagging such a thinly supported Formula 1 sub-strata with those exalted names was as a travesty. Tyrrell sold his sponsorship on the basis that he was accumulating technology for the forthcoming across-the-board return to naturally-aspirated power. In fact, when the time came, the technical stakes would remain just as daunting in 1989, with Honda, Renault and Ferrari all sustaining the pace at the front of the field.

The role of the also-ran was destined to change very little, but at least the 3.5 litre rules in 1987 allowed the resurgent March team to climb back on the Grand Prix bandwagon.

amongst today's Grand Prix drivers. I honestly cannot think of anybody I would have preferred to take my record...'

However, it is fair to say that Bernie Ecclestone had his own reasons for possibly not agreeing with that assessment. The season had started with a threat of a drivers' strike at Rio, a squabble in which Prost and Ecclestone played leading roles. It centred round FISA's decision to charge the Formula 1 drivers for their super licences on a sliding scale based on the Championship points they had earned during the previous year. The basic fee was pitched at £512, plus £102 per point. On that basis Prost's bill added up to £7,800, which at that time equated to just over $12,000.

One might have been forgiven, of course, for wondering what on earth all the fuss was about. A quick glance across the tarmac of European airports adjacent to a Grand Prix venue during a race weekend would reveal more private jets than at the Farnborough air show – many of them belonging to top drivers. And while separating most Grand Prix drivers from their money is a task akin to scaling Mount Everest in sneakers, their indignation over the super licence fees was not based on claims of penury.

Prost made it clear that the drivers' complaints centred round the arbitrary manner in which FISA had applied the new fees. They refused to pay. FISA responded with characteristic sympathy, threatening any driver who did not cough up the fee, with suspension both from this race and the World Championship.

In the end the drivers had to pay, although they exacted a promise from FISA that the licence fees would be index-linked in the future. It was a hollow victory.

Bernie Ecclestone took the opportunity to tear into the drivers. 'Some of these people are earning millions of dollars a year and they are not prepared to pay for the tools of their trade. Who the hell do they think pays for Professor Watkins to look after them and the emergency helicopters to stand by all weekend. With some of them, it's all take and no give. They wouldn't even buy you a cup of coffee...'

To some extent he had a point. However, he blew the credibility of this argument by adding: 'This race was close to being cancelled and I, for one, wouldn't have been sorry if it had been. We would have gone back to Europe, signed up a new set of drivers and, within three races, who would remember Alain Prost?' Ecclestone continually laboured under the assumption that it was the cars, not the men, which the public came to see. Most people agreed this was a delusion...

Bernie adopted this conciliatory stance in his newly assumed role as FISA vice president of public affairs, a position to which

The Ligier JS29 was originally intended to be propelled by the new Alfa Romeo 415T 4 cylinder turbo from the start of 1987, but some strong criticism in public from driver René Arnoux gave Alfa the excuse to pull out at the last minute. This forced Ligier to use Megatron/BMWs instead.

he had been appointed during February 1987. On the face of it, this was a case of Daniel not only poking his head into the lion's den, but sitting down to a three-course lunch with his old adversary. In fact, having established pretty conclusively that Balestre was not going to go away, or be defeated, it was a shrewd move by both men. Balestre could see what Bernie was up to, while Bernie's presence as a newly recruited member of the 'Establishment' might reasonably have been expected to soften some of Balestre's asperities.

Off-season, Jean-Marie had been at the centre of the stage in a right old brouhaha. In December 1986 he had theatrically quit the FISA presidency saying he had had enough 'of the lies and defamations for which the authors are never punished.' His main gripe was with the author of a book, *Les Bolides En Or*, which made some very specific allegations of malpractice against the sport's governing body. FISA would subsequently win a libel action against its author and, by February 1987, Balestre had re-assumed his role of 'acting' president of FISA. 'Acting' was something he was rather good at!

Gerhard Berger switched from Benetton to Ferrari at the start of 1987, battling against Williams and McLaren with this John Barnard-modified, Gustav Brunner-originated F187. Now powered by a 90 degree twin turbo engine, this 4 bar/195 litre contender was good enough to carry Berger to victories at Suzuka and Adelaide.

Practice for the second round of the Championship, the San Marino Grand Prix at Imola, very nearly produced a disaster when Nelson Piquet's Williams-Honda crashed at high speed coming off the fast Tamburello double right-hander just beyond the pits. Although Nelson was extremely fortunate to impact against the barrier travelling backwards, most people agreed that the high standards of passive safety reflected in the best carbon-fibre composite chassis designs had been demonstrated to quite spectacular effect. It was a very lucky escape indeed for the Brazilian, but he was very badly shaken and eventually accepted medical counsel that it would be better if he missed the race.

Mansell won easily in the surviving Williams-Honda entry, his confidence boosted by Goodyear's extremely responsible decision to replace all the tyres from the batch they had been using during Friday. The erratic skid marks on the track surface just before Piquet's accident-spot pointed the finger of suspicion at their products and an overnight airlift was arranged to replenish stocks.

Qualifying had seen Ayrton Senna squeeze every last drop of potential from the Lotus 99T-Honda to edge Nigel away from pole position, but it was a different story come the race. Constrained by ominously high fuel consumption, Senna at one point had to drop back behind Michele Alboreto's Ferrari F1/87 before again moving through to take second place before the finish. It was a turning point for the team, for although the active suspension machine had scored its first Championship points, in his heart of hearts Senna already knew that it was not good enough.

The development of the Team Lotus active suspension system went back to the early 1980s immediately in the wake of the Lotus 88 fiasco. During the pioneering days of ground-effect technology, Lotus developed sophisticated systems for both recording and monitoring under-car airflow and, at around the same time, the team's development engineer Peter Wright became intrigued by some of the possibilities offered by the Flight Instrumentation Group at the Cranfield Institute of Technology.

Cranfield was developing a 'variable feel' control system for the British Aerospace Hawk, the RAF's sophisticated training aircraft, by means of which the handling qualities of a wide range of other aeroplanes could be simulated, enabling a trainee pilot's experience to be dramatically widened. It was felt, with some confidence, that this technology could be applied to produce an 'active' suspension system for a Grand Prix car. Peter Wright instantly realised the implications and possibilities.

Wright would liken the fledgeling system to the way in which

Big guns wielding the influence. The three most powerful men in professional motor racing – Bernie Ecclestone, Jean-Marie Balestre and Enzo Ferrari – at a FIA press conference held at Maranello in 1987. To Ecclestone's right is Aleardo Buzzi, top man at Philip Morris; to the Commendatore's left his son Piero Lardi-Ferrari.

the brain sends messages to the human muscular system; legs are not springs, so when the brain senses a change in the surface on which a human being is walking, it makes instant adjustments and minuscule compensations. If this sensitivity and response could be applied to a racing car suspension system, ride quality could be improved dramatically, tyre wear reduced and driver fatigue minimised.

In 1981, Lotus built a prototype system into a turbo Esprit road car and first signs were extremely encouraging. Colin Chapman instantly became enormously enthusiastic about the concept and the go-ahead was given to produce an 'active' Formula 1 prototype. This was just the sort of high technology engineering, pushing back the frontiers of knowledge, to which the Lotus chief was so committed. It enabled him to recapture some of his dynamic enthusiasm for the Formula 1 business which had been so diluted as a result of the setbacks experienced with the twin-chassis development.

Young British Formula 3 aspirant Dave Scott was entrusted with much of the routine preliminary testing of the system installed in a Cosworth-engined Lotus 91. The team was at Snetterton, that fateful morning in December 1982, when Peter Warr arrived unexpectedly in the paddock to bring them the tragic news of Colin's sudden death. But work on the system progressed and, while it was put on the back burner after a few preliminary race outings in Mansell's hands during the early part of 1983, Wright was convinced that the potential existed to produce a really worthwhile performance advantage.

However, the active system was registered as a Group Lotus patent, so when the road car manufacturing arm of the empire passed into the hands of General Motors in the post-Chapman period, the racing team (still owned by Hazel Chapman) had to reach a commercial agreement for its adaptation for Formula 1 use.

It had originally been decided to build up one 'active' Lotus-Honda for development purposes at the start of the 1987 season, but a detailed re-evaluation of the system, together with a discussion with Ayrton Senna, prompted Lotus to pursue the system wholeheartedly for their racing programme. Senna was absolutely intrigued by its possibilities. Being just the sort of intelligent driver who could capitalise on its advantage if it could be made to function correctly, the Brazilian relished this dramatic new challenge.

Basically, the system, as installed in the Lotus 99T, relied on a small computer installed beneath the driver's seat which accepted impulses from a series of potentiometers and acceler-ometers mounted on and around the suspension arms. The computer then signalled a response to a series of hydraulic jacks which replaced the conventional coil spring/damper units.

In addition, a system of back-up springs was fitted to enable a driver at least to get home to the pits in the event of the computer system malfunctioning in some way, thereby shutting down the active system. In fact, when Senna had a major hydraulic failure during the 1987 German Grand Prix at Hockenheim, although the 99T collapsed on to its secondary springs, he was still able to wrestle it home to third place.

Inevitably, of course, there were some snags with the system. This added about 12kg to the all-up weight of the 99T and slightly more than 10bhp was sliced off the Honda V6's usable power in driving the hydraulic pump. There was also another crucial consideration, namely that the team was being absolutely deluged with information when they 'dumped' data from the on-board computer into a larger capacity unit installed in the pit garages at races.

It was all extremely convienient to be able to plug an engineer's keyboard into the system while the car was stationary in the pits, providing the facility to instantly re-set ride heights, adjust the damping or whatever, but, in practice, there was just too much to deal with. Lotus could only scratch the surface of the information which was now available.

Senna, however, would win two Grands Prix with the 'active' Lotus. Monaco was the first such success, but only after Mansell's retirement; his success through the bumpy streets of Detroit provided a more telling testimomy to the system's success.

Gordon Murray in the drawing office at McLaren International where he took over as technical director in 1987.

Piquet and Prost struggled home second and third, utterly exhausted, but Senna looked as though he could do it all over again. This was one spectacular occasion when the boulevard ride afforded by the computer-controlled suspension really paid dividends.

There were other occasions, though, when the 99T looked less than the ideal tool for the job. In the British Grand Prix at Silverstone, highlighted by Mansell's heroic pursuit of Piquet which saw the Englishman's Williams-Honda surge through to snatch a brilliant victory with just over a lap to go, Senna found the 99T's aerodynamic shortcomings constraining his fuel consumption to the point where he could only finish in a lapped third place. In terms of comparative ability between Piquet, Mansell and Senna, that was absolutely nonsense and a savage indictment of the Lotus 99T's negative points.

As a footnote to the Lotus active suspension development, a host of complaints from drivers about the bumpy nature of the Mexico City circuit prompted Jean-Marie Balestre to host a press briefing for a handful of journalists at which he announced that active suspension would be banned as from the end of the season. As one of those writers present, I found myself recalling the episode in the Fawlty Towers television comedy series when John Cleese bangs his head firmly on the hotel reception counter and says, 'No, it's not a dream – we're stuck with it . . .'

A couple of us sought to point out, with suitable deference, that M le President had got his wires crossed, surely? It was the other way round . . . active suspension actually was better, safer even, over the bumps. Did M Balestre really mean that he was going to make active suspension compulsory? It would certainly have made more sense. Subsequently, it seems that Balestre told Lotus technical director, Gérard Ducarouge, that he had not said he was going to ban active suspension. Well, at least, not definitely. Nothing more was heard on the subject . . .

Despite the limitations of his Lotus-Honda's potential, Senna would retain a mathematical outside chance of winning the Championship all the way through to the Mexican Grand Prix. The last vestige of those hopes would evaporate in that event when, grappling with an inoperable clutch in third place, he locked his brakes and spun. When the marshals proved less than totally committed to giving him a push-start, he vented his fury by leaping from the cockpit and thumping one of them. Television cameras nearby picked up this little altercation and Senna was later fined $15,000 for his trouble . . .

It is hard to imagine Prost, or even Mansell, responding to disappointment in such a spontaneous hair-trigger fashion. An individual's behaviour under that sort of dramatically intense

Nelson Piquet and his Criticism of Williams

Nelson Piquet has always been a driver who liked to work away developing a technical advantage in private testing before springing it on his unwitting rivals without warning at the start of a Grand Prix. The way he harnessed the resources of the Williams team prior to the 1987 Italian Grand Prix is a classic example.

Although early, unsettling experiences with the Team Lotus active suspension system left his team-mate Nigel Mansell feeling distinctly lukewarm when confronted with a similar system at Williams, Piquet instantly saw the possibilities. During the week before the Monza race, he completed a race distance test at Imola taking over a minute off Mansell's race winning time established in the San Marino Grand Prix.

It was sufficient to convince Piquet that the reactive system should be raced at Monza, so while Mansell opted for a standard specification car, the Brazilian took the gamble. It paid off. He won from Senna's Lotus 99T – also fitted with computer-controlled suspension – and Mansell's Williams. It was a classic Piquet victory, achieved by guile and tactics rather than out-and-out speed.

By this time, though, Piquet had determined to leave Williams and join Lotus for 1988. He firmly believed that the team had not adhered to the fundamental nature of its agreement with him. The team fumbled the Drivers' Championship in 1986 and Piquet won it in 1987 possibly only because Mansell missed the last two races after crashing in practice at Suzuka.

'I didn't come into this team to compete with another driver,' Piquet insisted firmly. 'I had a contract as number one driver and they screwed up the whole thing. Technically they were the best team I worked with, but I didn't join them to apply my experience to setting up cars for a team-mate who then made it difficult for me to win races.'

pressure often provides a telling index of their underlying character. So it was with Senna, just as the same temperament had been revealed by Piquet back in 1982 when his Brabham-BMW tripped over tail-end-charlie Eliseo Salazar's ATS in the German Grand Prix and Nelson started kicking and punching the the hapless Salazar once they had both climbed from their cars.

Senna and Mansell were like-minded individuals in one crucial sense, namely their towering commitment and determination. Inevitably, perhaps, this was going to lead to the same sort of trouble as had been seen on the opening lap of the 1986 Brazilian Grand Prix. On the opening lap of the restarted Belgian Grand Prix at Spa, just such an incident took place.

The race was stopped after the opening lap following a collision between the Tyrrells of Philippe Streiff and Jonathan Palmer, Mansell having made easily the best start. Senna got away first at the restart and, when Mansell tried to ease inside him on a right-hander midway round the first lap, the two collided.

Senna spun off on the spot, becoming bogged down in a sand trap and taking no further part in the proceedings. Mansell's car sustained damage to its undertray and, although he resumed the chase, he eventually retired. Each blamed the other, predictably, and in the relative seclusion of the Lotus garage they squared up to each other, but the confrontation was happily defused by the intervention of the Lotus mechanics.

Mansell's progress with the Williams FW11B was superb for most of the season. In addition to his victory at Imola, Nigel added commanding victories at Paul Ricard, Silverstone, Osterreichring, Jerez and Mexico City to his tally. Yet Piquet's stealth and good fortune meant that the Brazilian went into the penultimate round of the title chase, in Japan, with an eight point lead over Mansell, even though his victory tally amounted to half that of his arch-rival.

Mansell drove the whole year with a tantalising blend of speed and daring, balancing on the fine line between success and disaster until he put a wheel slightly off-line during qualifying at Suzuka. That minuscule error of judgement produced a terrifying high-speed accident from which he was fortunate to emerge with excruciating painful back injuries which, thankfully, resulted in no long-term damage. But his championship challenge was spent and Piquet, standing in the Williams garage at Suzuka, realised that the mantle of a third world title had dropped on to his shoulders.

It was an unsatisfactory conclusion to a season which had also seen Prost win three races. Back in 1958, when Stirling Moss won four races and Tony Brooks three, Mike Hawthorn took the title with a single race victory to his credit. 'That's when I decided that the World Championship really did not mean an awful lot,' Brooks later reflected. Mansell could have been forgiven for sharing that view at the end of 1987.

On the other hand, the Piquet fans would echo their man's argument that, like it or not, success in the World Championship is all about stringing together a larger total of points than the next man. But, that said, Nelson's success in the 1987 Championship was as much down to good luck as Mansell's failure to win was down to bad.

It was all very well for Nelson to say that he took a strategic approach, knowing that Mansell would over-drive into retirement, but such an argument simply does not stand up to detailed scrutiny. It is difficult to say Mansell's retirements, at Monaco and in Hungary, were his own responsibility. They were due to a faulty weld on an exhaust pipe and a loose wheel retaining nut respectively. Accepted, Mansell's crash at Suzuka was his own fault, but up to that point he had clearly been quicker than Piquet, notwithstanding Nelson's attempts to drive him off the road during the Mexican Grand Prix.

It was in late August that Honda informed Williams that it would not be continuing to supply the team with engines through until the end of 1988, when the existing contract ran out. Honda and Williams have kept private the precise reasons behind this split, the Japanese company repeating the phrase, 'It was by mutual agreement', whenever asked to comment on the matter.

The concept of anybody – by mutual agreement – opting to use an unproved Judd V8 at a time when Honda's turbo V6 was riding the crest of the winning wave is asking the dispassionate commentator to believe in Father Christmas. But you can read in the next chapter the convoluted sequence of events leading up to the split.

Either way, when the international press corps sat down to be told by Honda's po-faced Formula 1 manager, Yoshitoshi Sakurai, that Williams were being dropped in favour of McLaren 'by mutual agreement' the announcement had a strangely unreal ring to it. Only an hour earlier, Mansell and Piquet had taken the front row of the Italian Grand Prix grid by storm with their Williams FW11Bs, so one was bound to wonder what McLaren could offer that Williams couldn't. The answer, it seemed, was Ayrton Senna. But that in itself would turn out to be something of a double-edged Samurai sword as events would subsequently prove.

Ferrari's apparent gain in competitiveness was in fact exaggerated by the fact that two out of the last four events took place on medium speed circuits (Estoril and Jerez), and, of course, Berger's task was made easier by there being no Mansell to tackle at Suzuka or Adelaide. There was a revised aerodynamic package for Hockenheim, the race which coincided with Harvey Postlethwaite's reappearance on the pit wall to engineer the cars in the field. Barnard, by now, had his head down at GTO, concentrating all his efforts on developing the type 639 concept, prototype of what would evolve into the 1989 3.5 litre V12 race car.

Only Berger's inexperience under acute pressure prevented him from fending off Prost's relentless advance at Estoril, but while both he and Alboreto abused their machinery quite dramatically in the Spanish Grand Prix at Jerez, Berger plucked that memorable victory from beneath Honda's nose in the Japanese race. Senna grabbed second place for Lotus-Honda on the last lap, displacing Johansson's McLaren, but it hardly compensated the Honda technicians for the sight of Piquet's Williams rolling into the pit lane with oil gushing from a terminally damaged engine. The highly-disciplined capacity crowd, which had camped outside the turnstiles all night to witness the first Japanese Grand Prix for ten years, could have been forgiven for not knowing what to make of this unexpected glitch . . .

Elsewhere in the turbo ranks, Ford's type TEC, Cosworth-built V6 was now installed in the back of a sleek, tailor-made Benetton B187, a partnership which prompted Williams designer Patrick Head to remark that he expected the team to win at least one

The Steve Nichols-designed Honda-engined McLaren MP4/4 won fifteen races in the final season of the turbo era.

Grand Prix during the course of the year. It was an understandably over-optimistic assessment.

The engine was moderately quick, although beset by major throttle response problems which were addressed by modifications to the Garrett turbos in time for Detroit. But neither Teo Fabi nor Thierry Boutsen were quite out of the top drawer and you really did need every variable in the Formula 1 book to be absolutely outstanding to cope with the Williams-Hondas and McLaren-TAGs during the 1987 season.

In general terms the engine proved highly promising, but Cosworth and Ford took the joint decision not to pursue the 2.5 bar/150 litre regulations for the final year of the turbo era, with the result that Benetton found itself using the great grandson of the DFV, the Cosworth-Ford DFR 3.5 litre naturally-aspirated V8, in 1988. In retrospect, Cosworth's ultra-conservative engineering approach allied to Ford's stop-go, will-we-won't-we ambivalence to its Formula 1 programme, resulted in the wrong route being pursued.

Of course, BMW was still on the scene, but it had become clear that the Munich company was pretty disillusioned with Brabham after the spectacular failure of the low-line BT55. Gordon Murray had now left to join McLaren, while BMW plodded on through the final season of its contract with the Ecclestone *equipe*. They continued supplying the 72 degree canted M12/13/1 engine, which was now installed in the more conventional BT56 chassis to be driven by Patrese and Andrea de Cesaris.

Rights to the 'upright' BMW engine had passed to the Arrows team, under the Megatron label, and these were also used by the Ligier team after plans to use Alfa Romeo's suckling 4 cylinder 415T engine fell into acrimonious disarray. After the semi-works Euroracing Alfa V8s had failed to score a single Championship point through 1985, the Italian team effectively took a sabbatical in 1986 as 415T engine designer Gianni Tonti developed what looked like quite a reasonable power unit.

Using a single KKK turbo installation, the Alfa 415T had a claimed output of 830bhp at 10,300rpm using 3.8 bar boost pressure and was intended for installation in the Ligier JS29 chassis as a fully stressed member. But whilst Arnoux made suitably encouraging noises about the new engine on its preliminary test outing, its continuing unreliability prompted a very different response from the Frenchman after an abortive Imola test uncomfortably close to the start of the 1987 season.

Unfortunately, Rene's remarks gained plenty of media coverage, causing Alfa Romeo to withdraw from the agreement after accusing the Frenchman of making unnecessarily disparaging remarks. Alfa must have breathed a sigh of corporate relief at being presented with such a convienient escape route, for Fiat management changes had now decreed that Ferrari would be the group's sole representative in the Formula 1 arena. Alfa's competition role was to field production saloon cars, Lancia's to mount an international rally programme.

Any lingering Alfa Romeo Formula 1 programme would seem embarrassingly out of line with this overall strategy. Court action followed, for Ligier was not to be placated with an interim, short-term supply arrangement while he made alternative plans. Like so many other partnerships in the Formula 1 milieu, this Franco-Italian alliance ended up benefiting nobody but the lawyers.

THE TURBO YEARS' RESULTS 1987

Winner's average speed

April 12, BRAZILIAN GRAND PRIX, Rio

1	Alain Prost	McLaren-TAG MP4/3 turbo	(114.699mph)
2	Nelson Piquet	Williams-Honda FW11B turbo	
3	Stefan Johansson	McLaren-TAG MP4/3 turbo	
4	Gerhard Berger	Ferrari F187 turbo	
5	Thierry Boutsen	Benetton-Ford B187 turbo	
6	Nigel Mansell	Williams-Honda FW11B turbo	

May 3, SAN MARINO GRAND PRIX, Imola

1	Nigel Mansell	Williams-Honda FW11B turbo	(121.29mph)
2	Ayrton Senna	Lotus-Honda 99T turbo	
3	Michele Alboreto	Ferrari F187 turbo	
4	Stefan Johansson	McLaren-TAG MP4/3 turbo	
5	Martin Brundle	Zakspeed 871 turbo	
6	Satoru Nakajima	Lotus-Honda 99T turbo	

May 17, BELGIAN GRAND PRIX, Spa

1	Alain Prost	McLaren-TAG MP4/3 turbo	(127.8mph)
2	Stefan Johansson	McLaren-TAG MP4/3 turbo	
3	Andrea de Cesaris	Brabham-BMW BT56 turbo	
4	Eddie Cheever	Arrows-Megatron A10 turbo	
5	Satoru Nakajima	Lotus-Honda 99T turbo	
6	René Arnoux	Ligier-Megatron JS29 turbo	

May 31, MONACO GRAND PRIX, Monte Carlo

1	Ayrton Senna	Lotus-Honda 99T turbo	(82.08mph)
2	Nelson Piquet	Williams-Honda FW11B turbo	
3	Michele Alboreto	Ferrari F187 turbo	
4	Gerhard Berger	Ferrari F187 turbo	
5	Jonathan Palmer	Tyrrell-Cosworth DG/016	
6	Ivan Capelli	March-Cosworth 871	

June 21, DETROIT GRAND PRIX, Michigan

1	Ayrton Senna	Lotus-Honda 99T turbo	(85.69mph)
2	Nelson Piquet	Williams-Honda FW11B turbo	
3	Alain Prost	McLaren-TAG MP4/3 turbo	
4	Gerhard Berger	Ferrari F187 turbo	
5	Nigel Mansell	Williams-Honda FW11B turbo	
6	Eddie Cheever	Arrows-Megatron A10 turbo	

July 5, FRENCH GRAND PRIX, Paul Ricard

1	Nigel Mansell	Williams-Honda FW11B turbo	(117.16mph)
2	Nelson Piquet	Williams-Honda FW11B turbo	
3	Alain Prost	McLaren-Honda MP4/3 turbo	
4	Ayrton Senna	Lotus-Honda 99T turbo	
5	Teo Fabi	Benetton-Ford B187 turbo	
6	Philippe Streiff	Tyrrell-Cosworth DG/016	

July 12, BRITISH GRAND PRIX, Silverstone
1	Nigel Mansell	Williams-Honda FW11B turbo	(146.2mph)
2	Nelson Piquet	Williams-Honda FW11B turbo	
3	Ayrton Senna	Lotus-Honda 99T turbo	
4	Satoru Nakajima	Lotus-Honda 99T turbo	
5	Derek Warwick	Arrows-Megatron A10 turbo	
6	Teo Fabi	Benetton-Ford B187 turbo	

June 26, GERMAN GRAND PRIX, Hockenheim
1	Nelson Piquet	Williams-Honda FW11B	(136.94mph)
2	Stefan Johansson	McLaren-TAG MP4/3 turbo	
3	Ayrton Senna	Lotus-Honda 99T turbo	
4	Philippe Streiff	Tyrrell-Cosworth DG/016	
5	Jonathan Palmer	Tyrrell-Cosworth DG/016	
6	Philippe Alliot	Lola-Cosworth LC87	

August 9, HUNGARIAN GRAND PRIX, Budapest
1	Nelson Piquet	Williams-Honda FW11B turbo	(95.21mph)
2	Ayrton Senna	Lotus-Honda 99T turbo	
3	Alain Prost	McLaren-TAG MP4/3 turbo	
4	Thierry Boutsen	Benetton-Ford B187 turbo	
5	Riccardo Patrese	Brabham-BMW BT56 turbo	
6	Derek Warwick	Arrows-Megatron A10 turbo	

August 16, AUSTRIAN GRAND PRIX, Osterreichring
1	Nigel Mansell	Williams-Honda FW11B turbo	(146.28mph)
2	Nelson Piquet	Williams-Honda FW11B turbo	
3	Teo Fabi	Benetton-Ford B187 turbo	
4	Thierry Boutsen	Benetton-Ford B187 turbo	
5	Ayrton Senna	Lotus-Honda 99T turbo	
6	Alain Prost	McLaren-TAG MP4/3 turbo	

September 6, ITALIAN GRAND PRIX, Monza
1	Nelson Piquet	Williams-Honda FW11B turbo	(144.55mph)
2	Ayrton Senna	Lotus-Renault 99T turbo	
3	Nigel Mansell	Williams-Honda FW11B	
4	Gerhard Berger	Ferrari F187 turbo	
5	Thierry Boutsen	Benetton-Ford B187 turbo	
6	Stefan Johansson	McLaren-TAG MP4/3 turbo	

September 21, PORTUGUESE GRAND PRIX, Estoril
1	Alain Prost	McLaren-TAG MP4/3 turbo	(116.95mph)
2	Gerhard Berger	Ferrari F187 turbo	
3	Nelson Piquet	Williams-Honda FW11B turbo	
4	Teo Fabi	Benetton-Ford B187 turbo	
5	Stefan Johansson	McLaren-TAG MP4/3 turbo	
6	Eddie Cheever	Arrows-Megatron A10 turbo	

September 27, SPANISH GRAND PRIX, Jerez
1	Nigel Mansell	Williams-Honda FW11B turbo	(103.67mph)
2	Alain Prost	McLaren-TAG MP4/3 turbo	
3	Stefan Johansson	McLaren-TAG MP4/3 turbo	
4	Nelson Piquet	Williams-Honda FW11B turbo	
5	Ayrton Senna	Lotus-Honda 99T turbo	
6	Philippe Alliot	Lola-Cosworth LC87	

October 18, MEXICAN GRAND PRIX, Mexico City

1	Nigel Mansell	Williams-Honda FW11B turbo	(120.17mph)
2	Nelson Piquet	Williams-Honda FW11B turbo	
3	Riccardo Patrese	Brabham-BMW BT56 turbo	
4	Eddie Cheever	Arrows-Megatron A10 turbo	
5	Teo Fabi	Benetton-Ford B187 turbo	
6	Philippe Alliot	Lola-Cosworth LC87	

November 1, JAPANESE GRAND PRIX, Suzuka

1	Gerhard Berger	Ferrari F187 turbo	(119.82mph)
2	Ayrton Senna	Lotus-Honda 99T turbo	
3	Stefan Johansson	McLaren-TAG MP4/3 turbo	
4	Michele Alboreto	Ferrari F187 turbo	
5	Thierry Boutsen	Benetton-Ford B87 turbo	
6	Satoru Nakajima	Lotus-Honda 99T turbo	

November 15, AUSTRALIAN GRAND PRIX, Adelaide

1	Gerhard Berger	Ferrari F187 turbo	(102.299mph)
2	Michele Alboreto	Ferrari F187 turbo	
3	Thierry Boutsen	Benetton-Ford B87 turbo	
4	Jonathan Palmer	Tyrrell-Cosworth DG/016	
5	Yannick Dalmas	Lola-Cosworth LC87	
6	Roberto Moreno	AGS-Cosworth JH22	

DRIVERS' WORLD CHAMPIONSHIP

Posn	Driver	Points
1	Nelson Piquet	73
2	Nigel Mansell	61
3	Ayrton Senna	57
4	Alain Prost	46
5	Gerhard Berger	36
6	Stefan Johansson	30
7	Michele Alboreto	17
8	Thierry Boutsen	16
9	Teo Fabi	12
10	Eddie Cheever	8
11	Jonathan Palmer	7
	Satoru Nakajima	
13	Riccardo Patrese	6
14	Andrea de Cesaris	4
	Philippe Streiff	
16	Derek Warwick	3
	Philippe Alliot	
18	Martin Brundle	2
19	René Arnoux	1
	Ivan Capelli	
	Roberto Moreno	

CONSTRUCTORS' CHAMPIONSHIP

Posn	Constructor	Points
1	Williams	137
2	McLaren	76
3	Lotus	64
4	Ferrari	53
5	Benetton	28
6	Tyrrell	11
	Arrows	
8	Brabham	10
9	Lola	3
10	Zakspeed	2
11	March	1
	Ligier	
	AGS	

1988

John Watson recalls attending a dinner party in Germany hosted by Mercedes-Benz public relations man, Gerd Cramer, during 1987 at which he found himself in conversation with Ayrton Senna. The Brazilian was working out his final season at Team Lotus prior to joining McLaren for 1988, so the conversation inevitably worked round to Ayrton's future prospects. Logically, the question of how Ayrton would handle Alain Prost, McLaren's sitting tenant, also came up.

Watson, drawing on his experience of dealing with Niki Lauda, offered Senna his view that the best way to beat Prost would be by stealth rather than engineering a head-to-head confrontation. Ayrton listened politely, but then surprised John by telling him, in no uncertain terms, that he had other ideas.

'He told me that he would beat Prost by being fitter, more motivated and more dedicated,' John recalls, obviously impressed. 'He said he would make sure he was in a position to drive faster, more consistently, for longer than Prost could do. He meant to beat him convincingly from the front. I remember thinking, well, that seems a little optimistic!'

For the 1988 season, it was not just a question of Senna being with McLaren, it was the prospect of Honda supplying their engines to the powerful British team that worried the hell out of the opposition. It was widely forecast that the turbos, now strangulated with 2.5 bar boost pressure and limited to only 150 litres of fuel, would be outclassed by the faster naturally-aspirated cars, but this theory turned out to be an illusion.

It might have been different had, say, Renault or Ferrari come forward with their new generation 3.5 litre multi-cylinder engines in time for the 1988 Championship battle, but, as it was, there were no truly advanced atmospheric engines available. In reality, there was little chance of Cosworth's DFR (used by Benetton) or the Judd CV V8 (shared by Williams, March and Ligier) producing the necessary power, no matter how agile or efficient the chassis in which they were installed.

Of course, the McLaren team's alliance with Honda had taken over a year to get into place. After witnessing the Williams débâcle at Adelaide at the end of 1986, when Nigel Mansell and

*Family snap. McLaren Old Boys'
Reunion in the foyer of the team's
Woking factory, early 1988.* From left
to right, *James Hunt, Keke
Rosberg, John Watson, Stefan
Johansson and Alain Prost.*

Nelson Piquet fumbled a vital catch and allowed the World Championship to fall into Alain Prost's lap like an over-ripe plum, Sochiro Honda returned to Japan very much in two minds about his feelings towards Frank Williams's team.

It had been privately speculated ever since Frank's near-fatal road accident that Honda may have become uncomfortable about the prospect of a paraplegic running its front-line Grand Prix operation. In reality, of course, the operation of a Formula 1 team in the 1980s had expanded far beyond the scope of one key individual and Williams had a sound management structure in place long before Frank was incapacitated. But, either way, Honda certainly felt a degree of unease, exacerbated by the failure of either Williams driver to take the Drivers' title.

Now Honda sent out the word: 'get Alain Prost at all costs'. This more or less coincided with Ron Dennis concluding that the days of the TAG turbo project were numbered. It was all very well to employ Porsche as a sub-contractor, and there could be no doubting the excellence of the German-built turbocharged engines which propelled Lauda and Prost to a hat-trick of Championship titles. But Honda's involvement in Grand Prix racing reminded Dennis very forcibly that a hand-in-glove partnership with a major motor manufacturer was the best way to attack the future.

Towards the end of 1987, Frank Williams began dropping hints that it looked as though Honda would be supplying three teams the following year – his own, Lotus and McLaren. Prost and

Dennis journeyed to Tokyo for preliminary discussions on the matter, but the arrangement fell through. In the meantime, Honda had attempted to foist their nominee Satoru Nakajima on the Williams team, but the management would have none of it, Frank and Patrick Head taking the view that it was the team's responsibility to recruit the drivers they felt were best capable of gaining success. With the best will in the world, Nakajima did not fill this particular bill.

The deal came to nothing for 1987, although pinpointing the precise reason is no easy task. Dennis had said that, by waiting another year, they got a better deal out of Honda involving an exclusive engine supply agreement for 1989. Other sources have hinted that McLaren's managing director was a little too brusque for the Japanese company's taste. Either way, Prost was probably in his strongest position vis-a-vis Honda at this stage in the story, perhaps even capable of steering future events very much more to his advantage than they would eventually unfold.

McLaren remained with TAG turbo power for another season while Piquet headed for his third Championship title. But Prost's advantage in Honda's eyes was now diluted by the quite extraordinary technical and personal rapport which developed between the Japanese company and Ayrton Senna during his one season driving the Lotus 99T. By the time Ayrton concluded that there was no future for him with Lotus, Ron Dennis had him firmly targeted in McLaren's sights. Or, as has intriguingly been suggested, Senna had McLaren targeted in his sights – and wanted Honda to join him in a partnership with what he regarded as the best team in the Formula 1 business. In other words, was Senna calling the shots?

At the start of 1987, McLaren's new technical director, Gordon Murray, canvassed strongly to get Nelson Piquet included in the team alongside the French driver. Murray had worked with Nelson for many years and retained a high regard for the Brazilian driver who had also built up a satisfactory working relationship with Honda throughout 1986, to the point where he was perceived as 'their man'. Mansell, who had perhaps been too candid for his own good when it came to publicly highlighting what he regarded as Honda's shortcomings, had definitely become alienated from them.

Prost made it extremely clear that, notwithstanding Murray's high regard for Piquet, he was the one driver that he specifically did not want to drive alongside him at McLaren. Alain has kept his peace on this matter, reluctant to raise specific objections on the subject. However, I understand that from my researches that Marlboro's John Hogan, the key man behind the contemporary Philip Morris motor racing involvement, cared little for the cut of

Riccardo Patrese was Formula 1's one-time enfant terrible, but by the end of the 1980s the Italian had proved himself much underrated, asserting himself as an accomplished and consistent performer.

Nelson's jib and was also implacably opposed to his joining McLaren.

Back in 1978, Piquet ran a handful of races as a Formula 1 newcomer in a Marlboro-backed McLaren M23, fielded by an independent team, and fell out with Hogan at this early stage when, having agreed to join the late Ronnie Peterson in the planned 1979 McLaren line-up, he is alleged to have changed his mind and signed for Brabham. This resulted in the Marlboro door being slammed very firmly behind him for, alone amongst the top line drivers of the 1980s, Piquet never again came close to a Marlboro personal contract, let alone the chance of joining one of their sponsored teams.

When Senna came on to the scene, Prost raised no objection at all, perhaps feeling he could hardly raise any more objections. But there must have been times over the following couple of years when he wished he had raised objections to Senna's arrival. Of course, as far as the Piquet veto was concerned, it was not a case of McLaren bowing to Alain's every whim, merely a sane and sensible strategy to keep a good relationship with the man who had won them a record number of races since the start of 1984. As things turned out, Piquet was quickly snapped up by Team Lotus the moment Senna's lawyer informed the Norfolk-based team that his client would not be staying on for 1988.

For Lotus, this seemed at first glance, something of a master stroke. Piquet arrived on their doorstep as reigning World Champion, one of Honda's golden boys. He was finally rid of the internecine battles with the demonstrably faster Mansell which had spoiled his spell driving for Williams. Recalling the way in which he thrived during his heyday at Brabham, where the team was moulded round him alone, supported by a makeweight number two driver, many expected him to become revitalized in his new position. Honda nominee Satoru Nakajima, continuing as Lotus number two for a second season, would prove no threat.

Taking a broad over-view, grabbing Piquet may have looked like a major political coup which ensured a continued supply of Honda engines for another year. But, to judge by the dejected faces amongst some of the engineering personnel the weekend after they learned they would be losing Senna, if taking Piquet meant keeping Honda engines most would have opted to forego that privilege. Keeping Senna, even with a Judd V8 engine, would have been preferable in their eyes for 1988.

There were only four serious turbo teams in 1988: McLaren and Lotus using the RA168E version of Honda's 80 degree twin V6; Ferrari, with the latest development of its 90 degree V6; and Arrows with the Megatron-badged BMW M12/13 4 cylinder prepared exclusively by Swiss engine specialist Heini Mader. The

They seek him here, they seek him there ... The compact, dynamic and influential Bernard Ecclestone leans against Ken Tyrrell's transporter whilst chatting with Arrows team director Jack Oliver.

previous year the turbos had been permitted 4 bar boost and 195 litres of fuel. Now the fuel allowance was being slashed by a draconian 23 per cent, so the number one priority became a correspondingly dramatic improvement in fuel efficiency.

Honda also attempted to enhance its turbo response by the use of such refinements as ceramic turbine wheels and opted for a bore and stroke of 79 × 50.8mm, the former being quite long for a racing engine. In conjunction with a compression ratio of 9.4:1 and almost flat-headed pistons, an extremely compact combustion chamber was produced which made a major contribution towards the sought-after fuel efficiency.

Inevitably, the Honda engine management system was developed to its most sophisticated and complex with the intake air temperature being of absolutely paramount importance to the efficient functioning of the engine. The temperature of the air flowing into the engine was controlled as close to 40°C as possible by opening the intercooler's by-pass valve at the appropriate moment. There was also a temperature control system which utilised a heat exchanger fed by water from the cooling system, the flow controlled by a solenoid valve.

The amount of fuel remaining in the tank at any point in the race was calculated by a computer and displayed to the driver throughout the event, enabling Senna and Prost to select the correct balance of boost pressure, intake air temperature, fuel temperature and air/fuel mix during the course of the race. The maximum power output developed by the Honda RA168E engine during the course of the year was a quite remarkable 685bhp, and even in conditions of marginal fuel consumption produced around the 620bhp mark. With Ferrari never getting on top of its fuel consumption problems and the best Cosworth DFR developing in the region of 585bhp, the McLaren-Honda partnership was set fair from the outset.

Another winter of intensive development work saw Honda produce a smaller diameter clutch which enabled the crankshaft level to be dropped by 28mm, McLaren matching this by introducing a three-axis gearbox which raised the drive line sufficiently to facilitate an efficient upswept aerodynamic rear undertray, as well as reducing potentially wearing driveshaft angularity. Lotus, by contrast, were strapped for cash and unable to finance such an elaborate new transmission; they opted to angle the entire engine/transmission package towards the rear. It proved a far less effective solution.

Although John Barnard was by this stage long gone from the McLaren stage, he had left a fine legacy of design methodology and it was no surprise that the Woking-based chassis design team, led by Steve Nichols, produced a package which bore a strong

Dawn of an explosive new partnership. McLaren-Honda team-mates Ayrton Senna and Alain Prost shake hands across test driver Emanuele Pirro for the purposes of a publicity shot prior to the 1988 season. McLaren boss Ron Dennis cunningly arranged it so Ayrton would stand on the left, his right arm thereby blanking out his personal sponsorship patch below the Honda identification on his stomach!

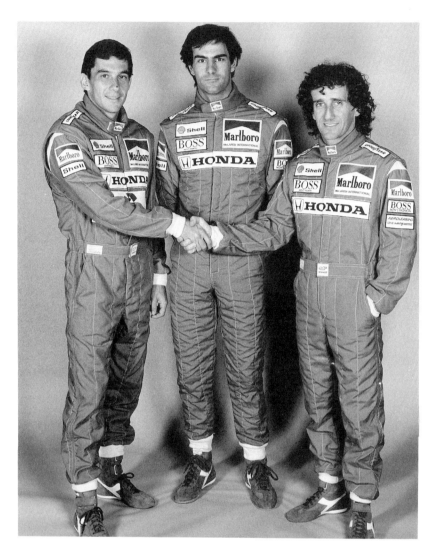

generic likeness to the TAG-propelled cars which had gone before, but incorporating a sharply reclined driving position as pioneered by Gordon Murray in the Brabham BT55 concept.

The first Honda engine tests were carried out with an adapted MP4/3, one of the chassis used by Prost and Stefan Johansson throughout the 1987 season. This adaptation was a bigger job than it might have seemed from the outside, because switching from the 'twin 3 cylinder' configuration of the TAG to the Honda V6 with its common induction tract, oil and water systems for both banks of cylinders called for an enormous amount of chassis re-plumbing.

One can only speculate how McLaren might have fared with

the TAG turbo running under the 2.5 bar, 150 litre regulations. In that connection, it is interesting to record that, in a 2.5 bar test, the Porsche-built V6 developed more power than the team ever saw from the Honda RA168E, although the fuel consumption figures with its relatively low compression head did not look so promising. But the Bosch and Porsche personnel privately felt that this was a problem that could have been surmounted had not the engine been destined for museum duties.

Those teams running turbocharged cars into this transitional season were permitted to use their 1987 machines, as long as these were materially unchanged and – crucially – featured the same engine mountings as those used in the last three races of the 1987 season. Interestingly, not only did Ferrari, Arrows, Zakspeed and Osella indicate their intention to avail themselves of this rule, but McLaren also considered doing likewise.

At one point the TAG turbo-engined MP4/3s were to have run the final races of the 1987 season fitted with additional engine mounts to cater for the Honda engine. This would have covered the unlikely eventuality of perhaps having to race these older cars, fitted with Honda engines, at the start of 1988 should any unforeseen problems have arisen with the new MP4/4. In the event, the idea was not pursued.

Ayrton Senna: an Enigmatic Champion

When rumours that Ayrton Senna might retire from racing at the end of the 1989 season swept the paddock at Jerez during that year's Spanish Grand Prix, it was Martin Brundle who reflected the blend of frustration and awe which the Brazilian driver exerted over his peers.

'I wish he bloody well would push off back to Brazil,' said Brundle. 'It might give the rest of us a chance ... there's no question about it, he's a great driver, damn him!' Truth was, Senna had become the most admired and resented man in the paddock. Admired for his towering skill, resented for the iconoclastic approach he brought to bear on his racing. Here was a man who conformed to none of the familiar stereotypes attaching to a top-line Grand Prix driver. People disliked his ascetic personality, the tight rein he held over his emotions.

Senna was the product of a close-knit Brazilian family upbringing in Sao Paulo, privileged in both the emotional and material sense. His father was a wealthy and successful businessman who clearly managed to balance the challenge of making a fortune with providing a secure home base for his offspring. In turn, their eldest son's appreciation of his parents' contribution to his considerable success became the most attractive feature of a complicated, private character.

Study all the contemporary group photographs of Grand Prix drivers taken during the second half of the 1980s. Ayrton is present, but seems to stand apart. He looks nervous, perhaps not aloof, but definitely not one of the boys. For better or worse, he carved a lone niche as a unique individualist.

Yet, out on the race track, he displayed no such insecurities. If anything, his consummate skill triggered an over-confidence which produced as many accidents as Grand Prix victories. His was a rare, if uniquely flawed, talent.

Such an option was not available to entrants pursuing the new 3.5 litre naturally-aspirated regulations, all of whom had to build brand new chassis in which the pedals had to be positioned behind the front axle line. For this new breed of chassis, a static impact test was also stipulated for the side of the cockpit and fuel cell areas, in addition to the established test involving a frontal impact on the nose box. As a totally new turbo contender, the McLaren MP4/4 was also subject to these revised constructional requirements.

The non-turbo brigade also theoretically benefited from a 500kg minimum weight limit, some 40kg below that set for the turbos. Yet there was a delightful paradox implicit in these new regulations which would help tilt the balance in favour of the McLaren-Hondas. A 150 litre fuel capacity meant that they would be carrying a significantly lighter fuel load than the naturally-aspirated cars, most of which were going to need in the region of 200 litres to perform over the average race distance, thereby negating much of their notional weight advantage.

The way in which the 1988 season developed was destined to be somewhat embarassing for Jean-Marie Balestre. Some eighteen months earlier, he had presided over a meeting of Formula 1 designers at Estoril during the 1986 Portuguese Grand Prix weekend where FISA's so-called 'strategy' for phasing out turbo power over the ensuing two seasons was disclosed.

'I promise you, gentlemen, in 1988 there will be no way for the turbos,' he announced majestically. As things turned out,

Right and opposite: *The imposing headquarters of the TAG/McLaren team in Woking, Surrey, from where the McLaren-Hondas sallied forth to win the 1988 and 1989 Constructors' Championship in overwhelming style. The foyer contains many of its greatest racing cars.*

there would be no way for anything but. Another case of egg on the face for the FISA president...

As usual, McLaren kept the opposition waiting until the last possible moment before showing its hand. The definitive MP4/4 was tested for the first time at Imola only ten days prior to the start of first qualifying for the Brazilian Grand Prix. Instantly, it caused a sensation. The official lap record had been established by Nelson Piquet on 1min 28.667sec, set at the wheel of an 'unrestricted boost' Williams-Honda FW11 in 1986.

Now, with substantially less power, but admittedly two years additional aerodynamic refinement, both Senna and Prost were lapping the MP4/4 in the low 1min 28sec bracket straight out of the box. There were problems, though, consequent on the new 2.5 bar boost limit. Whereas in 1987 the 4 bar limit was sustained by a straightforward valve which would open and bleed off excess pressure, the new French-made 'blow down' valves used in 1988 displayed different characteristics altogether.

From now on it became fairly disastrous to trip the boost

Frugal Fuel Consumption: a Crucial Factor

The basic requirements of a Grand Prix fuel are that it should combine good combustion performance, resistance to detonation, close control of temperature within the combustion chambers, excellent throttle response and adequate fuel efficiency. The need for these qualities in abundance was considerably enhanced by the 150 litre fuel capacity maximum prevailing during 1988. Working in close collaboration with Honda, Shell successfully developed a product to meet those wide-ranging requirements.

In general terms, it is worth bearing in mind that the difference between an engine running on ordinary fuel and tailor-made Formula 1 fuel can be as much as 10bhp. This additional output is achieved by the selective harnessing of the 200 or so hydrocarbons which are present in commercial fuel.

In 1988, under such draconian capacity restrictions, the priority was for high density fuel which would unlock as much energy per litre as possible. The easy route to boost power was perceived to be by using nitro-compounds, alcohols or other power-enhancing additives, but these have been specifically prohibited by the regulations for several years.

The use of aromatics was a major factor in achieving the desired result, these also offering extremely good combustion and anti-knock performance in turbocharged engines.

---

control valve, so much so that Honda installed a secondary valve within the inlet tract which was tripped before the FISA valve. If the 'official' valve was opened, a massive loss of boost pressure ensued before it closed. This would then take a couple of seconds to build up again, in contrast to the effect of the 4 bar valve which was more akin to that of a rev limiter.

There was also the question of 'pressure spikes' to be dealt with; these were surges of boost pressure which would build up in the inlet logue when the drivers were off the throttle, with the result that the driver found himself with no power when he went back on to the loud pedal. To cure this problem, Honda revised their inlet system mid-season, moving the throttle butterflies to the tube between the intercooler and the inlet logue, upstream from the valve, and the problem was solved.

Senna stole the show during qualifying at Rio, predictably taking pole position, although Nigel Mansell's efforts with the new reactive suspension Williams-Judd FW12 initially suggested that a good, naturally-aspirated 3.5 litre machine might keep the McLarens on their toes. Mansell lapped a mere 0.6sec slower than Senna, pushing Prost back to the second row. But this had been achieved by dint of a truly mighty effort on the part of the Englishman, one of those laps which make onlookers hold their breath. It was doubtful whether he could keep up that sort of pace in race conditions.

Senna's efforts to win in front of his home crowd were thwarted on the parade lap when his McLaren's gear linkage went awry, but he shrewdly led the pack back on to the grid before throwing his hands into the air, resulting in an aborted start which gave him a second chance. He duly took the second start from the pit lane at the wheel of the spare MP4/4, but was later deemed to have changed cars after the green flag was shown, so he was duly black-flagged out of the race after 30 laps.

Prost, meanwhile, drove serenely away to lead every lap, his delicate touch on the abrasive Rio track surface enabling him to survive the race with only one routine tyre change, as opposed to the two each needed by Gerhard Berger's Ferrari and Nelson Piquet's Lotus 100T, second and third place finishers in his wake. Berger subsequently remarked that, by the end of the Rio race, he had come to terms with the futility of the task which lay ahead of him throughout 1988.

'Alain was about twelve seconds ahead with fifteen laps to go when I started to make my counter-attack,' he remembers. 'I reckoned I was in a slightly stronger position because I'd made my second stop and had fresher rubber than he did. I set the fastest lap of the race, but Alain just speeded up. That's when I realised just what a difficult job Ferrari was facing . . .'

Piquet complained that his new Lotus 100T understeered too much, but he was not too dejected. Not yet, at least. Mansell's Williams ran briefly third, eventually succumbing to engine overheating, after heat, radiated from the exhaust system, melted a plastic sleeve protecting a lead from the ignition box during a

After BMW withdrew from Formula 1 at the end of the 1987 season, the upright M12/13 4 cylinder units continued in service with the Arrows team through to the end of the turbo era. The Megatron badging reflects the outside funding which under-pinned the Arrows team's technical programme.

The Ducarouge-inspired Lotus 100T should have given Lotus a great chance of getting on terms with McLaren, sharing as it did the same RA168E 2.5 bar turbo V6. But its aerodynamic qualities were seriously lacking, leading to a thoroughly disheartening season for Nelson Piquet (right).

Below: British rising star Johnny Herbert tests the car at Monza a week before breaking his ankles in a Formula 3000 accident at Brands Hatch.

pit stop. The lead short-circuited, defying all attempts to restart the engine.

The die was cast, although Piquet and Lotus were not about to capitulate at this early stage in the year. As they pointed out with some frustration, they had the same Honda engine, for heaven's sake, as McLaren. It was not possible to be so far off the pace. But they were . . .

Prior to the start of the European season at Imola, Senna crashed one of the McLaren MP4/4s during a test at Monza where Piquet concluded that he and Lotus had finally worked out a chassis set-up which would prove a match for the McLarens at the next race. Again, this would prove to be an illusion. Piquet ran to third place in the San Marino Grand Prix, but was lapped by Senna and Prost who finished in 1-2 formation. It just did not seem possible.

A matter of days later, Honda privately told Lotus that they would not be continuing their engine supply agreement for 1989, although for some reason both parties subsequently engaged in a bewildering charade, lasting many months, each saying that no decision had yet been reached. It was only when former Williams aerodynamicist Frank Dernie joined Team Lotus at the end of the year to design the new Judd V8-engined car for 1989 that the true shortcomings of the Lotus 100T became identified.

Dernie quickly concluded that the Lotus-Honda's aerodynamics had been lacking, due at least in part to erroneous test results produced in an incorrectly calibrated wind tunnel employed on a contract basis by the team. Of course, Gerard Ducarouge, Lotus's technical director for the previous five years, carried the can for this failure and left the team at the end of 1988.

There was not much about aerodynamics anybody could teach Dernie, who had been responsible for setting up the Williams team in-house wind tunnel almost a decade earlier, so his conclusions could hardly be challenged. Significantly, early in his design regime, the ex-Williams man would transfer the team's aerodynamic development programme to a fresh location.

Such retrospective reassurance could hardly compensate for Team Lotus's catastrophic 1988 season, of course, and Piquet reacted badly to finding himself in an uncompetitive situation, as team manager Peter Warr explained:

'With Nelson, we found ourselves dealing with a very different driver from Senna. During his years with Brabham and Williams, he had thrived on testing behind the scenes, developing a competitive edge, be it connected with the engine or chassis performance, and then going out on to the starting grid knowing that he could look across at the guy next to him in the knowledge that he had the potential to beat him even before the green light came on. We proved unable to offer Nelson that sort of leg-up, so he became slightly dejected by it all.'

Piquet, in truth, seldom looked better than his car and the momentum of the Lotus effort dwindled as the season wore on. The McLarens, meanwhile, took the season by its throat and never relinquished their grasp . . .

Prost won three out of the first four races. After Rio, he played second fiddle at Imola, won Monaco after Senna crashed, and beat his team-mate in Mexico City where the Brazilian ended the day concerned at higher-than-expected fuel consumption. The luck ran with the McLaren teamsters too; only after the finish in Mexico was a discarded 'tear off' visor strip from another driver's helmet found lodged in one of his McLaren's radiator ducts. That explained the ominously high water temperature which alarmed Alain so much in the closing stages of the race . . .

In the North American races, at Montreal and Detroit, Senna was absolutely in a class of his own when it came to ducking through traffic, particularly during qualifying when it is necessary to run absolutely on the limit to achieve a handful of really quick laps. Prost, with two World Championships and many more Grand Prix wins than had Senna already under his belt, could not motivate himself to take such risks, but there was no doubting his ability as a racer once the green light came on.

In Montreal, Prost got the jump on his team-mate at the start, but Senna eventually elbowed his way through by dint of a heart-stopping out-braking run manoeuvre up the inside of the other McLaren as they went into the tight, narrow hairpin. It was a move which reminded onlookers very forcibly of that pulled by Alan Jones on Gilles Villeneuve at the same point nine years earlier. And those two were driving for rival teams . . .

Detroit saw Senna score a hat trick of victories on this tricky street circuit, the McLaren team utterly depressing its rivals by going to the line with only 140 litres of fuel in their tanks – 10 litres less than they were permitted – and still destroying the opposition. Prost hated Detroit more than any other circuit on the Grand Prix trail. He inquired plaintively: 'Why do we have to race in this awful place when there are so many splendid race tracks in the US?'

Nobody had any immediate answer, but Prost later admitted he was happy to come out of this US street race with second place. His individualistic driving style, which involved turning into towards the apex of a tight corner with the brakes still applied, before releasing them and immediately returning his right foot to the throttle, was simply not practicable on a circuit where the track surface was crumbling. The build-up of gravel off-line made anything but braking and downchanging in a straight line potentially treacherous. Prost did his best to adapt, but to limited effect. He was just glad it was over.

Throughout the summer of 1988, the complexities of the relationship between Prost and Senna came to monopolise the headlines far more than the technical domination of the McLaren-Honda alliance. If that seemed unfair, it was merely a reflection of an inevitable trend. With media interest in Formula 1 running at an unprecedented level, it was personalities rather than machines which grasped the headlines.

In truth, McLaren made quite a fuss of Senna, going out of their way to nanny him in his new environment. That in itself provided a crucial key to the man's character. Although his outwardly cool countenance would earn him the 'Ice Man' soubriquet from many quarters, in reality Senna's genius was akin to a volcano on the verge of erupting. Once the lava flow was unleashed, there was every chance it could run out of control.

To get the best out of this overwhelmingly gifted young man, McLaren had to keep him simmering just below boiling point. And because he was so intensely wrapped up in his chosen profession, insulating him from the stifling commercial and media pressures away from the cockpit became as much a priority as providing him with competitive machinery. Senna was unquestion-

Return of the 'atmos'. The final season of the turbo era saw the re-introduction of naturally-aspirated cars, now with 3.5 litre engines. Here three essentially interim-engined 'specials' keep ahead of Gerhard Berger's stifled 2.5 bar Ferrari F187/88C during the 1988 Spanish Grand Prix at Jerez. They are Riccardo Patrese (Williams FW12-Judd V8), Ivan Capelli (March 881-Judd V8) and Alessandro Nannini (Benetton B188-Cosworth DFR V8).

ably a thoroughbred, but with all the moody temperament that label implies . . .

Getting a perspective on his relationship with Prost has become a fascinating exercises in retrospective analysis. That task has preoccupied those responsible for chronicling the Grand Prix scene during the two turbulent seasons in which this pair of great drivers raced together in the McLaren line-up. Even by the middle of the 1988 season, one could detect trouble coming, although circumstances obliged Prost to take a strategically deferential role towards the end of the summer.

After returning to Europe 'determined to go on to the attack', Prost scored a splendid victory from pole position in the French Grand Prix at Paul Ricard. But after this morale-boosting home triumph, Alain was forced to take a back seat as Senna reeled off four commanding consecutive victories at Silverstone, Hockenheim, Budapest and Spa. The Championship seemed all but over. Even Alain conceded, after the Belgian race, that it would be virtually impossible to catch Senna in the title chase. In effect, he doffed his cap to the new World Champion.

The men to beat in 1988, McLaren drivers Alain Prost and Ayrton Senna, confer with Honda technicians including Formula 1 project leader Osamu Goto (left foreground) who was the key engineer behind the development of the RA168E 2.5 bar turbo and the RA109E 3.5 litre V10 naturally-aspirated engine which replaced it in 1989.

At Monza, Senna made a crucial driving error which almost cost him a shot at the Championship. After Prost suffered a rare retirement with engine failure, Ayrton found himself well in the lead, but extremely marginal on fuel consumption, his advantage being gobbled up by the Ferraris of Berger and Michele Alboreto. On the penultimate lap, he collided with Formula 1 novice Jean-Louis Schlesser who was deputising for an unwell Nigel Mansell at the wheel of a Williams-Judd. The Brazilian ended the race straddling a kerb, handing a popular victory to Berger and ruining the possible symmetry of a grand slam, sixteen wins out of sixteen races for McLaren.

If I seem to labour this point in isolation, it is because I believe that it put on very public display a chink in Senna's armour. This deficiency would surface with increasing frequency throughout 1989 and play a major part in his failure to retain the Championship title which, after all, he would snatch from Prost's grasp in the last season of the turbo era.

Behind the wheel of a Grand Prix car, Senna increasingly displayed an arrogance which took little account of what others might be doing on any particular race track. To suggest that Schlesser was totally responsible for this episode was to misread the circumstances of the moment. He was a Grand Prix debutant and, as such, should have been given a wide berth by an experienced driver, particularly one with such a reputation for computer-like assessment of all the options available.

If Ayrton had been forced to follow Schlesser through that chicane before overtaking, he might have been obliged to settle for second place behind Berger. That, in itself, would have been no disgrace. But in Senna's philosophy, that would have been almost unthinkable . . .

I witnessed the confrontation between Schlesser and Senna after the race. It was cool, yet controlled and formally polite. Yet there was no apology from the Frenchman. He expressed regret over the episode, but did not accept responsibility for the collision. Ayrton just shrugged . . .

It seemed to me to emphasise that the qualities required to become world champion do not always correspond to those needed to establish a reputation as a great driver. Senna unquestionably falls into the latter category, just as Stirling Moss did. But while Britain's most celebrated non-champion failed to grasp the crown through a series of premeditated decisions to cast himself in the role of the underdog, Senna raced throughout 1988 and 1989 in the best team, with the best engine and the best back-up. He certainly did not always capitalise on that advantage to maximum effect.

Yet there were times when this dynamic, super-confident

approach paid dividends. Having qualified on pole position for the Japanese Grand Prix at Suzuka, Senna stalled his engine at the start. The World Championship was Prost's, surely. Yet Ayrton was not collected by any other car and, thanks to the slight downhill gradient, was able to pick up sufficient momentum to bump start his Honda V6 into life.

What followed was pure dynamite. As Prost stormed away from the pack, Senna was eighth at the end of the first lap, sixth on Lap 2, fifth on Lap 3 and fourth on Lap 4. He passed Berger's Ferrari to take third place on Lap 11 and, after Ivan Capelli's superb charge in the Judd-engined March 881 evaporated with electrical problems, he had a clear run at Prost.

With Suzuka now brushed by a fleeting rain shower, Senna's mind-numbing audacity came into its own. He slashed Prost's advantage to ribbons, forging ahead just after half distance. Although he would later whisper to his team that his car developed a slight gearchange problem, Prost had been beaten to the title. With a record eight wins now to his credit, Senna had broken Jim Clark's previous best of seven wins in a season, set in 1963.

Analysing Prost's 1988 season reveals that he was scarcely less eligible for a worthy World Championship title. Whereas Senna made major driving errors at Monaco, where he crashed whilst leading, and Monza, Prost's great strength was his ability to keep

The good old Cosworth V8 resurfaced in 1988 to power some of the smaller teams, enabling people to go racing on budgets which were small change compared with the front-line teams at the height of the turbo years. Andrea de Cesaris's Rial ARC1 (below), designed by Gustav Brunner, and Alex Caffi's Dallara Bms 188 (opposite), penned by Sergio Rinland, were just two examples of that breed.

out of trouble. Set against that was his decision to withdraw from the saturated British Grand Prix at Silverstone, his MP4/4 floundering along in the murk amongst the also-rans after only a couple of laps.

Although it was subsequently discovered that his car's chassis had lost some of its internal rigidity after Alain had whacked it over a high kerb on his glorious run to that French Grand Prix victory the previous weekend, his decision to come clean and quit at Silverstone put him in the firing line for a fusillade of venomous criticism. The French press, in particular, took up the torch in a big way. Come the German Grand Prix, most of them gave the bristling Prost a wide berth.

Senna's great skill, or complete lack of imagination – the choice is yours – made him a formidable contender in the wet. But the fundamental question now posed was whether Prost's self-confessed distaste for racing in the rain demeaned his status as a great Grand Prix driver. A tricky one, that.

Alain, unrepentant as ever, would repeat this stance at Adelaide in 1989, as we will see in the next chapter. Niki Lauda did this in 1976, when he abandoned the Japanese Grand Prix in similarly torrential conditions, thereby handing the Championship to James Hunt. Personally I believe that drivers should race, whatever the circumstances, yet I cannot bring myself to believe that either Prost or Lauda are anything less than Great Racing

Drivers. The record speaks for itself. And, ultimately, it is the record books that tell the tale.

Prost's Achilles Heel consistently proved to be his caution in traffic during qualifying. Time and again he was to discover you could not give Senna an inch, let alone the fifteen feet or so which separated pole position from second place on the starting grid. Yet Prost probably produced the most sensational race win of 1988 when he led the Spanish Grand Prix at Jerez from start to finish, a race where the potential fuel consumption of the McLaren-Hondas looked too marginal for him to finish.

Alain led all the way. Senna was fourth. The previous week at Estoril, Prost had won the Portuguese Grand Prix. Senna was sixth. Again, Alain seemed to make better use of his fuel allowance in circumstances less suited to Senna's throttle-blipping, keep-the-revs-up-at-all-costs, cockpit style.

As far as Ferrari was concerned, Monza offered the only moment of glory, and even then it proved to be a fortuitous victory on a day that saw the Arrows-Megatron partnership produce its best result with Cheever and Warwick finishing 3-4 in the Ferraris' wake. For Maranello, the 1988 season could best be summed up by Berger's performances at Silverstone and Adelaide.

McLaren had stumbled slightly during a rain-spoiled practice for the British Grand Prix, relinquishing the front row to Berger and Alboreto. But, knowing he had no chance in the race, Gerhard simply went out to enjoy himself, leading the early stages before being forced to back off drastically in order to conserve his fuel. He did the same at Adelaide, just to ensure that he went down in history as the man who, if nothing else, at least led the last race of the turbo era!

Not since the Ferrari Formula 2 domination of 1952/53 had any one team taken the opposition apart so comprehensively, reducing the other teams to the role of insignificant also-rans. True, there were moments of promise and events which would have far-reaching significance into 1989. For the most part, the rest of the cars were not competitors. Just traffic.

THE TURBO YEARS' RESULTS 1988

Winner's average speed

April 3, BRAZILIAN GRAND PRIX, Rio
1	Alain Prost	McLaren-Honda MP4/4 turbo	(117.08mph)
2	Gerhard Berger	Ferrari F187/88C turbo	
3	Nelson Piquet	Lotus-Honda 100T turbo	
4	Derek Warwick	Arrows-Megatron A10B turbo	
5	Michele Alboreto	Ferrari F187/88C turbo	
6	Satoru Nakajima	Lotus-Honda 100T turbo	

May 1, SAN MARINO GRAND PRIX, Imola
1	Ayrton Senna	McLaren-Honda MP4/4 turbo	(121.63mph)
2	Alain Prost	McLaren-Honda MP4/4 turbo	
3	Nelson Piquet	Lotus-Honda 100T turbo	
4	Thierry Boutsen	Benetton-Ford B188	
5	Gerhard Berger	Ferrari F187/88C turbo	
6	Alessandro Nannini	Benetton-Ford B188	

May 15, MONACO GRAND PRIX, Monte Carlo
1	Alain Prost	McLaren-Honda MP4/4 turbo	(85.51mph)
2	Gerhard Berger	Ferrari F187/88C turbo	
3	Michele Alboreto	Ferrari F187/88C turbo	
4	Derek Warwick	Arrows-Megatron A10B turbo	
5	Jonathan Palmer	Tyrrell-Cosworth 017	
6	Riccardo Patrese	Williams-Judd FW12	

May 29, MEXICO GRAND PRIX, Mexico City
1	Alain Prost	McLaren-Honda MP4/4 turbo	(122.34mph)
2	Ayrton Senna	McLaren-Honda MP4/4 turbo	
3	Gerhard Berger	Ferrari F187/88C turbo	
4	Michele Alboreto	Ferrari F187/88C turbo	
5	Derek Warwick	Arrows-Megatron A10B turbo	
6	Eddie Cheever	Arrows-Megatron A10B turbo	

June 12, CANADIAN GRAND PRIX, Montreal
1	Ayrton Senna	McLaren-Honda MP4/4 turbo	(113.18mph)
2	Alain Prost	McLaren-Honda MP4/4 turbo	
3	Thierry Boutsen	Benetton-Ford B188	
4	Nelson Piquet	Lotus-Honda 100T turbo	
5	Ivan Capelli	March-Judd 881	
6	Jonathan Palmer	Tyrrell-Cosworth 017	

June 19, DETROIT GRAND PRIX, Michigan
1	Ayrton Senna	McLaren-Honda MP4/4 turbo	(82.22mph)
2	Alain Prost	McLaren-Honda MP4/4 turbo	
3	Thierry Boutsen	Benetton-Ford B188	
4	Andrea de Cesaris	Rial-Cosworth ARC1	
5	Jonathan Palmer	Tyrrell-Cosworth 017	
6	Pierluigi Martini	Minardi-Cosworth M188	

July 3, FRENCH GRAND PRIX, Paul Ricard
1	Alain Prost	McLaren-Honda MP4/4 turbo	(116.49mph)
2	Ayrton Senna	McLaren-Honda MP4/4 turbo	
3	Michele Alboreto	Ferrari F187/88C turbo	
4	Gerhard Berger	Ferrari F187/88C turbo	
5	Nelson Piquet	Lotus-Honda 100T turbo	
6	Alessandro Nannini	Benetton-Ford B188	

July 10, BRITISH GRAND PRIX, Silverstone
1	Ayrton Senna	McLaren-Honda MP4/4 turbo	(124.14mph)
2	Nigel Mansell	Williams-Judd FW12	
3	Alessandro Nannini	Benetton-Ford B188	
4	Mauricio Gugelmin	March-Judd 881	
5	Nelson Piquet	Lotus-Honda 100T turbo	
6	Derek Warwick	Arrows-Megatron A10B turbo	

July 24, GERMAN GRAND PRIX, Hockenheim
1	Ayrton Senna	McLaren-Honda MP4/4 turbo	(120.01mph)
2	Alain Prost	McLaren-Honda MP4/4 turbo	
3	Gerhard Berger	Ferrari F187/88C turbo	
4	Michele Alboreto	Ferrari F187/88C turbo	
5	Ivan Capelli	March-Judd 881	
6	Thierry Boutsen	Benetton-Ford B188	

August 7, HUNGARIAN GRAND PRIX, Budapest
1	Ayrton Senna	McLaren-Honda MP4/4 turbo	(90.56mph)
2	Alain Prost	McLaren-Honda MP4/4 turbo	
3	Thierry Boutsen	Benetton-Ford B188	
4	Gerhard Berger	Ferrari F187/88C turbo	
5	Mauricio Gugelmin	March-Judd 881	
6	Riccardo Patrese	Williams-Judd FW12	

August 28, BELGIAN GRAND PRIX, Spa
1	Ayrton Senna	McLaren-Honda MP4/4 turbo	(126.41mph)
2	Alain Prost	McLaren-Honda MP4/4 turbo	
3	Ivan Capelli	March-Judd 881	
4	Nelson Piquet	Lotus-Honda 100T turbo	
5	Derek Warwick	Arrows-Megatron A10B turbo	
6	Eddie Cheever	Arrows-Megatron A10B turbo	

September 11, ITALIAN GRAND PRIX, Monza
1	Gerhard Berger	Ferrari F187/88C turbo	(142mph)
2	Michele Alboreto	Ferrari F187/88C turbo	
3	Eddie Cheever	Arrows-Megatron A10B turbo	
4	Derek Warwick	Arrows-Megatron A10B turbo	
5	Ivan Capelli	March-Judd 881	
6	Thierry Boutsen	Benetton-Ford B188	

September 25, PORTUGUESE GRAND PRIX, Estoril
1	Alain Prost	McLaren-Honda MP4/4 turbo	(116.21mph)
2	Ivan Capelli	March-Judd 881	
3	Thierry Boutsen	Benetton-Ford B188	
4	Derek Warwick	Arrows-Megatron A10B turbo	
5	Michele Alboreto	Ferrari F187/88C turbo	
6	Ayrton Senna	McLaren-Honda MP4/4 turbo	

October 2, SPANISH GRAND PRIX, Jerez
1   Alain Prost   McLaren-Honda MP4/4 turbo   (104.13mph)
2   Nigel Mansell   Williams-Judd FW12
3   Alessandro Nannini   Benetton-Ford B188
4   Ayrton Senna   McLaren-Honda MP4/4 turbo
5   Riccardo Patrese   Williams-Judd FW12
6   Gerhard Berger   Ferrari F187/88C turbo

October 30, JAPANESE GRAND PRIX, Suzuka
1   Ayrton Senna   McLaren-Honda MP4/4 turbo   (119.23mph)
2   Alain Prost   McLaren-Honda MP4/4 turbo
3   Thierry Boutsen   Benetton-Ford B188
4   Gerhard Berger   Ferrari F187/88C turbo
5   Alessandro Nannini   Benetton-Ford B188
6   Riccardo Patrese   Williams-Judd FW12

November 13, AUSTRALIAN GRAND PRIX, Adelaide
1   Alain Prost   McLaren-Honda MP4/4 turbo   (102.04mph)
2   Ayrton Senna   McLaren-Honda MP4/4 turbo
3   Nelson Piquet   Lotus-Honda 100T turbo
4   Riccardo Patrese   Williams-Judd FW12
5   Thierry Boutsen   Benetton-Ford B188
6   Ivan Capelli   March-Judd 881

DRIVERS' WORLD CHAMPIONSHIP

Posn	Driver	Points
1	Ayrton Senna	90
2	Alain Prost	87
3	Gerhard Berger	41
4	Thierry Boutsen	27
5	Michele Alboreto	24
6	Nelson Piquet	22
7	Ivan Capelli	17
	Derek Warwick	
9	Alessandro Nannini	12
	Nigel Mansell	
11	Riccardo Patrese	8
12	Eddie Cheever	6
13	Mauricio Gugelmin	5
	Jonathan Palmer	
15	Andrea de Cesaris	3
16	Pierluigi Martini	1
	Satoru Nakajima	

CONSTRUCTORS' CHAMPIONSHIP

Posn	Constructor	Points
1	McLaren	199
2	Ferrari	65
3	Benetton	39
4	Lotus	23
	Arrows	
6	March	22
7	Williams	20
8	Tyrrell	5
9	Rial	3
10	Minardi	1

BYE-BYE TURBO...

Below and opposite*Below and opposite: Championship clincher! The return to the era of naturally-aspirated Formula 1 produced a highly controversial finish to the 1989 World Championship with McLaren drivers Alain Prost and Ayrton Senna locked together in the middle of the circuit following a collision in the Japanese Grand Prix at Suzuka. This was only the start of the controversy . . .*

The 1989 season was to remind us just how the turbo era had dramatically increased the Formula 1 stakes. Those who believed that Grand Prix racing would revert to a situation where domination was shared by a handful of special builders, using off-the-shelf Cosworth engines, were, in my view, either stupid or deceitful. Stupid in the sense that they could not read the writing on the wall, deceitful in the sense that some may have attempted to sell sponsorship on a totally false premise.

No, the first message heralded by the new naturally-aspirated era was, if you have not got a deal with a major engine manufacturer, then you play amongst the supporting cast. Honda, Ferrari and Renault held sway at the front of the field, Ford's new V8 only gaining a lucky win in Japan after Senna's McLaren-Honda, first past the chequered flag, was subsequently disqualified.

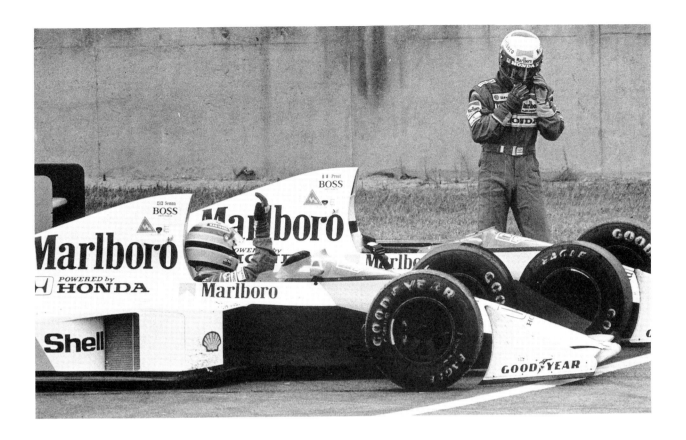

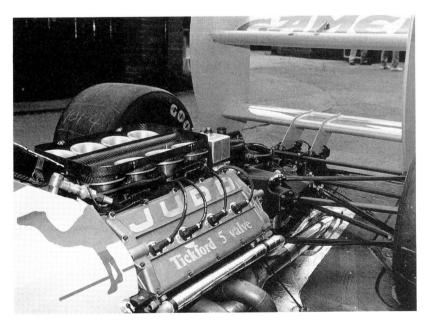

Left: *During 1989, Team Lotus attempted to enhance the performance of its Judd CV 3.5 litre V8s by collaborating with Aston Martin Tickford for the development of a five-valves per cylinder head. It proved abortive and was effectively shelved mid-season.*

*Williams technical director Patrick Head (*right, *in sunglasses) was delighted to renew a programme of technical collaboration with a major manufacturer when Williams concluded an agreement to use the RS1 3.5 litre V10 cylinder engine in 1989. Drivers were Riccardo Patrese, seen here in an FW12 in the Silverstone pit lane.*

However, more worryingly, the 1989 season provided an uncomfortable taste of *deja-vu*. You might have thought that, through that decade of turbo domination, FISA and the teams would have learned a little about living together in a vaguely congenial atmosphere. Not a bit of it. The 1989 season was plagued by more rancour and bitterness than at any time since the dispute over sliding skirts. Which is just about where we came in . . .

An objective analysis of the facts available must reveal that Balestre's hair-trigger temper and the lack of any cohesion among the teams contributed to this damaging state of affairs. The most celebrated episodes were Mansell's suspension from the Spanish Grand Prix after allegedly ignoring a black flag during the previous week's Spanish race, and the Senna/Prost collision in the Japanese Grand Prix at Suzuka, after which Ayrton was disqualified for missing a chicane.

It is just possible that FISA might have got away with disqualifying Senna from Suzuka if Balestre and his colleagues had left it at that. But no, they just could not resist turning the knife in the wound. At the FIA Appeal Court hearing, they introduced a host of new evidence, branded Senna as a fundamentally dangerous driver and effectively put him on probation for six months with a ban for that period, albeit suspended.

Touchline observers saw this as little more than a worried over-reaction to the manifest injustice involved in suspending Mansell from the Spanish race. However, Nigel exaggerated his own plight by infringing the rules in the first place when he snicked his Ferrari's electro-hydraulic gearbox into reverse after over-shooting his pit whilst leading the Portuguese race by a country mile.

As a further exacerbating factor, the collective lack of respect for FISA's authority engendered by its own unpredictable

Team-mate Thierry Boutsen is caught negotiating the Monaco chicane in his similar car, an uprated version of the previous year's Judd-propelled chassis which the Belgian driver used to win the 1989 Canadian Grand Prix. Later Boutsen won in Australia with the new Williams-Renault FW13 on only its fourth outing.

Frank Williams in company with Renault Sport chief engineer Bernard Cassin and a mock-up of the Renault V10 engine on the day the Anglo-French partnership was formally announced.

behaviour had plumbed fresh depths by the end of 1989. The suspicion that the governing body was being less than even-handed prompted McLaren to seek legal advice on the subject of suing FISA in the civil courts, something which had never previously been done with any success. At the time of writing it remains to be seen whether McLaren will be the first to succeed. Certainly they seem to have marshalled a stronger case than most, centred not round challenging FISA's authority to govern, but accusing them of mis-application of their own regulations. As things turned out, having attempted to marshal considerable media support in the dying weeks of the 1989 season, McLaren had made no progress at all on this front by the start of the 1990 season.

Senna, meanwhile, took it upon himself to be so outspokenly critical of FISA that he had to make amends with a public withdrawal before the sport's governing body would issue him with his licence for 1990.

Taken as a whole, though, FISA and the constructors learned virtually nothing about living with each other throughout the turbo years. Tensions ran deep, like a splinter beneath the skin, ready to send searing pain through the system at the slightest touch. The racing was superb, sometimes sensational, but the human relationships were every bit as fragile, unpredictable and highly stressed as the machinery.

INDEX